THE FUNDAMENTALIST PHENOMENON

S · I · E

Starkoff Institute Studies
in Ethics and
Contemporary Moral Problems

Series Editor
Barry S. Kogan

THE FUNDAMENTALIST PHENOMENON

A View from Within;
A Response from Without

Edited by Norman J. Cohen

WILLIAM B. EERDMANS PUBLISHING COMPANY
GRAND RAPIDS, MICHIGAN

Copyright © 1990 by Wm. B. Eerdmans Publishing Co.,
255 Jefferson Ave. S.E., Grand Rapids, MI 49503.

First published 1990 by Wm. B. Eerdmans Publishing Co. in cooperation with
The Starkoff Institute of Ethics and Contemporary Moral Problems as a volume
in the Starkoff Institute Studies series.

The views expressed in this volume are those of the authors and participants
and do not necessarily reflect those of The Starkoff Institute of Ethics and Contemporary Moral Problems

All rights reserved
Printed in the United States of America

Library of Congress Cataloging-in-Publication Data

The Fundamentalist phenomenon: a view from within, a response from
    without / edited by Norman J. Cohen.
        p.   cm.
    Revised version of papers presented at a conference, held Nov. 14-16,
1989, at the Brookdale Center, Hebrew Union College, New York School.
    ISBN 0-8028-0447-0
    1. Fundamentalism—Comparative Studies—Congresses.   I. Cohen,
Norman J.
BL238.F85   1990
291′.09′04—dc20   90-31018
                                                      CIP

Contents

LINCOLN CHRISTIAN COLLEGE AND SEMINARY

v

Introduction

The Fundamentalist Phenomenon: A View from Within; A Response from Without

Norman J. Cohen

The Hebrew Union College is the oldest rabbinic seminary in North America. As a liberal Jewish academic institution, its mandate has always been to encourage and foster discussion of the pressing, difficult issues of the day. No issue could be more important on the American scene, as well as globally, than religious fundamentalism. By bringing together academicians, theologians, clergy, and writers at a conference held on November 14-16, 1988, at the Brookdale Center of the College's New York School, we hoped to contribute to the general understanding of fundamentalism and to assess its impact on our social, political, and religious life. In addition to learning from scholars who have studied the nature of religious fundamentalism, we also wanted to hear from liberal thinkers concerning how they might respond to the challenges posed by fundamentalists.

The papers included in this volume, which are revisions of those presented at the conference, shed much light on the phenomenon, even as many of them raise difficult problems regarding its characterization and a determination of its future. One of the most focused concerns was the latitude of the usage of the term "fundamentalism" itself. Does such a term denote a loosely organized cluster of militant evangelicals, or is it descriptive of individuals who possess particular religious beliefs, such as the inerrancy of Scripture and the use of Scripture as the sole source of moral authority? Moreover, can such a term, which was spawned in the context of American Protestantism in the early twentieth century, be used to describe parallel trends in other religions? Can we speak of Muslim or Jewish fundamentalists, and do such appellations convey the same meaning as the label "fundamentalist" within the American Protestant milieu? The difficulty associated even with the use of the term is exacerbated by its often negative connotation as a shorthand for the hostile characterization of someone more orthodox than oneself who is totally out of touch with modern culture.

Although it is very difficult to determine what fundamentalism is and who fundamentalists are, we must ask whether it is possible to arrive at some generally accepted characteristics of the phenomenon. How should fundamentalism, at least on the American scene, be identified? Perhaps three more specific questions, which are raised by several of the authors, can help us delineate more clearly its contours. First, what is the relationship of religious orthodoxy and fundamentalism? Can they be distinguished, or does the fundamentalist believe nothing that is not already shared by his religious orthodox counterpart? If the latter, then the only difference between them would be the degree of militancy with which the fundamentalist presses the fight against modern culture and tries to save souls. This leads to the second concern. To what extent is the American Protestant fundamentalist movement characterized by its desire to restore traditional values based on Scripture and to call the society back to its religious, moral heritage? Concomitantly, is this negative response to and struggle with the general culture present in its counterparts in other societies and religions? Finally, though Protestant fundamentalism was shaped in the context of opposition to societal values and culture, and in isolation from the general polity, has it now been totally co-opted into the political process? What is the changing role of fundamentalists in American public life?

Fundamentalists have been both insiders and outsiders in American politics, but the 1970s saw their return to an insider posture with the shift from political passivity to electoral activity. Yet, with the increased political involvement of fundamentalists, do liberals exaggerate the influence and political challenge of fundamentalism? Ten years ago, the moral majority was formed due to the growing fundamentalist sociopolitical agenda. As they saw the courts asserting minority rights, they felt that they were losing control of their destinies and as a result they organized to promote traditional values. But Jerry Falwell's recent disbanding of this loosely bound umbrella organization prompts us to reassess the future direction of the fundamentalist movement. Will fundamentalists continue to be a political force, or will they be increasingly limited by their tendency to fragment and withdraw into a more passive political posture? Will the alliance of fundamentalists and right-wing Republicans, which was shaped in this decade, continue to exert the influence that it has had in recent years? Finally, whether or not fundamentalists continue to play a dominant role in the political system, they have clearly placed on the public agenda crucial issues of conscience, including religion and public education, and matters of personal choice, with which all Americans must grapple.

Liberals cannot abandon the public arena to the views of the religious right. As fundamentalists moderate the manner in which they express their views as well as their political techniques, liberals must be willing to participate in public dialogue. Is such dialogue feasible and will a politics of inclusiveness further moderate the fundamentalists' stance? As liberals interact with fundamentalists, they will be challenged to clarify their religious responses to them over the range of pressing issues. In addition, now that fundamentalists are a part of the political infrastructure, liberals will have to galvanize their strength on the local and state levels in order to counteract the gains of the religious right. Only time will tell whether liberals are able to respond to these challenges in an effective and organized manner.

These, then, are some of the crucial questions to which the participants at the conference on fundamentalism responded.

The questions easily fall into two categories, and as a result, the essays in this volume are arranged in two parts.

Part One focuses on a description of the fundamentalist phenomenon from a variety of perspectives. Jaroslav Pelikan analyzes the original claims of American Protestant fundamentalism against the backdrop of the classical orthodox teachings of the Church. In so doing, he helps us understand fundamentalism's basic thrust. George Marsden describes at length the history of fundamentalism and its many traits, and emphasizes that a fundamentalist is an evangelical who is militant in his opposition to modern liberalist theology and the secularity of modern culture. In contrast, Clark Pinnock cites the movement for its tenacious faith, for its courage to stand up for classic Christian beliefs, and for placing on the society's agenda many key moral issues. He also raises the matter of the appropriateness of the use of the term "fundamentalism" itself, which is discussed in several of the other papers as well.

Three papers attempt to analyze the phenomenon from either a sociological, political, or psychological perspective. James Davison Hunter characterizes fundamentalism as an embattled form of orthodoxy that resists modernity, seeks to reinstate the course of sacred history which modernity has derailed, and ties religious ideology to national identity. A. James Reichley traces the changing participation of fundamentalists in American politics. He stresses that evangelical Protestants have already shifted the balance of American politics and believes that they will continue to be a force with which to be reckoned. They have come to enjoy the power that emanates from political participation and remain dedicated to achieving their unfulfilled social agenda. Looking at fundamentalism from the viewpoint of modern psychology, Mortimer Ostow characterizes its adherents as being reluctant to tolerate doubt, uncertainty, and ambiguity. The world seems dangerously chaotic to them and they can only achieve certainty by looking to the Bible for guidance. After noting that fundamentalists see the world as wicked, depraved, and doomed to apocalyptic destruction, Ostow underscores that one of the main aspects of fundamentalism is its zeal, which is usually expressed in divisive militancy.

In a more sympathetic portrait, Richard Neuhaus draws extensively on the writings and philosophy of James Madison to describe the veritable *Kulturkampf* over the definition of the American enterprise that has been triggered by fundamentalist political involvement. Of greatest concern are issues related to religion and public education that will continue to be agitated and that raise the question of where to draw the line between teaching about religion and teaching religion. Taking a harsher view of fundamentalism's involvement in politics, James M. Dunn terms the fundamentalist–right-wing Republican partnership "the strongest alliance of religion with power since the Puritans." Most distressing to Dunn is the fundamentalists' dogmatic insistence on their being the sole possessors of truth, though from his perspective their involvement in politics has shown them to be less than idealistic.

Part One concludes with descriptions of the impact of fundamentalism on the Islamic, Catholic, and Jewish worlds. Riffat Hassan presents a strongly worded statement decrying the use of the term "fundamentalism" to describe any facet of the Muslim life. No such term exists in Arabic and therefore she rejects the very negative stereotyping implied by the idea of Islamic fundamentalism. The impact of fundamentalism outside American Protestantism is also addressed by Patrick Arnold, who characterizes fundamentalism as an emerging negative force in Catholicism whose rage is focused primarily on coreligionists who have adapted to modernity and its values. He charges that the fundamentalist movement is crippling the rest of the Catholic community by inhibiting its ability to respond to social problems, obscuring its image of outreach and hope, and setting groups within the Church against each other. Finally, Leon Wieseltier argues that there is no such thing as Jewish fundamentalism since Judaism has always fostered development and adaptation. Yet he does not deny that something significant has happened since a new relationship between religion and politics has been fostered. In the Jewish community this has resulted in the dangerous mingling of religion and nationalism in Israel.

Having described the fundamentalist phenomenon and delineated the many challenges it poses, we turn in Part Two to how liberals should respond to it. The responses begin with Donald Shriver, who calls for greater understanding for and acceptance of religious differences between liberals and fundamentalists. Shriver believes that people of religion with causes equally sincere can meet in the public arena and compromise. He urges liberals to foster greater dialogue with their fundamentalist counterparts.

David Saperstein agrees that greater dialogue must be fostered with fundamentalists, who need to be included in the public debate over the crucial issues of the day. Through the interaction of more mainstream groups with the religious right, the latter will continue to moderate their views and their social agenda, which were shaped in their effort to call America back to classic religious values. The political activism of the religious right is the result of their desire to protect their community from the outside political, social, and cultural environment.

Eugene Borowitz contrasts the positions of the orthodoxies of Western religion with liberal religious beliefs. Describing the central difference as a question of the proper balance between God's sovereignty and human will, Borowitz claims that what most concerns liberals about fundamentalists is their potential to generate extremism, zealotry, and fanaticism because of their beliefs. Despite the recent attractiveness of orthodox religions and of a more fundamentalist approach which rejects modernity and its values, Borowitz believes that the overwhelming majority of people who have tasted the personal dignity which modernity has conferred will continue to reject religious orthodoxy and fundamentalist fanaticism.

Finally, Preston Williams, like Donald Shriver, recognizes that fundamentalism is a changing phenomenon and that dialogue with fundamentalists will create greater understanding and cooperation. Williams is convinced that fundamentalism is not as great a threat to the polity as liberals tend to think, and that through a greater toleration of doctrinal differences, stereotypes can be overcome. The ensuing dialogue will foster even more change within the fundamentalist camp.

Williams's remarks are synonymous with the hopes of those who organized the conference on fundamentalism at the Hebrew Union College. Our agenda was to analyze the phenomenon of fundamentalism and the response of liberals to it in order to foster greater understanding and dialogue. The conference was the inaugural program sponsored under the auspices of the Starkoff Institute of Ethics and Contemporary Moral Issues. We are indebted to the generous support of Mr. Bernard Starkoff and to the work of Dr. Barry Kogan, director of the Starkoff Institute, which is housed on the Cincinnati campus of Hebrew Union College–Jewish Institute of Religion. The conference was also supported in part by a gift from the Lily Foundation.

We, the members of the faculty and administration of Hebrew Union College, were proud to host this extraordinary conference. Through the publication of its proceedings we aspire to make a small contribution to the discussion of the nature of fundamentalism and its impact on the religious, political, and social life of the American polity. We hope that we have analyzed enough of its many facets to provide a fair picture of this important phenomenon and in so doing to advance our understanding of it.

New York, N.Y.   Hebrew Union College
July 3, 1989

PART ONE

1. Fundamentalism and/or Orthodoxy? Toward an Understanding of the Fundamentalist Phenomenon

Jaroslav Pelikan

Beginning in 1910—thus as near to the opening of the twentieth century as we are to its close—a group of American Protestant laymen published a set of twelve small books bearing the overall title, *The Fundamentals: A Testimony of the Truth*.[1] Those books, which circulated in millions of copies, gave their name to a movement that had been developing within several denominations of American Protestantism during much of the nineteenth century.[2] But, rightly or wrongly, "fundamentalism" seems by now to have become instead, in the secular media and even in the believing public, a designation for any and every kind of orthodoxy within all the world religions, with the result that there is great confusion about fundamentalist teaching.

Because it was interdenominational in its provenance, fundamentalism did not adhere to any one of the classic confessional statements by which the Protestant churches coming

---

1. *The Fundamentals: A Testimony of the Truth*, 12 vols. (Chicago: Testimony Publishing Company, 1910-15); hereafter cited as *The Fundamentals*.
2. The most useful recent introduction, with a bibliography for further study, is George M. Marsden, "Fundamentalism," in Charles H. Lippy and Peter W. Williams, eds., *Encyclopedia of the American Religious Experience: Studies of Traditions and Movements*, 3 vols. (New York: Charles Scribner's Sons, 1988), 2:947-62.

out of the Reformation and post-Reformation controversies had identified themselves. In that sense, there is no "fundamentalist creed." Its place and function have been taken by what the first historian of the movement, Stewart Grant Cole, called "the famous Five-Points statement of doctrine, in which they insisted upon universal Christian acceptance of the Inerrancy of the Scriptures, the Deity of Christ, his Virgin birth, the Substitutionary Atonement of Christ, and his physical Resurrection and coming bodily Return to earth."[3] Although this set of doctrines never did, and still does not, have any official standing within fundamentalism, it acquired one in the secondary literature, thanks in large measure to Cole's historical constructs. "Whenever Fundamentalist beliefs have been discussed in the past," one of its most perceptive historians has lamented, "a prominent place has inevitably been given to what are called the five points of Fundamentalism."[4] Thus the five-point formula found its way into the article on fundamentalism by the pioneer historian of American religion in a standard reference book of the last generation.[5] And despite its lack of confessional standing, it does provide a convenient summary of some of the most important distinctive emphases of the movement.[6]

For a historian of Christian doctrine who deals chiefly with the history of how the confessions and creeds of orthodox Christian dogma have developed in both East and West, the topic in-

---

3. Stewart Grant Cole, *The History of Fundamentalism* (New York: R. R. Smith, 1931), p. 34.

4. Ernest Robert Sandeen, *The Roots of Fundamentalism: British and American Millenarianism, 1800-1930* (Chicago: University of Chicago Press, 1970), p. xiv; see also pp. 140-41.

5. William Warren Sweet, "Fundamentalism," in Vergilius Ferm, ed., *An Encyclopedia of Religion* (New York: Philosophical Library, 1945), pp. 291-92; hereafter cited as "Fundamentalism."

6. I am indebted to my colleague, Professor George M. Marsden of Duke University, for his helpful suggestions about the historical status of the "five points of Fundamentalism" and for other critical comments. His book, *Fundamentalism and American Culture: The Shaping of Twentieth-Century Evangelicalism, 1870-1925* (New York: Oxford University Press, 1980), is a solid historical contribution of lasting worth.

dicated in the subtitle of this essay, "Toward an Understanding of the Fundamentalist Phenomenon," must be approached from that perspective;[7] hence the arrangement of the title and the subtitle. That title would seem here to call for a review of fundamentalist doctrines—specifically of the five doctrines just enumerated, despite their ambiguous status—as each of them had originally developed in the history of orthodoxy, followed by an analysis of the differences between that orthodox development and the version of each doctrine propounded by fundamentalism and equated by it with the mainstream of the orthodox Christian tradition. As it will be used here, "orthodoxy" refers to the mainstream of the development of Christian doctrine, both its pluralism and its underlying consensus, as that was formulated, perhaps a bit overconfidently, by Vincent of Lerins in the fifth century: what has been believed "everywhere, always, by all [*ubique, semper, ab omnibus*]"[8]—with the stipulation added by John Henry Newman in the nineteenth century, that "the Rule of Vincent is not of a mathematical or demonstrative character, but moral, and requires practical judgement and good sense to apply it."[9] Because such an analysis is in the first instance a historical and descriptive task (although it does, of course, have normative consequences, as well as normative presuppositions), most of its validity should not depend upon whether one existentially shares the orthodox Christian tradition, or the fundamentalist position, or for that matter the Christian faith itself. As it happens, each of the five doctrines in the quasi-creedal statement fathered on fundamentalism lends itself to the consideration of a distinct aspect of orthodoxy in which such differences between orthodoxy and fundamentalism come clearly into focus.

---

7. Throughout this paper I shall, for the sake of convenience, be referring to that history: Jaroslav Pelikan, *The Christian Tradition: A History of the Development of Doctrine*, 5 vols. (Chicago: University of Chicago Press, 1971-89); hereafter cited as *Christian Tradition*.

8. See *Christian Tradition*, 1:33-39; 4:281.

9. See *Christian Tradition*, 5:80-81, 259.

I

As everyone inside or outside the movement would probably agree, the third of these fundamentals, "the inerrancy of Scripture in every detail," with its corollary of the literalistic interpretation of the Bible, is basic to all the others and could therefore be termed the *articulus fundamentalissimus* of all the fundamentals. In one essay after another of *The Fundamentals*, that is the question to which the discussion returns. For example, the article on the hypothesis of multiple authorship in the book of Isaiah, while seeking to show on literary grounds that such a hypothesis is not necessary to explain the relation between chapters 1–39 and chapters 40–66 of the book, leaves no doubt in the reader's mind that it is the a priori doctrine of plenary verbal inspiration, not the a posteriori outcome of such literary-critical investigation, that has determined the conclusion that the book had only one author, namely, the prophet Isaiah—or, to be completely precise and correct, only one *writer,* God the Holy Spirit being in the strict sense the only Author of all the biblical books.[10] During the third of a century between the trial of Charles Augustus Briggs in 1892 and the trial of John Thomas Scopes in 1925, the dispute over Darwinian evolution frequently resolved itself into a controversy over the doctrines of biblical inspiration and inerrancy, on the assumption that these were the chief doctrines at stake in the dispute: if the creation narrative (which was taken to be a single and consistent narrative) in the book of Genesis was not literally true, nothing in the Bible could be ultimately credible.

Within the orthodox Christian tradition, however, the affirmation of biblical authority and credibility was itself part of a larger and more complex system of authority. But on the details of biblical interpretation itself, orthodoxy had, repeatedly if not quite consistently, manifested and tolerated a hermeneutical pluralism that could not easily be accommodated to the fundamen-

---

10. *The Fundamentals,* 7:70-87.

talist mold.[11] Orthodoxy was based on a total and unquestionable consensus on the doctrine of creation itself, as articulated in the opening sentence of the Niceno-Constantinopolitan Creed,[12] with its paraphrase of the *Shema:* "We believe in one God, the Father, the Almighty, Maker of heaven and earth, of all visible and of all invisible beings."[13] But concerning the mode and the time-table of that creation, the Creed was silent.

Concerning the specifics of the exegesis of the creation narrative (or narratives), moreover, the fundamentalist assumption that there has been a homogeneous orthodox position is seen to be mistaken, as becomes evident from a comparison of the two most influential orthodox theologians of the Latin West, Augustine of Hippo and Thomas Aquinas. Augustine took the six "days" of the Genesis account to be a symbolic expression for a creation that was in fact instantaneous, arguing that "the second day, the third, and the rest are not other days, but the same 'one' day is repeated to complete the number."[14] Although he composed a massive commentary with the title *De Genesi ad litteram* (now finally available also in English translation),[15] the phrase "the literal meaning of Genesis [*ad litteram*]" in the title apparently did not mean interpreting the "days" literally as periods of twenty-four hours each.[16] Thomas Aquinas, in Question 74 of the First Part of the

11. On the problems of interpretation, see the comments of Gabriel Herbert, *Fundamentalism and the Church* (Philadelphia: Westminster Press, 1957), pp. 84-98.

12. Also in its Western recension, to which the notorious *Filioque* was added: in Heinrich Denzinger, ed., *Enchiridion symbolorum definitionum et declarationum de rebus fidei et morum,* 36th ed. (Barcelona, Freiburg, and Rome: Herder, 1976), § 150; hereafter abbreviated as "Denzinger," with the paragraph number.

13. Text in Joseph Alberigo, et al., eds., *Conciliorum oecumenicorum decreta,* 3d ed. (Bologna: Istituto per le scienze religiose, 1973), p. 24; hereafter abbreviated as "Alberigo."

14. Augustine, *The City of God* XI.9.

15. Augustine, *Literal Meaning of Genesis,* tr. John Hammond Taylor, 2 vols. (New York: Newman Press, 1982).

16. See also Augustine, *Confessions XII.* xiii.16.

Summa Theologica, took issue with the Augustinian interpretation of the "days," in which, as he put it, "Augustine differs from
other expositors," and he came out in favor of seven distinct
and literal days. But there is not even a hint in Saint Thomas
that Saint Augustine should be declared a heretic for holding
to this atypical interpretation of the creation story.[17]

This exchange between Augustine and Aquinas has at
least two implications for our consideration of the differences
between orthodoxy and fundamentalism. The obvious one is
that, unlike the definition of fundamentalism, the definition of
orthodoxy does not seem to have included the obligation to
agree on the literal exegesis of the creation story in Genesis, but
instead seems to have been able to comprehend both the
Augustinian and the Thomistic interpretations within the range
of the ecclesiastically and dogmatically permissible. Orthodoxy
was not a straight line, but a circle drawn around a variety of
permissible views, excluding other views. The other and
broader implication involves the very nature of the exegetical
enterprise as such. Historic Christian orthodoxy was able to
speak about biblical "inerrancy" only because its hermeneutic
was sensitive to the multiple senses of a biblical text. Medieval
theory sometimes distinguished four such senses, sometimes as
many as seven; but the multiple sense enabled the exegete to
have recourse to another level of meaning when it became obvious that a literal interpretation of the text did not make
sense.[18] An interesting example was Origen's exegesis of the
text from Joshua 4:9: "And Joshua set up twelve stones in the
midst of the Jordan . . . and they are there to this day." Since
the stones were, quite clearly, not there to his own day, Origen
argues, the text must have meant something else: *Iēsous,* the
name for Joshua in the Septuagint, was of course also the name
for Jesus in the New Testament; and the twelve stones were the
twelve apostles, who, Origen maintained, truly "are there to this

17. Thomas Aquinas, *Summa Theologica,* Pars Prima, Q. 74, art. 2.
18. A masterful study is that of Beryl Smalley, *The Study of the Bible in the
Middle Ages* (Notre Dame, IN: University of Notre Dame Press, 1964).

day" through the Church.[19] We may smile at this exegetical alchemy as quaint or fanciful or, in the British phrase, "too clever by half "; but it was, through most of the history of Christian orthodoxy, the way to be able to speak about an "inerrancy in every detail." Therefore, when the multiple meaning or *sensus plenior* was declared illegitimate, the possibility of inerrancy was—inadvertently, to be sure—invalidated as well in the process.

II

The doctrine of the Resurrection of Christ is listed second among the tenets of fundamentalism, and it is of course a fundamental tenet of any Christian orthodoxy as well. "If Christ has not been raised," the apostle Paul declared, "your faith is futile and you are still in your sins."[20] But when fundamentalism insisted, as it sometimes (though not always) did, that this referred only to what it called the *physical* resurrection of Christ, this evidenced an inability to come to terms with the pluralism that makes its presence felt even within the New Testament witness itself. That term "physical resurrection" may be appropriate for one or another of the resurrection accounts in the Gospels, though even here there is variety.[21] But "physical resurrection" as some fundamentalists defined it is not an accurate, or at any rate not an adequate, way to summarize Pauline language. For having made the declaration just quoted, Paul went on later in the same chapter to explain to the Corinthians what he meant: "So it is with the resurrection of the dead. It is

19. Origen, *In Jesu Nave* 4:9.
20. 1 Cor. 15:17.
21. The historical, literary, and theological problems have been well analyzed (regardless of whether one accepts his conclusions) by Hans von Campenhausen, "The Events of Easter and the Empty Tomb," in *Tradition and Life in the Church: Essays and Lectures in Church History*, tr. A. V. Littledale (Philadelphia: Fortress Press, 1968), pp. 42-89.

sown a physical body [*sōma physikon*], it is raised a spiritual body [*sōma pneumatikon*]. It is not the spiritual which is first but the physical, and then the spiritual. I tell you this, brethren: flesh and blood cannot inherit the kingdom of God."[22] Those distinctions would seem to have applied both to the Resurrection of Christ and to the general resurrection, which were so interconnected in this chapter that Paul could argue: "If the dead are not raised, then Christ has not been raised."[23]

It is, however, another aspect of the resurrection faith that is of even greater interest here. Fundamentalism treats the Resurrection of Christ as a corollary of the doctrine of biblical inerrancy: since Scripture cannot teach an untruth, its announcement of the Resurrection of Christ must also be true. The authentication of that announcement is taken to consist in the divine revelation to the New Testament writers, which was followed by (and was to be distinguished from) their divine inspiration. Therefore when Paul introduced the various verses just quoted with the formula, "I delivered to you as of first importance *what I also received*,"[24] and then went on to confess the Crucifixion and the Resurrection of Christ, that is regarded as his way of laying claim to such divine revelation and inspiration for himself in his apostolic authority as the writer of the Epistle. Now Paul was indeed careful to insist that the risen Christ, having appeared to Peter and the other original disciples, had subsequently appeared "last of all, as to one untimely born, . . . also to me."[25] But when he came to specify the content of "what I also received," he did not recite the mysteries communicated in any private revelations and "things that cannot be told, which man may not utter,"[26] as he might have received them when Christ appeared to him, perhaps on the road to Damascus (although the details of that version appear in the Book of Acts

22. 1 Cor. 15:42, 44, 46, 50.
23. 1 Cor. 15:16.
24. 1 Cor. 15:3.
25. 1 Cor. 15:8.
26. 2 Cor. 12:4.

written by Luke, but not in the writings of Paul himself)[27] or in some other ecstatic experience. On the contrary, he made use of formulas that were in fact part of the tradition of the early Church. The disclaimer in his words to the Galatians, "I did not receive it [the gospel] from man, nor was I taught it, but it came through a revelation of Jesus Christ,"[28] would seem to pertain, then, to the event of his conversion directly at the hands of the risen Christ; but evidently it does not apply to the details of the *kerygma* about the risen Christ, which he "did not receive from man," that is, from mere human opinion but did receive from normative church tradition.

Those details are, consequently, of a piece with the details introduced earlier in 1 Corinthians, and with a similar formula, "I received *from the Lord* what I also delivered [*paredoka,* the verb from which comes *paradosis,* the word for 'tradition'] to you,"[29] which was followed by the words of institution of the Eucharist, similar to, though not quite identical with, the words of institution in the three synoptic Gospels.[30] Both the similarity and the difference among the accounts of the Eucharist are important evidence for the way the institution of the Eucharist and the Resurrection had been transmitted in the tradition of the Church, transmitted also to Paul "as to one untimely born." That tradition existed earlier than the Gospels, also earlier than the Epistles of Paul; and the Epistles as well as the Gospels drew from the tradition and stood upon the tradition. It was, then, transmitted also to Paul "from the Lord," but from the Lord through the Church. The verification of the doctrine of the Resurrection of Christ shows, therefore, that it was an essential part of Christian orthodoxy to acknowledge the authority of tradition, whatever answer one may give to the persistently controverted question of tradition's relation to the authority of Scripture. When the authority of tradition was eliminated, even

27. See Acts 9:1-22; 22:4-16; 26:9-18; cf. Gal. 1:11-24.
28. Gal. 1:12.
29. 1 Cor. 11:23.
30. Matt. 26:26-29; Mark 14:22-25; Luke 22:15-20.

when this was done in the name of asserting the sole authority
of Scripture, *sola Scriptura* in the Reformation formula, the
eventual victim proved to be the very authority of Scripture itself. And that, too, represents a basic difference between orthodoxy and fundamentalism.

III

From several of the articles in *The Fundamentals* and from the
recurring emphasis upon it in the polemical literature of the
fundamentalist movement, it seems fair to assert that the doctrine of redemption as vicarious atonement through the death
of Christ was seen to be one of the most important issues at stake
in the controversy. Albrecht Ritschl's monumental three-
volume work of 1882-1883, *The Christian Doctrine of Justification
and Reconciliation,* was probably the outstanding theological formulation of the widespread conviction within liberal Protestantism that the theory of the death of Christ on the cross as an
act of vicarious satisfaction, with its emphasis upon the vindic-
tive justice of God demanding capital punishment through the
crucifixion of Christ, was both an unworthy picture of the God
of biblical revelation and a distortion of the true meaning of the
life, teaching, and work of Jesus Christ: Christ the Example and
the Teacher were seen, by the fundamentalist critics of Ritschl
and of his American followers, as having eclipsed Christ the Redeemer. Because it was taken to be the essential content of the
Christian gospel as the message of salvation and therefore also
the sine qua non of any authentic orthodoxy, the substitutionary theory of the atonement belonged among the "fundamentals" that wanted defending against modern, liberal distortions
of that gospel.

Upon closer historical inspection, however, the status of
the substitutionary theory of the atonement within orthodoxy
proves to have been far more complex. To begin with the most
massive fact about it: while the doctrine of the *person* of Christ

and of his two natures was the subject of legislation by church councils and of creedal formulation over a period of several centuries, there was no similar legislation and formulation concerning the doctrine of the salvific *work* of Christ. The first ecumenical council of the Church, held at Nicea, after specifying in considerable detail how the Son of God was related to the Father within the mystery of the Holy Trinity, went on to speak of his incarnation, passion, resurrection, and ascension. The creed explained *that* this (presumably all of this) had happened "for the sake of us human beings and for the purpose of our salvation [*di' hēmas tous anthrōpous kai dia tēn hēmeteran sōtērian*],"[31] but it did not specify in similar detail *how* this salvation took place. It employed the Greek preposition *dia* with the accusative, which tells "the reason why someth[ing] happens, results, exists" but does not, as would the Greek preposition *anti*, necessarily indicate substitution:[32] "for us" did not have to mean any more than "for our benefit" or at most "on our behalf." Those closest to the Council of Nicea, chronologically and theologically, did not in fact take its formulas to be speaking about "vicarious atonement," but went on employing an abundance of metaphors for the involvement of God the Father, Christ the Son, the human race, and the devil in the redemptive transaction.[33]

What came to be interpreted, in fundamentalism and elsewhere, as the only orthodox doctrine of the atonement was in fact the formulation that was developed by Anselm of Canterbury at the end of the eleventh century, in his speculative masterpiece, *Cur Deus homo*.[34] Reasoning, so he claimed, "as though

31. In Alberigo, p. 5.
32. See Walter Bauer, *A Greek-English Lexicon of the New Testament and Other Early Christian Literature*, 2d ed., trans. William F. Arndt and F. Wilbur Gingrich, rev. F. Wilbur Gingrich and Frederick W. Danker (Chicago: University of Chicago Press, 1979), pp. 181 *(dia)*, 73 *(anti)*; hereafter this work is abbreviated as "Bauer-Arndt-Gingrich."
33. Jaroslav Pelikan, Foreword to Gustaf Aulen, *Christus Victor: An Historical Study of the Three Main Types of the Idea of the Atonement*, trans. A. G. Herbert (New York: Macmillan, 1969), pp. xi-xix.
34. *Christian Tradition*, 3:129-44.

Christ had never existed [*remoto Christo*]," Anselm constructed a rational argument to prove that, even without revelation, both mercy and justice were necessary attributes of God, and that such a God, in dealing with human sin, had to devise a method by which simultaneously mercy could be accomplished and justice could be satisfied. That method was the death of one who was human (to satisfy divine justice) but also divine (to render a satisfaction that was universally applicable). Although Anselm's theory enjoyed widespread acceptance, it was not legislated into church dogma. As a theory about the work of Christ, it could not have developed as it did if orthodoxy had not first, from the fourth to the seventh century, elaborated its dogmas about the person of Christ. It depended, moreover, on a more general theory of the relation between sin, guilt, and satisfaction, which (whether or not one accepts the explanation that it was a theological adaptation of a feudal view of the relation between lord and vassal) had been lodged in the practice and teaching of the Church through the evolution of penance, where "satisfaction" was, after contrition and confession, the third of the steps by which the repentant sinner was reconciled with God. It is noteworthy that when, for example, at the fourteenth session of the Council of Trent,[35] the official language of the Church did make use of the metaphor of "satisfaction" in speaking about redemption through Christ, it was usually as part of an affirmation about this sacramental-penitential meaning of the word.

All of that makes the metaphor of substitutionary atonement as "satisfaction" a particularly fascinating case study in the development of Christian doctrine. Ironically, despite Luther's misgivings about it,[36] the metaphor managed to establish itself within Reformation Protestantism; indeed, one can argue that the atonement as vicarious satisfaction has had a stronger hold on Protestantism than on Roman Catholicism, perhaps even that its hold has been strongest of all precisely where both penitential satisfaction and development of doctrine are re-

35. In Alberigo, pp. 708-9.
36. See *Christian Tradition*, 4:160-65.

pudiated.[37] That irony manifests itself with special poignancy in fundamentalist interpretations of the atonement. Seen in the context of the development of doctrine, the Anselmic theory may be said to have gathered into one a number of ideas and themes that had developed in orthodox Catholic theology and to have made consistent sense of them. Some of these ideas (e.g., the dogma of Christ as the God-man) were retained in fundamentalism; others (e.g., penitential satisfaction) were cast aside. What was chiefly cast aside, however, was the principle of development of doctrine. In the second half of the nineteenth century, at the very time that the beginnings of fundamentalism were stirring in various Protestant denominations, that principle of development, articulated by Schaff, Möhler, and Drey, and above all by John Henry Newman, was beginning to recast the very definition of orthodoxy.[38] Thus the fundamentalist insistence on the doctrine of vicarious satisfaction as a "fundamental" removed that doctrine from its context just at a time when orthodoxy was finding the context of development to be absolutely necessary, not only for the doctrine of the atonement but for every other Christian doctrine.

IV

Usually listed last among the "fundamentals"—last because it deals with eschatology, the doctrine of last things—is "the imminent, physical second coming of Christ."[39] In part, its place on the fundamentalist agenda is due to the premillennial orientation of many of the theologians who participated in the founding of the movement.[40] But to the extent that fundamentalism

---

37. See *Christian Tradition*, 4:359-61; 5:212-13.
38. See *Christian Tradition*, 5:272-81.
39. Sweet, "Fundamentalism," p. 291.
40. This has been well documented in Timothy P. Weber, *Living in the Shadow of the Second Coming: American Premillennialism 1875-1982* (New York: Oxford University Press, 1979).

claimed, also in this respect, to reflect generic Christian orthodoxy, it is not the premillennial aspect of the doctrine that will claim our attention here,[41] but once again the larger orthodox context and the place of the Church's language about the *parousiai* and "comings" of Christ within that large context. For the plural form "coming*s*" is crucial—indeed, one is tempted to say "fundamental"—to the entire question.

From the beginning, Christianity set itself apart from Judaism by a claim about the "coming" of Jesus as the Christ—not, however, the "second coming," but the "first."[42] Thus, the Gospel of Luke describes the beginning of the ministry of Jesus as having taken place in the synagogue at Nazareth when, after reading the familiar prophecy from Isaiah 61, "The Spirit of the Lord is upon me," he declared: "Today this scripture has been fulfilled in your hearing."[43] Because the historical life of Jesus of Nazareth had, however, left so many of the prophecies about the Coming One unfulfilled, Christians early began to distinguish two "comings" and to classify those prophecies as to whether they had already become history in the first coming (so the account of the Suffering Servant in Isa. 53) or were yet to come true in the second coming (so the opening words of Ps. 110 about the future reign of the Messianic King).[44] It seems incontrovertible, moreover, that they regarded this "second coming" as imminent: in 1 Corinthians 15:51, Paul assured his readers that "we shall not all sleep," that is, die, and to the Thessalonians he even wrote that "we who are alive, who are left until the coming of the Lord, shall not precede those who have fallen asleep."[45] Of course, in addition, many passages in the

---

41. See the comments of Milton L. Rudnick, *Fundamentalism and the Missouri Synod: A Historical Study of Their Interaction and Mutual Influence* (St. Louis: Concordia, 1966), pp. 49-51.

42. For an exposition of the distinction between the two comings, see Cyril of Jerusalem, *Catechetical Lectures* XV.1-3.

43. Luke 4:16-30; despite the parallels in Matt. 13:53-58 and Mark 6:1-6, the reference to Isaiah is unique to Luke's account.

44. See *Christian Tradition*, 1:18-19.

45. 1 Thess. 4:15.

Gospels attribute this expectation to Jesus himself. Despite repeated disappointments of that expectation in each successive generation of Christian history, this belief in "the imminent, physical second coming of Christ" has repeatedly (as it is now once again in fundamentalism) been seen as a mark of authentic Christian teaching.

In the development of the orthodox Christian tradition, however, that distinction between "first coming" and "second coming" has been expanded: *parousia* really means "presence,"[46] and therefore the manifestation of a presence (as in the English verb "to put in one's presence"), and thus a "coming." But into the interim between the first *parousia*/presence/coming and the second the orthodox Catholic tradition has interposed another *parousia*/presence/coming, in the liturgy and specifically in the Eucharist. To *this* coming, moreover, it attached many of the words and other symbols that had been initially applied to the "first" and especially to the "second" coming. In the story line of all four Gospels, the entry of Jesus into Jerusalem on Palm Sunday was not only the prelude to the events of Holy Week, but also a kind of dress rehearsal for the second coming; therefore, in each of the versions he was greeted with the eschatological shout, "Blessed is he who comes in the name of the Lord!"[47] That shout was then echoed in the Apocalypse, in the penultimate verse of the New Testament: "He who testifies to these things says, 'Surely I am coming soon.' Amen. Come, Lord Jesus!"[48]

In the development of the early Christian liturgy, as first attested by Caesarius of Arles in the early sixth century, these apocalyptic words of the Palm Sunday narrative, "Blessed is he who comes in the name of the Lord," came to be applied not primarily to the first and historical, nor to the second and eschatological, *parousia*/presence/coming, but explicitly to the sacramental one. The Latin verb *venit* in the Benedictus, "Bene-

---

46. Bauer-Arndt-Gingrich, pp. 629-30.
47. Matt. 21:9; Mark 11:9; Luke 19:38; John 12:13.
48. Rev. 22:20.

dictus qui venit in nomine Domini," could be either in the perfect tense or in the present tense; but the two mean the same,
because "Christ is always the one who is still coming [Christus
ist immer noch der Kommende]."[49] That "coming" was also
called "the real presence," as a *parousia* no less real than the first
or the second; and just as the "memorial" carried out in the Eucharist was not the commemoration of an absent figure from
the past but the celebration of one who was believed to be present here and now in the sacramental reality and within his
Church, so his eucharistic "coming in the name of the Lord"
was no less real than his coming through birth from Mary had
been or his final coming to judgment would be. When Christian orthodoxy, therefore, spoke about a "second coming," it
was referring to the coming, at the end of history, of the very
same one whose "coming" had not merely taken place in the
days of Caesar Augustus, but was taking place daily in the eucharistic liturgy. And if that "second coming" was postponed, as
it was over and over, the disappointment, genuine though it
was, did not in any way alter the daily reality of the sacramental *parousia*/presence/coming promised in his final words: "And
lo, I am with you always, to the close of the age."[50] When, in
fundamentalist theology, this sacramental and liturgical framework of both the memory and the hope was repudiated, not
only the memory but also the hope was basically redefined; and
that redefinition constitutes another far-reaching distinction
between orthodoxy and fundamentalism.

V

Some of the bitterest conflicts in the fundamentalist controversy
were those waged over the doctrine of the Virgin Birth of Christ.

49. J. A. Jungmann, *Missarum Sollemnia: eine genetische Erklärung der
römischen Messe*, 3d ed., 2 vols. (Vienna: Verlag Herder, 1952), 2:170-73.
50. Matt. 28:20.

In part, this was because one of the central issues in the debates over biblical inerrancy was the status of biblical miracles, among which the Virgin Birth held a special place. But the Virgin Birth was more important than, for example, the long day of Joshua, because of its implications for the orthodox Christian doctrine of the person of Christ. That importance was made clear in the classic fundamentalist defense of it, J. Gresham Machen's book *The Virgin Birth of Christ,* which was published shortly after the author's resignation from the faculty of Princeton Theological Seminary over the liberal-fundamentalist schism.[51] In this book Machen argued that the Virgin Birth was a necessary doctrine not only because of "the general question of the authority of the Bible," but also because "the virgin birth belongs logically with the Cross" and Jesus Christ could not have been the Savior if he had been conceived and born in the normal manner.[52] Now although an argument from silence lacks probative force in logic, it should perhaps be noted that if this were indeed so utterly fundamental a teaching, it could be expected to appear in more places of the New Testament than the opening chapters of the Gospels of Matthew and Luke:[53] one cannot imagine John the evangelist or Paul the apostle ignoring the doctrine of the Resurrection of Christ as they both do ignore the doctrine of the Virgin Birth of Christ.

That does not, of course, negate the undeniable consensus of all the orthodox teachers, councils, and creeds of the undivided Church on the doctrine of the Virgin Birth. But in the systems of those orthodox teachers, councils, and creeds of the undivided Church, the doctrine of the Virgin Birth developed as part of a far larger and deeper consensus—devotional, liturgical, iconographic, and thus also doctrinal—about the place of

51. Ned Bernard Stonehouse, *J. Gresham Machen: A Biographical Memoir* (Grand Rapids: Eerdmans, 1954), pp. 462-65.

52. John Gresham Machen, *The Virgin Birth of Christ* (New York: Harper and Brothers, 1930), pp. 382, 391.

53. See Krister Stendahl, "Quis et unde? An Analysis of Mt. 1–2," in Walther Eltester, ed., *Judentum Urchristentum Kirche: Festschrift für Joachim Jeremias* (Berlin: A. Töpelmann, 1960), pp. 94-105.

Mary, as Virgin and *Theotokos*, in the history of salvation. The primary venue of that development, moreover, was the Christian East.[54] It was in the East that devotion to her had taken hold in the orthodoxy of the earliest Christian centuries; it was at the Council of Ephesus in 431 that the title of *Theotokos* was made official and orthodox; and it was in Byzantium during the eighth century that the legitimacy of icons not only of Christ but of his Mother was established by orthodox teachers and then by the action of the Second Council of Nicea in 787. It is probably the case that on no other orthodox doctrine is the Eastern provenance (expressed in the very usage of "Orthodoxy" and *Pravoslavie* to mean "*Eastern* Orthodoxy") as decisive as it is on Mariology, and, conversely, that a definition of orthodoxy which loses sight of that provenance ends up with a truncated doctrine of Mary, including a truncated doctrine of the Virgin Birth.

That had already made itself evident in Western definitions of Marian orthodoxy quite apart from the modernist-fundamentalist controversy within American Protestantism. If one considers only officially promulgated dogmas of the Church, rather than private *theologoumena* of individual theologians, there have been only three such dogmas during the history of the modern Roman Catholic Church in its separation from the East: the infallibility of the Pope, as defined by the First Vatican Council in 1869/1870;[55] the Immaculate Conception of Mary, as defined by Pope Pius IX in the bull *Ineffabilis Deus* of 8 December 1854;[56] and the Assumption of Mary, as defined by Pope Pius XII in the apostolic constitution *Munificentissimus Deus* of 1 November 1950.[57] Two of the three, then, dealt with the doctrine of Mary. In part this emphasis on the Virgin Mary was directed against the Protestant break with the tradition of Marian doctrine and devotion, going back to the Reformation

54. See Jaroslav Pelikan, *Development of Christian Doctrine: Some Historical Prolegomena* (New Haven: Yale University Press, 1969), pp. 95-119: "Athanasius on Mary."

55. In Alberigo, pp. 815-16.

56. In Denzinger, §§ 2800-2804.

57. In Denzinger, §§ 3900-3904.

itself. But it was also symptomatic of the break between the Western Church, specifically the Roman Catholic Church, and the Orthodox East, out of which so much of that tradition of Marian doctrine and devotion had come to the West in the first place. Eastern Orthodoxy has objected to these Western dogmas about Mary partly on procedural grounds—because no one patriarchate of the Church, not even Rome, had the right to legislate on matters of doctrine binding upon the entire Church—and partly on substantive grounds as well.[58] Therefore, it is ironic that despite its vigorous polemic against Roman Catholicism and specifically against Roman Catholic Mariology, to which it regularly applied the epithet "Mariolatry," fundamentalism was in fact perpetuating a Roman Catholic pattern in its own doctrine of Mary when, in taking it upon itself to define what was "orthodox" and "fundamental" teaching on this doctrine, it did so in isolation from the Orthodox East.

Significantly, all four of the other components of the distinction between orthodoxy and fundamentalism also play a major role here in the doctrine of Mary: an exegesis that preserved a doctrine of inerrancy by stressing the *sensus plenior* of Scripture; an affirmation of the centrality of tradition to the preservation of orthodox doctrine; the acceptance of the ongoing development of doctrine in the Church as both a reality and a norm; and the principle that the *lex orandi* of the Liturgy should define the *lex credendi* of the Creed. Each of these took on an especially important function in Orthodoxy (note the capital *O*) as that has evolved in the Syriac, Greek, and Slavic branches of the Church. And any interpretation of orthodoxy (even with a lower-case *o*) that was not (if you will pardon the pun) oriented to these elements of the tradition would inevitably have difficulty either vindicating its own orthodoxy or preserving as "fundamental" those teachings that had taken their rise within that Oriental tradition and that pointed beyond themselves to that tradition.

58. See *Christian Tradition*, 5:208-9.

2. Defining American Fundamentalism

George M. Marsden

Since fundamentalism is primarily an American Protestant phenomenon, our definition of it should be derived from the experiences of self-described fundamentalists from that tradition. In this paper we shall consider such fundamentalists' definitions of themselves and also the features of the American experience that have defined fundamentalism in the sense of shaping it.[1]

My own offhand definition of a fundamentalist is "an evangelical who is angry about something." I have been gratified to find that Jerry Falwell now sometimes uses this same definition of fundamentalism, prefacing it with "some have said. . . ."

My more careful statement of this definition with regard to classic fundamentalism is that a fundamentalist is an evangelical Protestant who is militantly opposed to modern liberal theologies and to some aspects of secularism in modern culture. This definition refers to fundamentalism in its classic historical

1. Some of the paragraphs in this chapter are taken from my essay "Fundamentalism and American Evangelicalism," in *The Variety of American Evangelicalism*, ed. Donald W. Dayton and Robert K. Johnston (Chattanooga: University of Tennessee Press, forthcoming). I am grateful to the University of Tennessee Press for permission to republish these portions of my essay.

American sense, the Protestant evangelical movement that was so named in 1920. It also applies to those Protestants who call themselves fundamentalists today.

Let me unpack this definition briefly. A fundamentalist must be an evangelical. Essential to being an evangelical, in the dominant American sense, are at least three points, derived largely from the Reformation. First, one must be a "Bible believer," having a high view of the Bible as the highest authority on what God says. Second, one must believe that eternal salvation comes only through the atoning work of Jesus Christ for our sins. And third, the kindest thing one person can do for another is to tell him or her of this gospel promise of salvation. In addition, fundamentalists must be militant. They must not only believe these evangelical teachings, but they must be willing to fight for them against modernist theologies, secular humanism, and the like.

With this systematic definition before us, let us look at how fundamentalists define themselves. By so doing, we can elaborate on some of these themes.

Fundamentalist Self-Definitions

The one fundamentalist history of fundamentalism is George W. Dollar's *A History of Fundamentalism in America* published by Bob Jones University Press in 1973. Here is Dollar's definition of fundamentalism: "Historic fundamentalism is the literal exposition of all the affirmations and attitudes of the Bible and the militant exposure of all non-Biblical affirmations and attitudes."[2] In Dollar's definition, as in my own, militancy is one of the leading features that distinguishes fundamentalism from other forms of revivalist evangelicalism. A fundamentalist is ready to stand up and fight for the faith. Militancy is, of course, not a sufficient condi-

---

2. George W. Dollar, *A History of Fundamentalism in America* (Greenville: Bob Jones University Press, 1973), p. XV.

tion for distinguishing fundamentalists from other Christians; but it is a necessary condition. Central to being a fundamentalist is perceiving oneself to be in the midst of religious war. Fundamentalists are particularly fond of the metaphors of warfare. The universe is divided between the forces of light and darkness. Spiritually enlightened Christians can tell who the enemy is. In such war, there can be no compromise.

As Dollar's definition suggests, fundamentalists universally see the war as primarily a war over the Bible. To this extent they would agree with outside observers who claim that fundamentalism is, in its distinctiveness, a modern movement. To a large extent, fundamentalism is a militant reaction to modern higher criticism of the Bible and to the displacement of the Bible as a central culture-forming force in American life.[3] According to fundamentalists, this war was started by the modernists and secularists who attacked the Bible. As Dollar writes, "It was more deadly than military warfare, for it swept away the spiritual foundations of our churches, our nation, and our heritage."[4]

For fundamentalists, the battle for the Bible almost always has two fronts. They are fighting against modern interpretations of the Bible that they see as destroying most American denominations. At the same time, they are fighting to save American civilization, which they see as founded on the Bible.

Dollar's definition suggests in addition that the battle for the Bible is over a particular type of interpretation of the Bible, what Dollar describes as "the literal exposition of all the affirmations and attitudes of the Bible." Fundamentalists equate this literal interpretation of the Bible with belief in the Bible itself. They see people who claim to believe the Bible but who interpret it in other ways to be actually denying the truth of the Bible and putting their own standards of interpretation above the Bible.

The way of getting at this point that has become virtually

---

3. On the cultural role of the Bible and fundamentalist reactions see *The Bible in America*, ed. Nathan O. Hatch and Mark A. Noll (New York: Oxford University Press, 1982).

4. Dollar, *History of Fundamentalism*, p. 1.

universal for fundamentalists is to assert that the Bible is "inerrant." For fundamentalists, this claim means that the Bible is not only an infallible authority in matters of faith and practice, but it is also accurate in all its historical and scientific assertions. Of course, fundamentalists do not hold that everything in the Bible is to be interpreted literally (the mountains do not literally clap their hands). Rather "literal where possible" is their interpretative rule. Whatever in the Bible can reasonably be given a literal reference should be interpreted as literal and accurate.

Literal interpretations of the Bible for fundamentalists include defense of other doctrines fundamental to their tradition, such as the miracles or the bodily resurrection of Christ. The name of the movement is, in fact, derived from its defense of such fundamentals. John R. Rice, a revered fundamentalist and mentor to Jerry Falwell, wrote in a typical statement: "It is generally understood that the fundamentals of the Christian faith include the inspiration and thus the divine authority of the Bible; the deity, virgin birth, blood atonement, bodily resurrection, personal second coming of Christ; the fallen, lost condition of all mankind; salvation by repentance and faith, grace without works; eternal doom in Hell of the unconverted and eternal blessedness of the saved in Heaven."[5]

In addition to militancy in defense of the Bible and fundamental doctrines, which are the most distinctive traits setting off fundamentalism from similar movements, are some other traits that fundamentalists usually share with similar movements. Fundamentalists generally demand strict behavioral standards consistent with those of the American revivalist tradition. These involve avoidance of the barroom vices, such as smoking, drinking, dancing, card playing, immodest dress, and any sort of sexual license. These behavioral standards help set them off as a distinctive people, even though they may fully participate in other aspects of modern life, such as business or comfortable suburban living.

Fundamentalists, like other of the more sectarian evangel-

5. John R. Rice, *I Am A Fundamentalist* (Murfreesboro: Sword of the Lord Publishers, 1975), p. 9.

icals, also define themselves as aggressive evangelists. They must be "soul winners," or at least support aggressive soul winning.[6] Often this is their overriding concern.

A Broad or Narrow Definition?

Now, however, we come to the major interpretative problem in defining American fundamentalism. This is the problem of a broad or a narrow definition. What we have said so far provides a broad definition of fundamentalism, but it does not entirely distinguish fundamentalists from some similar evangelical sub-movements of the past century. Particularly it does not distinguish adequately between those subgroups who call themselves fundamentalists (whom we might call "card-carrying fundamentalists") and those who may be militant about the above issues but who do not call themselves fundamentalists.

Fundamentalist in the broad sense we have used so far can refer to anyone who takes a militant stance for the defense of a literally interpreted Bible, fundamental doctrines, and soul saving. For instance, many Holiness and Pentecostal groups and other revivalists, some white and some black, share these traits, and hence might reasonably be called fundamentalist in a broad sense.

The nature of this terminological problem becomes clearer if we look at fundamentalism in the American South. Fundamentalism as a self-conscious, more or less organized coalition of militants developed first in the North, and the word "fundamentalism" was invented in 1920 to refer to militant conservatives in the Northern Baptist Convention. Soon the term spread to similar groups fighting modernism. In the South, however, fundamentalism as an organized movement was largely redundant. The vast majority of southern evangelicals already were committed to soul saving and were firm Bible believ-

6. Ibid., p. 10.

ers, assuming literal interpretations. Moreover, many white southerners were militant in defense of their biblical faith, which since the Civil War they had contrasted with northern liberal Protestantism. Blacks remained firm Bible believers, but, even more than southern whites, they were kept isolated from both liberalism and wider cultural influences, and hence from most antiliberal campaigns.

In any case, with traditional evangelical attitudes so dominant in southern culture, there was little reason to organize as fundamentalists. Southern affinities to organized fundamentalism soon became apparent in the 1920s, however, especially in the antievolution crusades. Conservative white southerners had already taken stands against evolution, and they quickly adopted the national antievolution cause and promoted legislation banning the teaching of biological evolution in public schools. Southern majorities agreed that evolution conflicted with the Bible, literally interpreted. They viewed the preservation of the literally interpreted Bible in the public schools as essential to saving American civilization. Vast numbers of southerners could in this sense properly be designated as fundamentalists.

To return to the general point of broad and narrow definitions, fundamentalism thus can be traced on two tracks, one a broad militancy for soul-saving Bible-believing evangelicalism, and the other a more explicitly organized coalition of such militants, who call themselves fundamentalists and whom we are calling card-carrying fundamentalists.

A recent example of the problem of discriminating between card-carrying fundamentalists and similar groups is Jerry Falwell's attempt to take over the PTL ministry in 1987. One of the issues that made the attempt remarkable and the combination unlikely was that Falwell was a self-styled fundamentalist, while the PTL ministry was Pentecostal or charismatic. Part of the self-definition of most card-carrying fundamentalists is opposition to speaking in tongues and other Pentecostal gifts, which they consider heresy. Thus Falwell fundamentalists were as uneasy as the rest of us about Pat Robertson's claims to be able to control the weather or to receive direct messages from God.

Fundamentalists as Insiders or Outsiders

Keeping in mind the problem of the broad and narrow definition of fundamentalism, we can consider some of the other traits of the movement, especially as they have been defined by the American cultural and religious experience.

In mid-nineteenth-century America, revivalist evangelicalism was the culturally dominant religion in America. Essential for understanding fundamentalism is to see it as a reaction among some evangelicals to the decline of that cultural dominance. Between roughly 1880 and 1930, some of the most respectable American beliefs became objects of derision.

The collective fundamentalist experience was thus in some respects like the immigrant experience. Beliefs and traditions that had been sources of pride and respect for an older generation now made one an outsider. As in every such group, while some try to assimilate with the new culture, others raise walls of defense and fight against the changes—especially against their religion being displaced as a central culture-shaping force.

This experience of being displaced is very important for understanding fundamentalist views of politics. In the collective experience of the white northern European ethnic grouping that makes up most of fundamentalism, these people have been both insiders and outsiders in America. A hundred years ago, they were insiders; for the past half century and more they have been ridiculed outsiders.

When it comes to their view of the nation, however, they alternate between taking an outsider and an insider stance. Simply put, do they see the United States as more like Babylon or, like the Puritans, as a New Israel? More often than not, fundamentalists have taken an outsider stance. Seeing the United States as Babylon, they have despaired of political solutions, condemned the liberal social gospel, and emphasized saving souls. As Dwight L. Moody, the evangelist of the late nineteenth century and a progenitor of the movement, said, "I look on this world as a wrecked vessel. God has given me a life-boat and said to me, 'Moody, save all you can.'"[7]

One would wonder, then, if the United States is a sinking ship, why fundamentalists would get interested in politics. As they sometimes say, you do not fix up the staterooms of the Titanic after it has hit the iceberg. The answer, I think, is an inconsistency in the tradition that derives from their dual heritage of being both insiders and outsiders. The insider heritage still persists and can be revived if this group sees itself as getting closer to power. That is just what happened in the 1970s. *Newsweek* proclaimed 1976 the "Year of the Evangelical." Fundamentalists thought they could mobilize many of those evangelicals for their kind of politics. Soon they had a political agenda that was a revival of the old Puritan agenda to build a New Israel, based on God's law.

Dispensational Premillennialism

Such political fundamentalism, however, conflicts with the distinctive doctrine that has had most to do with shaping fundamentalism as a distinct movement in the narrow sense. This is the doctrine of dispensational premillennialism.

This kind of premillennialism became popular among American revivalists just during the era, after 1870, when revivalism was receding as a culture-shaping force. Dispensationalism teaches that world history is divided into seven dispensations. In each the human race fails a test from God and the era ends with dramatic divine intervention and judgment. The first

---

7. Dwight L. Moody, *New Sermons, Addresses, and Prayers* (New York: Henry S. Goodspeed, 1877), p. 535, quoted in James F. Findlay, Jr., *Dwight L. Moody: American Evangelist, 1837-1899* (Chicago: University of Chicago Press, 1989), p. 253.

was that of Adam and Eve. The second ended with the flood. The third ended with the tower of Babel. And so forth. We are in the sixth, the church age. It also is ending in failure as the mainline churches become apostate and civilization declines. The only hope, therefore, is not in current politics but dramatic divine intervention. The onset of the last age will be associated with the return of Jesus to set up a millennial kingdom to reign for a literal thousand years in Jerusalem.

In the meantime, our dispensation will end with destruction. Believers, however, will be exempted from this destruction by the secret rapture, when they will mysteriously be taken up to heaven while the rest of the earth goes through seven years of warfare and tribulation. The nation of Israel is central to the events of the last days (which is why fundamentalists strongly support Israel). During the last seven years, the Jews will be converted to Christianity. There will also be dramatic battles among world powers. Jesus will return again with the saints and defeat the forces of Antichrist at Armageddon and set up his millennial kingdom.

An essential part of this scenario is that biblical prophecies concerning Israel will be literally fulfilled. Unlike some other Christians, fundamentalists do not allow that the Israel of the prophecies can be interpreted figuratively (e.g., as the Church). So it is inconsistent with the fundamentalist hermeneutic to talk of the United States in the old Puritan fashion, as though it were a New Israel—God's chosen nation for the modern era.

Dispensationalist premillennialism is a view of history that would clearly have appeal to outsiders. Christians are not going to control history; rather, they will simply wait for God to act. The modern world is moving toward an inevitable doom.

Other Outsider Movements

Though it complicates the picture somewhat, I must add that dispensationalism was not the only revivalist innovation of the late nineteenth century that appealed to revivalist evangelicals who had a sense of being displaced culturally. The nineteenth-century Holiness movement responded to modernity by emphasizing a dramatic second blessing that would lead to a life of personal holiness. The best known of the Holiness denominations today is the Salvation Army, but there are many less conspicuous groups.

Of wider importance today is the early twentieth-century Pentecostal movement. This movement added to holiness teaching an emphasis on dramatic personal experience which marked the believers' separation from the world.

Both these movements emphasized separation from the so-called apostate major denominations and established their own denominations. Though they were similar to fundamentalists and took on some fundamentalist traits, they have remained distinct movements.

Organized Fundamentalism

Dispensationalism provided one important base for organized fundamentalism. Many of the early dispensationalists were originally in major Protestant denominations and were among the most militant opponents of modernist theologies which challenged their literal interpretations of the Bible.

In 1919, a dispensationalist Northern Baptist preacher in Minneapolis, William B. Riley, founded the World's Christian Fundamentals Association. The next year, Curtis Lee Laws, a religious journal editor and leading antimodernist in the Northern Baptist Convention, coined the word "fundamentalist" for his party. Laws was not a dispensationalist, and so fundamentalism was originally a fairly broad coalition of religious conservatives, especially in the Northern Baptist Convention and the (northern) Presbyterian Church in the U.S.A. The antievolution movement, led by William Jennings Bryan, another nondispensationalist, gave the coalition a broader political dimension.

Fundamentalism flourished between 1920 and 1925,

gained some antievolution legislation, and had some hopes of controlling the large Northern Baptist and Presbyterian denominations. During this era fundamentalism included a strong insider dimension, operating in some of the most respected Protestant denominations and wielding some political power. After 1925, however, these broader efforts to control the churches and the nation foundered.

The Division between Evangelicals and Fundamentalists

By the 1930s, a major tension within the fundamentalist camp was becoming apparent. On the one hand, many fundamentalists still had insider aspirations. Typically, such people thought that even though they were a minority, they should simply continue to champion their cause within the major denominations, building individual fundamentalist congregations that could resist liberal influences of denominational leadership.

On the other hand, another group of fundamentalists increasingly concluded that the submovement should form its own separate institutions, which could be freed from corrupting entanglements with the major denominations. Dispensationalists were especially inclined in this separatist direction since one of the dispensationalist teachings was that the major churches of this age would become apostate. Many, although not all, dispensationalists carried this teaching to the conclusion that Christians must separate themselves from any such apostasy. Often, such separatism led to the formation of independent local congregations, almost always baptistic, that might be loosely associated in fundamentalist associations or sometimes connected in small denominations.

Through the 1940s, however, separatism was still not necessarily a test of fundamentalist faith. For instance, William B. Riley did not separate from the Northern Baptist Convention until 1947, the year of his death. In the meantime, fundamentalism, whether of the separatist or nonseparatist variety, was growing through evangelistic agencies independent of any denominational affiliation (and thus not having to face the separatist question, since in practice they were largely independent anyway). During World War II, fundamentalists promoted successful revivalism, marked especially by the organization in 1945 of Youth for Christ. Billy Graham got his start as the first full-time evangelist for Youth for Christ and as Riley's handpicked successor to head his schools in Minneapolis.[8] Cardcarrying fundamentalism was thus growing through networks of interrelated agencies. Often Bible institutes, of which Moody Bible Institute in Chicago was the prototype, served virtually as headquarters for various fundamentalist subgroups.[9] The quip of Daniel Stevick that fundamentalism may be defined as "all those churches or persons in communion with Moody Bible Institute," while overstated, suggests a method of identification that worked fairly well during the 1940s and 1950s.[10]

In this context, the explicitly organized parts of fundamentalism began a process that led eventually to a split into two parts, evangelicals (originally neo-evangelicals) and strict separatist fundamentalists. An early sign of the impending crisis was the formation of two competing organizations in the early 1940s. The most important of these was the National Association of Evangelicals (NAE), founded in 1942. Some months earlier, in 1941, Carl McIntire established the smaller American

---

8. See Joel A. Carpenter, "From Fundamentalism to the New Evangelical Coalition," in *Evangelicalism and Modern America,* ed. George M. Marsden (Grand Rapids: William B. Eerdmans, 1984), pp. 3-16; idem, "Youth for Christ and the New Evangelicals' Place in the Life of the Nation," in *American Recoveries: Religion in the Life of the Nation,* ed. Rowland A. Sherrill (Urbana: University of Illinois Press, 1988).

9. See William Vance Trollinger, Jr., "One Response to Modernity: Northwestern Bible School and the Fundamentalist Empire of William Bell Riley" (Ph.D. diss., University of Wisconsin, 1984). See also Virginia Lieson Brereton, "Protestant Fundamentalist Bible Schools, 1882-1940" (Ph.D. diss., Columbia University, 1981).

10. Daniel B. Stevick, *Beyond Fundamentalism* (Richmond: John Knox Press, 1964), p. 45. My thanks to Joel A. Carpenter for suggesting the importance of this point.

Council of Christian Churches. The major difference was that, on the one hand, McIntire's organization demanded that member denominations be strictly separatist, having no connection with the Federal Council of Churches. On the other hand, the NAE accepted individual members who were in denominations associated with the Federal Council.

By the end of the 1950s, a major realignment brought a redefinition of fundamentalism. Essentially a breakup occurred within the coalition of card-carrying fundamentalists. The central event in this realignment was Billy Graham's New York crusade in 1957.[11] Rather than conduct his crusade with the sponsorship only of other fundamentalists, Graham accepted the sponsorship of the City Council of Churches. That relation meant that his converts would be guided to some liberal churches and denominations. This was the last straw for many stricter fundamentalists.

So the two parties split. Graham and the evangelicals, as they came to be called, tried to moderate the fundamentalist tradition and to bring it closer to the mainstream of the Christian tradition and of American culture. Since 1957, the simplest definition of an evangelical is someone who agrees with Billy Graham.

Fundamentalism Today

Card-carrying fundamentalists, who kept the name fundamentalist and who do not like Billy Graham, are a much smaller group. They are usually strict sectarians who have made separation from mainline denominations a test of the faith. They are also almost invariably dispensationalists (though not all dispensationalists are fundamentalists). They also insist on separation from Pentecostal and charismatic groups. Thus, those who call themselves fundamentalists belong to a rather precise movement.

11. See Butler Fraley Porter, Jr., "Billy Graham and the End of the Evangelical Unity" (Ph.D. diss., University of Florida, 1976).

Such card-carrying fundamentalists are separatists and dispensationalists. They are almost all Baptists, often belonging to independent Bible churches.

The one major exception is the fundamentalist party which, under the banner of the inerrancy of Scripture, gained a majority voice in the Southern Baptist Convention during the 1970s and 1980s.[12] These Southern Baptist fundamentalists are more like those of the first stage of the northern movement through the 1940s, when fundamentalism most often referred to militantly biblicist denominational conservatives who did not demand strict separation.

The stricter separatist fundamentalists have long since separated from the Southern Baptist Convention. They have also split among themselves over how separatist one must be. The strictest groups are "second-degree separatists." They not only will not associate in religious activities with theological liberals—they also will not associate with conservative evangelicals who associate religiously with liberals.

They are also split over degrees of political involvement. Many of the stricter fundamentalists have taught that Christians should stay away from political involvements. Jerry Falwell used to hold this view. Since Falwell and others have departed from that view in the last decade, they have been roundly condemned by the strictest fundamentalists. Bob Jones III, of Bob Jones University, calls Falwell a "pseudo neo-fundamentalist." George W. Dollar calls Falwell "the leading TV bishop of Compromise, Inc."[13]

The Falwell type of fundamentalist, however, seems to have become today's dominant type, tempering their separatism with a new political activism. Falwell resolves the tension between separatism and his political involvements by making a sharp distinc-

12. For an exposition of the fundamentalist or conservative viewpoint, see James Carl Hefley, *The Truth in Crisis: The Controversy in the Southern Baptist Convention* (Dallas: Criterion Publications, 1986). Cf. David O. Beale, *S.B.C.: House of Sand?* (Greenville, SC: Unusual Publications, 1985).

13. See *The Fundamentalist Phenomenon: The Resurgence of Conservative Christianity*, ed. Jerry Falwell with Ed Dobson and Ed Hindson (Garden City, NY: Doubleday, 1981), p. 160.

tion between his ecclesiastical and political affiliations. Ecclesiastically, he is a separatist Baptist. Politically, The Moral Majority was a coalition that included people from groups which fundamentalists normally condemn, such as Catholics and Mormons.

Insiders and Outsiders Again

The tension between separatism and political involvement once again reflects the tension that always has been present in the fundamentalist movement. Are they insiders trying to control the culture, or outsiders trying to separate from it? This tension was apparent in the original fundamentalist coalition of the 1920s, which combined dispensationalist teachings with campaigns such as William Jennings Bryan's to preserve evangelical control over American culture. Eventually this tension led to the split between evangelical and separatist fundamentalists.

For today's fundamentalists (the heirs to the separatist wing), the question is, Which focus will define their movement: theological traditions or practical politics?

As a separatist Baptist, Falwell is in a tradition that has strongly favored separation of church and state. Moreover, he is also a dispensationalist. He argues, for instance, that there cannot be a nuclear holocaust for at least 1,007 years because the events of the tribulation (which lasts 7 years) and the thousand-year reign of Jesus must well precede the destruction of the earth.[14]

Nonetheless, Falwell and political fundamentalists do not act as though they believe the dispensational teachings that all modern nations are hopelessly corrupt. Rather, they give unswerving support to American patriotism, and act as though they are on the verge of successfully setting the moral agenda for the nation. In so doing, they are defining themselves as in-

14. From a Jerry Falwell promotional tape, ca. 1983.

siders and appropriating the old Puritan-Republican agenda of setting a biblically based moral standard for the nation.

The essential tension in the movement, between its insider and outsiders stances, has already led to schism and is likely to do so again. This persistent tension should be kept in mind as qualifying the fundamentalist agenda. Fundamentalists are most likely not going to withdraw from American society and become simply a pietist sect. But they are essentially sectarian enough that neither are they likely to take over American society.

American and Other Fundamentalisms

The ambivalence in relation to American culture is one of the features that most distinguishes American Protestant fundamentalism from its alleged counterparts in other cultures.

At least one major side of the American Protestant fundamentalist mentality views the movement as preserving the best of the heritage of one of the most modern of nations. American Protestant fundamentalists are thus far more committed to many of the aspects of modernity than are religious militants who are trying to preserve traditional cultures. American Protestant fundamentalists are not only more or less traditional Protestants, they are also Americans. So they are committed to important dimensions of the modern eighteenth- and nineteenth-century American outlook, including professedly high regard for the scientific method,[15] for modern nationalism, and for separation of church and state. Although some of their theocratic rhetoric may be at odds with these traditions, their philosophy is, nonetheless, enough a product of the American heritage to be a long way from most other militant religious traditionalists.

---

15. See George M. Marsden, *Fundamentalism and American Culture: The Shaping of Twentieth-Century Evangelicalism, 1870-1925* (New York: Oxford University Press, 1980), for elaboration of this theme.

3. Defining American Fundamentalism: A Response

Clark H. Pinnock

Introduction

In response to George Marsden's interesting and informative paper defining fundamentalism "from within," my task is to reflect on some of his ideas and to add to the picture of fundamentalism we are painting. It is a privilege for me to do this, both because Marsden himself is a leading expert on the subject as well as a friend, and because I have as much of an appreciation for the contribution of fundamentalism to church and society as he does.[1] Out of my own experience and study, I will join Marsden in attempting to create genuine understanding of the nature of Protestant fundamentalism.

---

1. Marsden has succeeded Ernest R. Sandeen as the leading authority. See Sandeen's classic work, *The Roots of Fundamentalism: British and American Millenarianism, 1800-1930* (Chicago: University of Chicago Press, 1970). Now see George M. Marsden, *Fundamentalism and American Culture: The Shaping of Twentieth-Century Evangelicalism, 1870-1925* (New York: Oxford University Press, 1980); idem, *Reforming Fundamentalism: Fuller Seminary and the New Evangelicalism* (Grand Rapids: Eerdmans, 1987).

The Commentators

I think I should say something at the outset about George Marsden and myself as commentators on fundamentalism. Specifically, how can we possibly claim to be offering a view of fundamentalism "from within" when neither of us is actually a fundamentalist in a meaningful sense? Marsden's credentials include his reputation as a leading historian of fundamentalism who has immersed himself in the sources and can, as it were, let the fundamentalists speak for themselves. In addition, given his own religious background as a conservative Protestant, he has an element of insider status.[2]

How about myself? How can I write "from within?" Though I am not a historian of fundamentalism, I can claim a certain insider status as well. I began my spiritual pilgrimage as a fundamentalist. Converted in the early 1950s in the context of Protestant fundamentalism, I received instruction from the Peoples Church in Toronto, a large, independent, fundamental church. I enjoyed the ministry of Youth for Christ, which in those days had a fundamentalist profile. I sent away for literature from the American Prophetic League; I listened on the radio to Perry F. Rockwood, a fundamentalist pastor from Truro, Nova Scotia, to the early Billy Graham, and to dispensationalist Bible teacher Donald Grey Barnhouse of Philadelphia. I imbibed the theology of old Princeton early on, and would later be invited to deliver a commencement address at Dallas Theological Seminary, as well as to give lectures at Tennessee Temple in Chattanooga. I was part of the fundamentalist party in the Southern Baptist Convention in the 1960s, and a co-worker and confidant of

---

2. Nancy T. Ammerman is also an evangelical, and she mentions the fact that she was able to gain access to the fundamentalist community and way of thinking partly because they felt she understood what made them tick. Thus she was given participant status. See her *Bible Believers: Fundamentalists in the Modern World* (New Brunswick, NJ: Rutgers University Press, 1987), pp. 10-11.

Francis A. Schaeffer of the L'Abri Fellowship. Finally, I still think biblical inerrancy is important.

I relate this background simply to indicate that I have a feeling for the subject of fundamentalism and appreciate the positive contribution of fundamentalism both to myself and to the Church and society. In particular, I appreciate fundamentalism for its tenacious faith, for its courage to stand up for historic Christian beliefs when they have come under attack, and for taking a number of important moral stands in contemporary North American society. In short, I think I can present fundamentalism in an accurate and sympathetic light.

Verbal Abuse

Defining fundamentalism is a problem, for it is used in several different ways. It belongs historically to the movement which began early in the twentieth century among evangelical Protestants. But lately the media have adopted it to describe any orthodox religion in a struggle with secular modernity (Sikh, Muslim, Jewish, etc.). Let me begin with a very problematic use of the term "fundamentalism"—verbal abuse.

The term today is often one of opprobrium and abuse. It was not so in 1909 when the "fundamentals" referred to historic Christian convictions and when the first "fundamentalists" defended themselves with balance and scholarly integrity. But a lot of water has gone under the bridge since then, and the word, as it is generally used by nonfundamentalists nowadays, is more often than not a word of contempt, a theological swearword and not a precise category. James Barr, who has written an important book on what he calls *Fundamentalism*, first recognizes the problem and then adds to it: "Fundamentalism is a bad word: the people to whom it is applied do not like to be so called. It is often felt to be a hostile and opprobrious term, suggesting narrowness, bigotry, obscurantism and sectarianism.

The people whom others call fundamentalists would generally wish to be known by another term altogether."[3]

Barr is wrong when he says that people do not like to be called fundamentalists—in fact, real fundamentalists do like the label as well as the term. In this case, the people Barr is sharply and vehemently criticizing, the British evangelicals, do not like the term being applied to them because they are not, in fact, fundamentalists. They protest that Barr is unfair when he insists on applying that label to them. So Barr both understands and illustrates the problem very well. Fundamentalism is a verbal weapon one can use against one's enemies. He knows this full well and uses it skillfully to castigate nonfundamentalist evangelicals. Why would he do that? One can only guess, but it might have something to do with the fact that he was once an evangelical himself, when he was president of the Inter-Varsity Fellowship group in Edinburgh during his student days.

Granted, fundamentalists have done and said things which justify a measure of legitimate disapproval. There is an organization called "Fundamentalists Anonymous" to help people get over bad experiences in the movement. Many like Barr harbor hard feelings against the movement, often justifiably. But we must not let such experiences interfere with our effort to understand fundamentalism. No human group is without fault.[4]

I think Richard Quebedeaux is right: "For too long it has been the fault of mainstream ecumenical liberalism to lump together with pejorative intent all theological conservatives into the worn fundamentalist category."[5] It is high time to stop the

---

3. James Barr, *Fundamentalism* (London: SCM Press; Philadelphia: Westminster Press, 1977), p. 2.

4. Orthodox rabbis in Toronto at the moment (November 1988) are denying access to the ritual bath for Conservative and Reform rabbis to perform rites of conversion to Judaism—a Canadian version of the dispute in Israel to define who a Jew is. It is estimated that it will affect about 100 converts a year. See *Globe and Mail,* 9 November 1988.

5. Richard Quebedeaux, *The Young Evangelicals: Revolution in Orthodoxy* (San Francisco: Harper & Row, 1974), p. 19.

practice of using the label "fundamentalist" as a word to describe
believers more orthodox than oneself when one is displeased
with them. The strictly orthodox Jews in Israel are called fundamentalists by more liberal Jews. The Shiite Muslims of Iran
are called fundamentalists by more liberal fellow religionists.
Karl Barth has even been called a fundamentalist by those who
think he respects the Bible too much. It is a common experience
(certainly familiar to me) to be called a fundamentalist by those
to one's theological left.

Surely the issue of justice is involved here? Why should
millions of ordinary people who love their God be pilloried and
ridiculed? Fundamentalists must be one of the few remaining
minorities in our otherwise permissive society which one can
safely ridicule without fear of rebuke. (Perhaps they ought to
form an antidefamation league.) They deserve fairer treatment
from their critics. I hope one outcome of this volume will be a
determination not to abuse other people by an insensitive use
of this verbal weapon.[6]

Two Kinds of Fundamentalism

In my opinion, fundamentalism is orthodoxy in a desperate
struggle with secular modernity. It is a unique kind of orthodoxy, shaped by this conflict which it feels so keenly. Marsden has made several important distinctions in his definition of
Protestant fundamentalism—I would like to make one of my
own in order to provide an additional perspective.

Since World War II, two major conservative Protestant
movements have come to the fore in North America: fundamentalism and evangelicalism. In many respects they are very similar and must seem especially so to the outsider. They agree on

6. Fundamentalists themselves speak of the abuse factor in *The Fundamentalist Phenomenon*, ed. Jerry Falwell with Ed Dobson and Ed Hinson (Garden
City, NY: Doubleday, 1981), pp. 2-4.

the basic essentials of the Protestant faith and debate much the same issues among themselves. One can discern two subdivisions within each of these two movements: within fundamentalism there is one strict and one more open party, and within evangelicalism there is an establishment and a progressive alignment. Since our subject here is fundamentalism, let us look more closely at the two factions it comprises.

Strict Fundamentalism

On the one hand, there is a strict and separatist strain of fundamentalism which even fundamentalists like Jerry Falwell call hyperfundamentalism.[7] Its characteristics include complete separation from religious liberalism, as well as belief in the inspiration of the Bible by divine dictation, without the usual disclaimers, and frequently the view that the King James Version of the Bible is the inerrant text of Scripture. Strict fundamentalists hold to a strongly dispensational theology which implies the disintegration of society and therefore the uselessness of trying to improve conditions. It also involves a belief in the apostasy of the Church and thus the evils of ecumenism. Strict fundamentalists observe the familiar cultural taboos and support the anticommunist crusades of Hargis and Macintyre.[8]

Marsden mentions militancy as a prominent feature of strict fundamentalism, citing George Dollar's definition: "Historic Fundamentalism is the literal exposition of all the affirmations and attitudes of the Bible and the militant exposure of all non-biblical affirmations and attitudes."[9] (Dollar's book is one of the few scholarly works about fundamentalism by an ac-

---

7. Ibid., pp. 168-72.
8. For background and color, see C. Allyn Russell, *Voices of American Fundamentalism: Seven Biographical Studies* (Philadelphia: Westminster Press, 1976).
9. George Dollar, *A History of Fundamentalism in America* (Greenville: Bob Jones University Press, 1973), p. xiv.

tual member of the strict group. Because books about them tend
to be particularly hostile, it is useful to be able to consult Dollar
as a scholarly insider and an apologist of the movement.)

Dollar sees his fundamentalism as a response to an attack
on the authority of the Bible by critical scholars. Truth, and not
politics, is his entire focus. Fundamentalism arose in order to
defend the authority of the Bible, which is the epistemological
foundation of Christianity. On this point many evangelicals
would agree with him, but in regard to hermeneutics he is less
observant. For example, he does not seem to see the dispensational scheme of interpretation as a relatively modern reading of the Bible and hardly representative of the conservative
Protestant traditions.

Nancy Ammerman, a student of fundamentalism like
Marsden, has examined strict fundamentalists, and she finds
that separatism particularly identifies them.[10] These are people
who want to be different from the world and to separate from
those Christians who compromise their witness. They want to
be a distinct people, which means adopting a different way of
living in the world. It means refusing to cooperate with those
who do not observe the same strict standards of belief and behavior. Compromise and accommodation are what they want
most to avoid. Strict fundamentalism is a world in opposition,
a sacred world which offers meaning and direction in contrast
to the deteriorating world outside.

Open Fundamentalism

On the other hand, there is also a variety of fundamentalism
which one can only call open. This faction is trying to distance
itself from the strict, separatist type. It is epitomized by Reverend Jerry Falwell, well-known for his leadership of the

10. Nancy Ammerman, *Bible Believers: Fundamentalists in the Modern World*
(New Brunswick, NJ: Rutgers University Press, 1987).

Moral Majority, and by his colleagues at Liberty Baptist Church and Liberty Baptist University in Lynchburg, Virginia. Falwell and his circle are certainly "fundamentalists" and proud of the label; they are creationists, dispensationalists, inerrantists, and separatists. But, compared to strict fundamentalists, they have become relatively more open on a number of important issues.

For example, they are more open to higher education and the place of the intellect in Christianity.[11] They have done an about-face on public discipleship and are now committed to social reform. Open fundamentalists are even prepared to be self-critical, which is remarkable given the closed character of much fundamentalist thinking. For example, the authors of *The Fundamentalist Phenomenon* admit openly to having been too judgmental of others, to have overemphasized external spirituality, to have been too resistant to change, to have majored on the minor points of doctrine. They even confess to having been guilty of adding to the gospel, of having been overdependent on strong pastors, of having been excessively worried about labels and associations, of having had a black-and-white mentality, of having been too authoritarian and too exclusivist. They are critical of the tendency of fundamentalism to split and split again and to go to extremes. Falwell himself actually appeals to the strict fundamentalists to change their ways, to admit their weaknesses, and to reform themselves.[12]

Obviously, today we are encountering a more moderate expression of fundamentalism. Reading the list of self-criticisms that these fundamentalist authors provide, one must conclude that fundamentalism is changing in some important ways. Falwell himself sees his open fundamentalism as a middle path between strict fundamentalism and what he sees as compromis-

11. Harvey Cox noted their intellectual seriousness in *Religion in the Secular City: Toward a Postmodern Theology* (New York: Simon & Schuster, 1984), chap. 3.

12. Falwell, *Fundamentalist Phenomenon*, pp. 219-21.

ing evangelicalism: "Left-wing evangelicalism is extremely relativistic in its approach to truth, whereas hyper-fundamentalism
is overtly absolutistic."[13] These sentiments would not be important if they were the words of some unknown fundamentalist
leader. But they come from the Falwell camp, whose followers
are the most important fundamentalist group, both in terms of
numbers and influence. Thus Marsden has called them the
dominant type today.

We cannot leave this point without pausing in amazement
at the rise of open fundamentalism. It is remarkable to find the
original fundamentalists opening up and becoming more moderate at the very moment that elsewhere (in the Arab world and
even in Israel) the new so-called fundamentalists are harden-
ing. One can only call this phenomenon neo-fundamentalism
and note how far down the path which leads to evangelicalism
they have already traveled. The "open fundamentalists" seem
to be traveling the same liberalizing trajectory that led evangelicals out of fundamentalism in the first place.[14] It is becoming
difficult now to distinguish these fundamentalists from the post-
fundamentalist evangelicals.

The gap between open fundamentalism and establishment evangelicalism is also narrow if one looks at it from the
other side. Evangelicals, when they are under pressure from,
say, liberals, will respond just like open fundamentalists. When
they encounter theologically radical liberals of the type represented by Cupitt or Kaufman, Ogden or Hick, they tend to respond exactly the way a Falwell would respond. Militancy and
anger in the face of perceived unbelief is not foreign to evangelicals either. Open fundamentalism is very difficult to distin-

13. Ibid., p. 169.
14. See Joel A. Carpenter, "From Fundamentalism to the New Evangelical Coalition," in *Evangelicalism and Modern America*, ed. George Marsden
(Grand Rapids: Eerdmans, 1984), pp. 3-16. (We need a book titled *Fundamentalism: The Coming Generation* analogous to James D. Hunter's *Evangelicalism: The
Coming Generation* [Chicago: University of Chicago Press, 1987], which would
trace the liberalizing process in fundamentalism.)

guish from evangelicalism under pressure. Many evangelicals, too, sympathize with Falwell's warnings about drifting and compromise. Some, like Harold Lindsell, are even considering taking up the fundamentalist label again as the term "evangelical" comes to mean less and less. We see a horizontal spectrum: strict fundamentalism, open fundamentalism, establishment evangelicalism, and progressive evangelicalism with movement in both directions.

The Primacy of Truth for Fundamentalism

I would like now to consider two matters of considerable importance in understanding fundamentalism from within.

First, I want to point out the primary importance of truth for fundamentalists, particularly the importance of truth rather than politics. Fundamentalists understand their movement to be a bulwark against error and theological compromise. Their critics have a tendency, possibly because politics means a great deal to them, to assume that fundamentalists organize in order to impose their will on society. This is an important misconception.

The fundamentalists' real concern, and what gave rise to their movement in the first place, is what they perceive to be the reductionism implicit in religious liberalism. In their own words: "Fundamentalism was born out of a doctrinal controversy with liberalism. The ultimate issue is whether Christians who have a supernatural religion are going to be overpowered by Christians [*sic*] who have only a humanistic philosophy of life. Fundamentalism is the affirmation of Christian belief and a distinctively Christian lifestyle as opposed to the general secular society."[15] Fundamentalists are bothered (and they are not alone in this) by an apparent loss of traditional theological grammar and Christian identity. They feel as an Or-

15. Falwell, *Fundamentalist Phenomenon*, p. 6.

thodox Jew must feel in the presence of revisionist Judaism. They feel they must protest.[16]

Truth is the real issue for fundamentalists. They care about fundamental beliefs such as the inspiration of the Bible, the deity of Jesus Christ, the substitutionary atonement, the bodily resurrection of Christ, and the return of the Lord in power and glory. They understand themselves to be preserving historic evangelical Christianity against a tide of unbelief. In their own words: "Doctrinally, fundamentalism is really traditional and conservative Christian orthodoxy. It arose as a defense of minimal doctrinal essentials, apart from which Christianity ceases to be Christian."[17] Their purpose in life is to contend for the truth once delivered to the saints. This is true of both the strict and open varieties of fundamentalism. In my judgment, they are sending a wholesome message to the mainline churches.

I appreciate their tenacity in standing up for precious traditions in an age when so many are discarding them. Though I wish that they made a few more distinctions between major and minor points, between essential and nonessential factors, I still admire their firmness of faith. Though I wish they were less dogmatic and harsh in their judgment of others, I have to admit they are not the only culprits in this regard. For dogmatism and militancy can be found on the left as well as on the right. In addition, I do not think the popular view of fundamentalists as irrational people is valid. Certainly they accept opinions which the public at large think are outrageous (e.g., that evolution is untrue). But even here it should be noted that the fundamentalists never accepted the post-Kantian legacy of subjectivism and are actually far more open to the positive role of reason in religion than most of their religious critics.

16. Thomas C. Oden's sharp call for a return to orthodoxy belongs to the same outraged mentality which takes offense at the surrender of Christian verities to placate some aspect of modernity; see his *Agenda for Theology: Recovering Christian Roots* (San Francisco: Harper & Row, 1979).

17. Falwell, *Fundamentalist Phenomenon*, p. 11.

The Place of the Political

If truth is primary, what about politics? Critics of fundamentalism are often especially interested in this side of the movement. Attacks leveled against them for their supposed political ambitions are often shrill and alarmist. What do the fundamentalists want?[18]

On this point the two types of fundamentalists definitely do not want the same thing. On the one hand, the strict party sticks to the letter of their dispensational theology and considers political and social action useless and wrongheaded. You do not polish the brass on a sinking ship. On the other hand, the open fundamentalists now believe in reforming society and in social involvement.

Falwell has explained his own change of mind on this question in these words:

> Back in the sixties I was criticizing pastors who were taking time out of their pulpit to involve themselves in the civil rights movement or any other political venture. I said you're wasting your time from what you're called to do. Now I find myself doing the same thing and for the same reasons they did. Things began to happen. The invasion of humanism into the public school system began to alarm us back in the sixties. Then the Roe vs Wade Supreme Court decision of 1973 and abortion on demand shook me up. Then adding to that gradual regulation of various things it became very apparent the federal government was going in the wrong direction and if allowed would be harassing non-public schools, of which I have one of 16,000 right now. So step by step we became convinced we must get involved if we're going to continue what we're doing inside the church building.[19]

The concern here is not to take over the United States and turn it into a religious theocracy. The idea is not to make the

18. See Richard J. Neuhaus, "What the Fundamentalists Want," *Commentary* 79/5 (May 1985): 41-46.

19. From *Eternity* 31 (July-August 1980): 18-19, cited in *Fundamentalist Phenomenon*, p. 144.

United States like the Iran of the Ayatollah, but to be responsible Christian citizens in a democracy. Falwell and his colleagues make this clear:

> Fundamentalists are not interested in controlling America; they are interested in seeing souls saved and lives changed for the glory of God. They believe that the degree to which this is accomplished will naturally influence the trend of society in America. As Christians, we should remember that we are not to be only the light of the world but also the salt of the earth. Christian influence in society has always been the moral stability that has held this nation together. In calling this nation back to moral sanity, we want to see freedom preserved so that the work of the gospel may go on unhindered in the generations ahead.[20]

The fundamentalists have not made moves comparable to groups in the Middle East, for example. Nothing among the fundamentalists can be compared with the religious parties of Israel or the theocratic movement in Iran. No doubt there is something to fear in these examples. But those moves are far more radical than even what the Christian reconstructionists in the United States suggest and far beyond anything the open fundamentalists have considered.

Thus Falwell states, of the Moral Majority: "We are not a political party. We are committed to work within the multiple party system in this nation. We are not a political party and do not intend to become one. Moral Majority is not a religious organization attempting to control the government. Moral Majority is a special interest group of millions of Americans who share the same moral values. We simply desire to influence government—not control government."[21]

This means that their goals are really prepolitical, not political. They want to improve the morals of American culture, not take it over.

In case one is skeptical of these testimonies, we should re-

---

20. Falwell, *Fundamentalist Phenomenon*, pp. 184-85.
21. Ibid., p. 191.

member the following: (1) These open fundamentalists are de-
nominationally mostly Baptists who believe in the separation of
church and state and do not want to impose their religious
beliefs on other people. (2) They have not, in fact, created political parties to gain power. Even Pat Robertson did not try to do
that but rather sought the nomination of a major pluralist party.
Even then the fundamentalists did not vote for him in large
numbers and his plan fell through.[22] (3) The reforms they seek
in society are prepolitical and moral in character. They want to
see America spiritually converted and morally renewed.
(4) Their premillennial theology protects them from the dark
side of theocratic postmillennialism even if it should tempt
them. Their eschatology does not lead them to expect evil to
disappear nor to achieve victory in worldly political terms. Not
being Calvinists, they are not tempted to be theocrats. One finds
the theocratic urge in Reformed theology, and, of course, in the
religions of Judaism and Islam, which bind religion and society
closely together, but not in Baptist premillennialists.

The political philosophy of the open fundamentalists
seems to be in the historic mainstream of American thinking.
They believe that the convictions on which the republic was
founded, such as a belief in human dignity, were grounded and
need to be rooted in transcendence and not left to fend for
themselves as though they were autonomous. They think the
American experiment was based upon religious beliefs and will
not work well if divorced from them.[23] Thus the fundamentalists make a great contribution to American culture. They are at

---

22. If the fundamentalists planned to seize power, the plan is not working. See Jeffrey K. Hadden and Anson Sharpe, *Televangelism: Power and Politics
on God's Frontier* (Toronto: Fitzhenry & Whiteside, 1987).

23. In his 1988 Thanksgiving Day statement, President Reagan cited
George Washington's proclamation which called upon the American people to
"be devoted to the service of that great and glorious Being, who is the benefi-
cent Author of all the good that was, that is, or that will be." Reagan added:
"The blessings that are ours must be understood as the gift of a loving God
whose greatest gift is healing," and he went on to call all Americans to offer
grateful praise to God for all his blessings (*New York Times*, 13 November 1988).

the very least in the historic mainstream—they may even be in the vanguard.[24] Is it not time that we stopped attempting to suppress knowledge about America's Christian heritage in our history textbooks, for example, and began to acknowledge the truth which the fundamentalists care so much about?

The shrill response to fundamentalists is more worrisome to me than the fundamentalists themselves. Frenetic writers solemnly warn us that the fundamentalists are leading us speedily to nuclear war. We see titles like *The Gospel Time Bomb* and *Thunder on the Right*. In my opinion, we greatly exaggerate the political challenge of fundamentalism, both in its importance to fundamentalists themselves and its supposed danger to a liberal society.[25] Neuhaus has remarked: "Those who compare our situation to that of the Weimar republic or the religious Right to the Nazis have fallen victim to polemical heat prostration." He also calls it "alarmist nonsense."[26] The danger to the United States is less from these fundamentalists than from the "blame America first" liberals.

I do not see much of a threat from fundamentalism, but rather the promise of a moral renewal we surely need. The naked public square needs all the moral and theological help it can get. North American society has always been a very religious and moral culture, and fundamentalists are making a valuable contribution to its heart and soul. They rightly deplore the way

24. I believe Richard J. Neuhaus would think so. The thesis of his book *The Naked Public Square* (Grand Rapids: Eerdmans, 1984) is that the American experiment is based on religiously grounded beliefs and depends upon them still. Thomas E. Buckley has recently argued that Thomas Jefferson himself held such a view (*The Virginia State for Religious Freedom: Its Evolution and Consequences in American History* [New York: Cambridge University Press, 1987]). See also Mark Noll, Nathan Hatch, and George Marsden, *The Search for a Christian America* (Westchester: Crossway Books, 1983).

25. See Grace Halsell, *Prophecy and Politics: Militant Evangelists on the Road to Nuclear War* (Westport, CT: Lawrence Hill, 1986); Lowell D. Streiker, *The Gospel Time Bomb: Ultrafundamentalism and the Future of America* (Buffalo: Prometheus Books, 1984); Gary K. Clabaugh, *Thunder on the Right: The Protestant Fundamentalists* (Chicago: Nelson Hall, 1974).

26. *Commentary* 79/5 (May 1985): 41.

the Bible has declined as a culture-forming influence, and they aim to restore it. They count our Christian heritage to be precious and well worth reinvigorating. I, for one, am thankful that the fundamentalists finally woke up to this necessity.

The Political and Social Agenda

What is the problem then? It is not that fundamentalists have begun to show an interest in public issues. Liberals had been pleading with them for decades to do just that. Which of the mainline churches is not up to its ears in politics in that sense? No, I think what bothers many critics is the political and ideological complexion and slant the fundamentalists usually have. The critics would have preferred Reverend Jesse Jackson to Reverend Jerry Falwell on matters of public policy. They do not easily forgive fundamentalists for choosing to be Republicans rather than Democrats. In fact, fundamentalists (like many other Americans) dislike political and social liberalism as it has developed in recent years. Fundamentalists see things differently, and some liberal values offend them. Let us take some examples from Falwell's "Agenda for the Eighties" to illustrate the point.[27]

Protestant liberals do not usually like the strong fundamentalist commitment to life. They do not like the recent demonstrations in Atlanta in front of the abortuaries. They prefer the evangelicals and even certain Roman Catholics who fudge on their commitment to life. Fundamentalists do not fudge.[28]

Protestant liberals also do not like the unabashed love fun-

27. Jerry Falwell, "Agenda for the Eighties," in *Fundamentalist Phenomenon,* pp. 186-223.

28. I am thinking of the JustLife/88 lobbying effort by evangelicals like Ron Sider and Catholics like Bernardin in which, by combining issues such as welfare and disarmament with the abortion question, they are able to support candidates who support pro-choice on abortion. See Neuhaus, *Religion and Society Report* 5/10 (October 1988).

damentalists have for their democratic society. Fundamentalists are at the opposite extreme from the "blame America first" mentality of many liberal and self-styled radical Christians. Fundamentalists are old-fashioned enough to think that Western civilization is worth protecting. Therefore, they are strongly anticommunist and support a strong national defense.

Many Protestant liberals do not like fundmentalists' unqualified support for Israel either. Jews may be puzzled by the theology that fundamentalists invoke to ground this support, but they have every reason to appreciate the political implications. It is surely a good deal better than the traditional Christian doctrine called "supercessionism," which writes the Jews off altogether.[29] As Irving Kristol has said: "It is their theology, but it is our Israel." Furthermore, support for Israel is theologically, and not only geopolitically, grounded, which strikes me as more secure.

On the subject of pornography, the critics are a little embarrassed. With the collapse of the sexual revolution, the fundamentalists have been vindicated for understanding all along that libertinism hurts people. Similarly, on homosexuality, the fundamentalists are not afraid to identify this alternate life-style with moral perversion and stand in the way of its gaining moral acceptance.

There is no need to go on. The moral issues raised by fundamentalism are well-known. I believe that open fundamentalism has been, on balance, an advantage for America and certainly not something to fear. It shares basic values with millions of other Americans. If fundamentalism has been influential, it is not because it is domineering, but because it is popular and, perhaps, correct on many issues.

In conclusion, I believe that fundamentalism, and especially open fundamentalism, is making a positive contribution to modern society and to the Church. It sends a clear and important message to mainline Protestantism: (1) to identify more

29. See the evangelicals debating this issue in *Christianity Today*, 7 October 1988, pp. 53-68.

clearly with the historic Christian faith and to stop dabbling with wild theological revisions, and (2) to start talking better sense in the area of politics and society, and to stop advocating radical positions and get back to fundamental values.

I close with an appeal. Tens of millions of Americans find faith and hope in the context of fundamentalism. They believe they are recovering biblical truth very nearly lost. They also long for the moral renewal of society. It would be ironic if, at the very moment when some are reaching out a hand of friendship to nonfundamentalists, the overture is spurned. Let us take the outstretched hand and walk together into a better future.

4. Fundamentalism in Its Global Contours

James Davison Hunter

Scholars very often wince when journalists, popular pundits, and political ideologues invoke the term "fundamentalism" as descriptive of a wide variety of religiopolitical movements in different parts of the world. Religious historians and area specialists are particularly aggravated by the cavalier use of the term. It is as though the word has evolved as just another synonym for religious dogmatism or ideologically rooted authoritarianism of any historical manifestation.

Their grievances cannot be easily discounted as mere academic pedantry. For one, the roots of the concept "fundamentalism" derive from the specific historical experience of American Protestantism in the late nineteenth and early twentieth centuries. The term, then, is context-bound. Simply to apply the term universally, without regard for the national setting, the particular history of a religious faith, whether the religion is a dominant or a minority faith, and a host of other factors, would seem to make its broad usage impossible. Such movements around the world are, perhaps, better understood as different forms of religious radicalism or religious revitalization, but certainly not as fundamentalism. Or so it is argued.

In the final analysis, these objections may carry the day. Certainly for every generalization that can be made about so-

56

called religious fundamentalism, one could probably find an exception. Given this probability, one might think it folly even to try to derive a unified conceptual understanding of the phenomenon. Nevertheless, important commonalities found in the experience of a wide variety of religions all over the world repeatedly press themselves upon our imaginations in such a way that it would seem imprudent to ignore them. Minimally, it would be appropriate to explore tentatively, within the various empirical cases typically called fundamentalist, the formal properties they seem to share. At the broadest level of generalization, then, the concept of fundamentalism may actually have a certain utility.

Fundamentalism and Orthodoxy: The Essential Difference

The great pretense of all fundamentalists, of whatever stripe, is their conviction that what they espouse and what they seek to promote is a basic, unaltered orthodoxy. This, I would argue, is not at all the case. Orthodoxy as a cultural system represents what could be called a "consensus through time"—more specifically, a consensus based upon the ancient rules and precepts derived from divine revelation. Its authority and its legitimacy derive from an unfaltering continuity with truth as originally revealed—truth in its primitive and purest expression.[1] It is fair to say that fundamentalism is something else: *Fundamentalism is orthodoxy in confrontation with modernity.*

The argument can be framed in this way. From a sociological perspective, all religious traditions confronting the modern world order—its rationality, its pluralism, its public/private dualism, its secularity—are faced with three options.

First, the religious community, as bearers of the tradition, can withdraw from engagement. In this option there is a prin-

---

1. See James Davison Hunter, *Evangelicalism: The Coming Generation* (Chicago: University of Chicago Press, 1987).

cipled refusal to deal with the outside world beyond what is absolutely necessary for survival. The community becomes, for all practical purposes, a closed and total world, caring for its own educational, medical, commercial, and spiritual needs. The archetypal examples of this approach are found among the Amish, the old order Mennonite and Brethren communities, and some forms of Hasidic Judaism, such as the Satmar Hasidism.

Second, the religious community can simply accommodate its traditions to the social and cultural forces of the modern world. Here the traditions come to conform increasingly to the cognitive and normative assumptions of contemporary secular society, be it materialism, scientism, humanism, or hedonism. The most obvious illustrations of this approach are found in those religious communities where the traditions are so liberalized and desacralized that the languages of traditional faith are translated into the languages of contemporary therapy, politics, or science.

Third, the religious community can resist modernity and the pressures that would dilute the purity of traditional religious expression. I would maintain that fundamentalism derives its identity principally from a posture of resistance to the modern world order. Of course, the sociological reality is that traditions that engage with modernity generally reflect a dialectical process which involves both accommodation (perhaps unwitting) and cultural resistance. Some accommodate, while others resist. Nevertheless, fundamentalist religion is defined principally by a defensive reaction to the "world-disaffirming" qualities inherent in the modern world. At root, then, there is no fundamentalism without modernity.

Fundamentalism: Making History Right Again

The argument that fundamentalism emerges out of the defensive interplay between orthodoxy and modernity can be crystallized through three simple propositions. Nearly everything else that distinguishes fundamentalism in its global contours derives from these, namely, *all fundamentalist sects share the deep and worrisome sense that history has gone awry. What "went wrong" with history is modernity in its various guises. The calling of the fundamentalist, therefore, is to make history right again.*

Take what may be the paradigmatic case of American Protestant fundamentalism. From the early colonial period, in New England, to the late nineteenth century, there was tremendous optimism that God was doing a wondrous work in this world through the heirs of the Reformation, particularly those who settled on American shores. America would be a "Christian commonwealth," a "righteous empire," a "redeemer nation" (to use Tuveson's phrase). The blessings of revivalistic awakenings, as well as the hardship of famine and war—first with the French and later with the British for independence, and even the Civil War in the mid-nineteenth century—were all viewed as part of a providential design. God's favor for America would continue so long as its people remained true to the faith. Yet the pernicious effects of modernism—in the forms of higher criticism, evolution, the social gospel, ecumenism, and the like— threatened not only the integrity of the true faith, as they saw it, but also the very hope of the cause of Christianity in America. History was going awry, and it was up to the faithful followers of the gospel to make it right again.

It is only in the light of this purpose that one can understand the emergence of dozens of Bible colleges and institutes, the founding of numerous fundamentalist periodicals, the establishment of the World Christian's Fundamentalist Association (in 1919), the wars within denominations (the Baptists and Presbyterians most notably) and denominational seminaries, and the fight between the creationists and evolutionists in the late nineteenth and early twentieth centuries.

It is also only in this light that one can properly understand, nearly a century later, their efforts to reverse the legal status of abortion, to delegitimate progressive sexual and familial attitudes, to return the practice of prayer in public schools, to elect Christian politicians, and so on. Nothing less than the course of American history was and is at stake.

The story of Islamic fundamentalism bears a strong resemblance in its general contours but is different, of course, in the details.[2] Early Islamic history was marked by tremendous success. The community of believers expanded numerically, grew in geopolitical dominance, and prospered in their cultural and religious accomplishments. In its first five centuries, it established a new and vibrant civilization. It was as though Allah was confirming the truth of the Islamic vision within history itself. Even after the Mongol invasion in the thirteenth century and the collapse of the growing Muslim dynasty, a revitalization and expansion of Arab civilization in its medieval period allowed Muslims to reinterpret this crisis as occurring within the divine pattern of historical development. Such a reinterpretation has not been possible for Muslims in the face of Islam's second major crisis: the confrontation with the modern world order.

This confrontation came as early as the seventeenth and eighteenth centuries with the expansion of Western capitalist economics into the Middle East, Mongol India, and the Ottoman empire. By the end of the eighteenth century, various Western powers had established direct economic, political, and military control over much of that region as a result of the region's deep economic, technological, and intellectual dependence on the West. European hegemony meant, among other things, the introduction of radical political and administrative reform and the subjugation of Islamic culture and ideals to Western traditions of rationalism, secularism, and dualism. Muslim society had indeed lost control over its collective destiny; history had, indeed, gone awry. Ever since, there has been a pervasive confusion over how to salvage that history— even fundamental doubt as to whether that history can be salvaged at all.

Yet this confusion and doubt have not impeded the effort.

2. See Wilfred Cantwell Smith, *Islam in Modern History* (Princeton: Princeton University Press, 1957); Marshall Hodgson, *The Venture of Islam* (Chicago: University of Chicago Press, 1974); and John Voll, *Islam: Continuity and Change in the Modern World* (Boulder: Westview Press, 1982).

From the earliest (proto-)fundamentalist reactions against the internal "deterioration" of Islam in the early eighteenth and nineteenth centuries (including the Wahhabi movement of Arabia, the Waliyulh movement in India, the Sansusi movement in Libya, the Madhi movement in the Sudan, and Sarekat Islam in Indonesia) to the twentieth-century movements (including al-Ikhwan al-Muslimun or the Muslim Brotherhood, Jund al-Rahman or Soldiers of God, Jamaat al-Muslmun or the Muslim Group, Shabab Mohamed or Muhammad's Youth, al-Takfir wa al-Hijra or Repentance and Holy Flight, and al-Jihad or Holy War), all share the common passion to recover the classical experience of Islam (a history without deviation) and the original meaning of the Islamic message (a faith without distortion).

In Hinduism, the clearest case of fundamentalism is Rashtriya Swayamsevak Sangh (RSS) or the National Pure Service Society. Once more the story is retold.[3] According to the Hindu revivalists of the late nineteenth century (those from whom the RSS derived inspiration), Hindu society had degenerated because Hindus had not observed *dharma* (a code of conduct for various social categories, situations, and stages of life). Its degeneration had created conditions conducive to foreign domination (by the "British and Muslim villains") which itself intensified the pollution and degradation of classical Hindu culture. Because, according to orthodox Hindu doctrine, the good society can exist only when it is rooted on correct principles of *dharma*, India could not regenerate itself—indeed, antiquity could not be recovered—until the rules of *dharma* were again properly observed. In this conviction was the central religious justification for all nationalist and independence movements of the twentieth century. It was a particularly powerful justifica-

3. See Dina Nath Mishra, *RSS: Myth and Reality* (Sahibabad, India: Vikas, 1980); K. R. Malkani, *The RSS Story* (New Delhi: Impex India, 1980); Walter K. Andersen and Shridhar D. Damle, *The Brotherhood in Saffrom: The Rashtriva Swayamsevak Sangh and Hindu Revivalism* (Boulder: Westview Press, 1987); Pranay Gupte, *Vengeance: India after the Assassination of Indira Gandhi* (New York: Norton, 1985); and S. Mark Heim, "Religious Extremism and Hindu Ecumenism," *Christian Century* 103 (1974): 1177-81.

tion for the RSS because of its fundamental passion to recover
the purity of Hindu antiquity. In the cyclical reality defined by
Hindu cosmology, "making history right again" meant returning to the pure forms of Hindu culture that had degenerated
during foreign rule.

    In Judaism, fundamentalism takes form within religious
Zionism. Its clearest expression is Gush Emunim or the Bloc of
the Faithful. Satmar Hasidism and the Agudath Israel bear a
strong resemblance in many ways, but Gush Emunim is paradigmatic.[4] But in this case a slight adjustment must be made to the
argument. For Jewish fundamentalists, it is not that history has
gone wrong, it is that history *could* go wrong. As in Protestant fundamentalism, the RSS, and Islamic fundamentalism, so for Gush
Emunim history has a sacral quality—history is God's means of
communicating with his people. Thus, the establishment of Israel
in 1948 and its military victories in the Six Day War of 1967 and
the Yom Kippur War of 1973 were signs of a providential process.
Israelis had a sacred duty (mitzva) to repossess and settle the land,
for the land itself contains an imminent holiness. Withdrawal,
therefore, would contravene God's will and represent a step backward in the messianic process of redemption. For this reason, the
men and women of Gush Emunim have made it their lifework to
ensure that the occupied West Bank and Gaza Strip are incorporated permanently into the state of Israel, thus hastening the
fulfillment of "Jewish destiny."

    The threat to the proper playing out of this redemptive
history is ever imposing. It is important to note that it does not
just come from the Arabs and Palestinians, but also from the
decadence of Western secular culture and from Israel's secular
state which, as the Camp David accords made clear, could compromise Jewish destiny for the sake of an ill-founded peace.

    4. See David Biale, "The Messianic Connection: Zionism, Politics, and
Settlement in Israel," *The Center Magazine* 18 (1985): 35-45; Yehuda Litani, "The
Fanatic Right in Israel: Linking Nationalism & Fundamentalist Religion," *Dissent,* Summer 1985, pp. 315-91; Ian S. Lustick, "Israel's Dangerous Fundamentalists," *Foreign Policy,* Fall 1987, pp. 118-39; and Ofira Seliktar, "The New Zionism," *Foreign Policy* 51 (1983): 118-38.

History, then, as narrative and as empirical process, is at the heart of all fundamentalism. Though each fundamentalist community has its own particular vision of the nature and direction it should go, all have engaged in a quest either to put sacral history back on course or to keep it on course. Significantly, in some places in the world fundamentalisms are in close proximity, each maintaining opposing and contradictory views about the course and content of sacral history. The Middle East, of course, is one such place. The northwest quarter of India is another. Such proximity is obviously a recipe for protracted and violent confrontation.

While the meaning of history may be at the heart of fundamentalist reaction, history is not an abstract ideal existing in the minds of theologians and philosophers. History is about a specific people in a specific place at a specific time. It is here where one may discern other characteristics of the fundamentalist phenomena.

Organized Anger

Largely because of the imperatives of the faiths themselves, fundamentalism is not just a theological reaction to modernity: orthodoxy is invariably linked to orthopraxy. In practical terms, this means that all fundamentalisms are characterized, to varying degrees, by a quality of organized anger.

The issue here is one of means—the mechanisms by which the truth is defended and the forces of modernity are kept at bay. Making history right again requires the methodical mobilization of a wide range of resources. The most important of these are the resources of cultural reproduction—schools, newspapers, magazines, political advertisements, radio, television, direct mail, and the like. The reason is very simple. Making history right again is, at heart, a matter of redefining the direction and meaning of history. The success or failure of a fundamentalist campaign, then, can be measured by the degree to which the cultural meanings imposed or reimposed are ac-

cepted as the official and legitimate public reality. Armed revolt
and terrorist intimidation may be useful ways of getting public
attention, but control over the mechanisms of cultural reproduction are, in the end, the most effective way of delegitimat-
ing the opposition's authority and legitimizing their own.

To single out the importance of symbols and the institutions that produce and disseminate them is not to suggest that
the struggle is only literary in nature. The fundamentalist challenge very often incorporates the violence of military or para-
military coercion, largely because of the special place given to
the concept and reality of war in the fundamentalist cosmology.

It is not as though warfare is either desired or eagerly
sought by different fundamentalists, though martyrdom on behalf of a sacred cause does have tremendous significance in
many of these traditions. War simply represents a time of testing, a sign of strength—a necessary means by which the will of
Providence is worked out. It is no accident that Muslim fundamentalists view their struggle as a *jihad* or holy war against
the great Satan of the United States, Israel, and the Soviet
Union. It is important to realize that Jewish fundamentalists
have the same view. Within Gush Emunim, war is a central component to the purgative process that will bring about messianic times. Some within the movement quite literally view Arabs
(including women and children civilians) as Amalekites or
Canaanites that contemporary Jews, in the tradition of Joshua
from biblical times, have a duty to destroy.[5] (In this case, the
settlement drive on the West Bank is viewed as nothing less than
a military campaign. Therefore, anyone who hinders its success
is considered an enemy.)

Sikh fundamentalists also view political violence as a necessary and legitimate part of a *Dharm Yudh* (or religious war).
Particularly after the breakdown of moderate leadership in the
Akali Dal party in the late 1970s, many Sikh fundamentalists felt
as though they had little effective recourse but to turn to political agitation. In the same country one may even find evidence

5. Ofira Seliktar, *Foreign Policy* 51 (1983): 118-38.

of paramilitancy among Hindu fundamentalists not only in the RSS but in such splinter organizations as Shiv Sena (Shiva's Army) and Bajrang Dal.

By comparison to other expressions of global fundamentalism, Protestant fundamentalism is curiously domesticated. Little evidence suggests any systemic orientation toward violent confrontation. There are many reasons for this accommodation to and integration with American political culture. Nevertheless, some random antiabortion violence and antisecular intimidation (such as book burnings) have long been associated with Protestant fundamentalism. Extremist groups are scattered about the country, such as the Fundamentalist Army in southern California.

The metaphor of warfare as applied not only to spiritual struggle but also to the struggle against the principalities and powers of this world remains one of the most potent metaphors within Evangelical Christianity. At the very least, the language and imagery of spiritual warfare provide the rhetorical context where its translation into actual militancy becomes feasible.

The ultimate resource for coercively realizing the fundamentalist agenda is the instrumentality of the state. It is in this relationship that one may discern another central feature of fundamentalism in its global contours.

Religious Ideology and National Identity

Within the various manifestations of fundamentalism, a close relationship seems to exist between religious ideology and national identity. In other words, the integrity of the faith and the future of the nation are entwined. The defense of one implies the defense of the other.

The case of Gush Emunim illustrates this dynamic clearly if not paradigmatically. In the religious ideology of the movement, national identity is not just a sociocultural reality, it is a geopolitical ideal. National identity is born both out of a cultural self-understanding and out of the actual land that the Jews inhabit.[6] The popular slogan of the movement reflects this: "The Land of Israel, for the people of Israel according to the Torah of Israel." Just as the covenant had been established with one particular chosen people, so too the covenant must be fulfilled in one particular chosen place. As Zvi Yehuda Kook, the undisputed leader of Gush Emunim until his death in 1982, put it, "The Land was chosen even before the people." Hanan Porat, one of the emerging younger leaders of the movement, echoed the solemnity of this perspective: "For us the Land of Israel is a Land of destiny, a chosen Land, not just an existentially defined homeland. It is the Land from which the voice of God has called to us ever since that first call to the first Hebrew: 'Come and go forth from your Land where you were born and from your father's house to the Land that I will show you.'"[7] Given this view, one is hardly surprised that questions of geonational border "automatically assume cosmic proportions." Through the fusion of eschatological vision and political power, Gush Emunim aspires not only to assume the leadership of Zionism (altering its presently pluralistic character) but also to assume control over the State of Israel itself. Thus it aspires to create a religious state.

The ideology of Sikh fundamentalism has much the same passion for the ideals of a distinct people and a distinct place, as seen in the nationalist rhetoric of its political arm, the Akali Dal. The division of the state of Punjab into Hindi-speaking (and Hindu) Haryana and Punjabi-speaking (and Sikh) Punjab in 1966 was the first step toward the recognition of Sikhs as a nation and not just a religious community, but it was enough. As a paid political advertisement in the *New York Times* in 1971 put it, "No power on earth can suppress the Sikhs. There are a people with a destiny. There will always be a Sikh nation. There always has been."[8] As a result, ever since the Anandpur Sahib

---

6. Ian S. Lustick, *Foreign Policy,* Fall 1987, pp. 118-39.

7. Ibid., p. 127.

8. Robin Jeffrey, *What's Happening to India? Punjab, Ethnic Conflict, Mrs. Gandhi's Death and the Test for Federalism* (London: Macmillan, 1986), p. 61.

Resolution of 1973, the focus of political and religious aspirations within significant factions of Sikh fundamentalism has been the creation of the independent state of Khalistan.

In the Indian subcontinent, the Sikh demand for a homeland is contrasted with the objectives of RSS and its Bharatiya Jana Sangh party in its own ambition to create a pure Hindu society. It is out of this same logic that one also sees, within Islamic fundamentalism, a quest for an Islamic state. The notion of the Islamic state revives, in some measure, the classical ideal of the caliphate, where spiritual and political power are unified in a single office, the *khalifa* or *imam*. So, too, one can hear in the rhetoric of many Protestant fundamentalists a call for a "return" to a Christian America. One can find an interesting variation among Christian theonomists, but virtually all view the establishment of this country, from its founding as a haven for religious dissenters to its originating documents, as the consequence of providential mediation in history. If one accepts this view, then the machinery of the state can be legitimately exercised to suppress sin and to advance the cause of righteousness and the cause of Christian faith. Among some extremists (such as the Christian Reconstructionists), the logic of theocracy extends even further, as seen in the effort to apply Old Testament law as the ideal form of governance.

In all of these cases, and in others, the dualism separating religion and politics (church and state) that has so long characterized political life in the West is openly repudiated. God's dominion is indivisible and far-reaching; spiritual purpose is one. Thus, fundamentalist ideology posits an organic unity between religious and political authority, its net effect being an essentially theonomic model of governance.

Scripturalism

The issue of religious authority needs to be pursued somewhat further, for it is conceived within various fundamentalist cos-

mologies in a fairly distinctive manner. In short, all fundamentalisms share a certain proclivity to base both religious
authority and the rejection of modernity upon a literal reading
of scriptural texts. The significance of scripturalism is that it establishes very clear symbolic boundaries between good and evil,
right and wrong. It also establishes the criteria for distinguishing the faithful from the unfaithful and infidel. In view of the
moral and religious ambiguities that seem intrinsic to modern
and postmodern thought and aesthetics, the text becomes the
source of all religious and moral authority, establishing safe,
definable, and absolute standards of life and thought.

In American fundamentalism, the textual compulsion initially came in the reaffirmation of the Reformational principle
of *sola Scriptura.* Here the context is critical to its proper understanding. Prior to the 1850s, American Protestants, even the
most pietistic, did not operate with a fully developed theology
of Scripture. At best, there existed a solid, unquestioned reverence and loyalty for the Bible as the ultimate source of spiritual,
religious, and moral truths. Yet the questions posed by literary
and biblical criticism, anthropology, biology, and the social sciences collectively undermined this popular reverence by challenging the truths assumed by this reverence. The only recourse
for those committed to the truth as inherited from earlier
generations was to defend the basis upon which these truths
were asserted. The logic was simple: if the faithful could successfully defend the notion that the Bible was the inerrant Word of
God, to be interpreted literally as such, then they would have
an adequate basis for rejecting all erroneous teachings. Modernism would be repudiated and what was going wrong with
Protestant history could be made right again. The problem was
that, in the effort to shore up the basic truths of Christian faith,
a relatively novel doctrine of Scripture evolved, the doctrine of
inerrancy. Within a few short decades, belief in inerrancy and
the hermeneutic of literalism had evolved as a para-theological
test of true faith.

Nowhere could this be seen more clearly than in the 1910
publication, *The Fundamentals.* Sponsored by two wealthy busi-

nessmen, the twelve volumes (ninety articles) were intended to check the spread of apostasy in the churches by clarifying and reaffirming the essentials of orthodox Christianity.

In Islam, the Koran (or Qur'an) plays a similar role. The very words of the Koran are not merely the constructed meanings of human beings but are actually "uncreated"—the literal dictations of the eternal thoughts of God. As such, they are not subject to modification either through translation or interpretation. For this reason, we again see an impulse toward literalism. The Koranic scriptures do not just point to ultimate truth but are, themselves, ultimate truth.

It is worth noting, by way of comparative-historical irony, that if anyone ever doubted the usefulness of the term "fundamentalism" as applied to the Islamic case, their doubts would have been allayed by the publication of *The Fundamentals of Islamic Thought* by the Ayatollah Murtaza Mutahhari.[9] This volume is reminiscent of the early twentieth-century Protestant tracts not only in name but in purpose. The net effect of this Ayatollah's apologetic is nothing less than to provide a doctrinal standard for rejecting all erroneous (and in particular, liberal and secular) teaching.

There are parallels in other faiths as well. In Theravadin Buddhism, the Pali Canon functions as a scripturalist base of fundamentalist reaction. In Gush Emunim the literal reading of Torah operates in much the same fashion. In Rashtriya Swayamsevak Sangh, religious authority derives from a literal and politicized reading of the Bhagavad Gita. The net effect of this kind of scripturalism is the creation and imposition of a sharp dualism and absolutism. These qualities not only characterize theological commitments but are also translated as moral imperatives in the conduct of social and political affairs.

---

9. Ayatullah M. Mutahhari, *The Fundamentals of Islamic Thought: God, Man and the Universe* (Berkeley: Mizan Press, 1985).

The Final Ironies

Most fundamentalisms seem to share several other general characteristics. For one, fundamentalism typically emerges among those faiths with a deep prophetic tradition. However, Soka Gakkai, if it can be labeled a form of fundamentalism in Japanese Buddhism, curiously does not fit that description. Another trait is that most fundamentalists are drawn from the lower middle classes, particularly those who are caught between the old order of traditional faith and the new order of modern secularity.

While important in their own right, these features are in many ways peripheral to the overriding and defining passion about the direction of history. Here we see two great ironies surrounding fundamentalist religion in its various permutations. The first irony is this: what justifies the fundamentalist impulse is the quest to overcome modernity—to put sacral history back on course or else to keep it on course; yet what ultimately triggers the fundamentalist reaction within religious traditions is a sense of crisis in the credibility of the faith for the fundamentalists themselves. In other words, though the fundamentalist reaction, of whatever religious stripe, is legitimized by the concern for the course and content of history, its ultimate motivation appears to be a crisis in the religious self-identity of the believers themselves. Thus modernity not only threatens to derail the course of sacral history but also threatens the very survival of orthodox faith. Fundamentalism, then, is not born out of great confidence and bravado but out of genuine fear about survivability.

A second irony follows from the first. In the attempt to shore up their own beleaguered faiths, the beliefs that they so passionately defend are themselves transformed into something that may be orthodoxy in name only. In more sociological terms, the moral boundaries that long defined orthodox faith shift in such a way that the faith would be unrecognizable to previous generations. More simply, in the effort to defend the truth, truth itself is transformed. This is seen, for example, in the struggle to establish an Islamic state (law, education, economy, etc.) in Iran and elsewhere in the context of global interdependence and the social, political, and cultural interaction that context assumes.

In Protestant fundamentalism it is seen in doctrinal innovation (in the creation of the test of inerrancy) and in their reification of the concept of the traditional family. In Orthodox Judaism it can be seen in the translation of religious Zionism into a new form of civil religion. These are just a few illustrations of a general tendency. In the end, the continuity with the past that fundamentalism strives so hard to maintain is broken, and it is broken in the very effort given to keep it from breaking.

Conclusion

While by no means exhaustive, the foregoing review does suggest that there may be an empirical and conceptual basis for a general theory of fundamentalism. At the very least, it suggests the need for further conceptual elaboration and empirical specification of the concept. On its own terms, then, there is legitimate call for further theoretical exploration of the fundamentalist phenomena. But there is, perhaps, another reason for further exploration. The ultimate significance of the fundamentalist phenomena, to the extent that one can generalize about it, may not be in what it tells us about religion as much as what it tells us about qualities intrinsic to the modern age. However one may disagree with fundamentalists theologically, morally, or politically—however one may fear their agenda— fundamentalism provides a window through which one can understand much about the modern world, particularly the pressures and strains it creates for ordinary people and the religious communities of which they are a part.

See also:

de Bary, William Theodore, Stephen N. Hay, and I. H. Gureshi, eds. *Sources of Indian Tradition.* Vol. 2 of *Introduction to Oriental Civilizations.* New York: Columbia University Press, 1958.

Bhacu, Parminder. *Twice Migrants: East African Sikh Settlers in Britain.* London: Tavistock, 1985.

Goldberg, Gloria, and Efraim Ben-Zadok. "Gush Emunim in the West Bank." *Middle Eastern Studies* 22 (1986): 52-73.

Jeffrey, Robin. "Grappling with History: Sikh Politicians and the Past." *Pacific Affairs* 60 (1987): 59-72.

Kapur, Rajiv A. *Sikh Separatism: The Politics of Faith.* London: Allen & Unwin, 1986.

Malik, Yogendra K. "The Akali Party and Sikh Militancy: Move for Greater Autonomy or Secessionism in Punjab?" *Asian Survey* 26 (1986): 345-62.

Newman, David. *Jewish Settlement in the West Bank: The Role of Gush Emunim.* Durham: Center for Middle Eastern and Islamic Studies, University of Durham, 1982.

————. *The Impact of Gush Emunim: Politics and Settlement in the West Bank.* London: Croom Helm, 1985.

————. "The Evolution of a Political Landscape: Geographical and Territorial Implications of Jewish Colonization in the West Bank." *Middle Eastern Studies* 21 (1985): 192-205.

Puri, Geeta. *Bharativa Jana Sangh: Organisation and Ideology.* New Delhi: Sterling, 1980.

Saiedi, Nader. "What Is Islamic Fundamentalism?" Unpublished manuscript. Los Angeles: University of California.

Schiff, Ze'ev. "The Spectre of Civil War in Israel." *The Middle East Journal* 39 (1985): 230-45.

Wallace, Paul. "The Sikhs as a 'Minority' in a Sikh Majority State in India." *Asian Survey* 26 (1986): 363-77.

Weiner, Myron, ed. *State Politics in India.* Princeton: Princeton University Press, 1968.

5. Pietist Politics

A. James Reichley

Socially conservative Protestants—whether they be labeled "fundamentalists," "evangelicals," or the "religious new right"—have already significantly shifted the balance of American politics. Movement of large numbers of white evangelical Protestants from the Democratic to the Republican side of the partisan lineup, and change from political passivity to at least sporadic bursts of electoral activity, were major contributors to the social and political swing to the right that characterized most of the 1980s.

    White evangelicals used to be a reliable, though usually quiescent, pillar of the dominant Democratic coalition that came out of the 1930s. This was partly because evangelicals were concentrated in the South, where the Democrats monopolized virtually all political power until the 1960s. But even in northern industrial states with sizable evangelical populations in their rural areas, such as Pennsylvania, Ohio, Indiana, and Illinois, evangelicals seem to have been more Democratic than other Protestants, probably because they were found disproportionately in relatively low-income groups. The political impact of the white evangelicals, who make up about one-fifth of the national population, was limited by their low level of electoral participation, caused in part by theological aversion to social action outside their church communities.

All of this has now dramatically changed. White evangelicals, after supporting Jimmy Carter, himself an evangelical Baptist, for president in 1976, switched in 1980 to give Ronald Reagan 60 percent of their vote. Four years later, white evangelicals went even further, supporting Reagan by a majority of slightly more than 80 percent. Some political analysts argued that evangelicals were attracted to Reagan personally rather than to Republicanism, and that many of them would again vote Democratic once Reagan was no longer on the ballot. But in the 1988 presidential election white evangelicals gave George Bush about four-fifths of their vote—a degree of social group unity surpassed only by blacks, who voted by an even larger margin for Michael Dukakis.[1]

In presidential years, the evangelicals' shift in partisan allegiance has been accompanied by a substantial increase in voter participation. In 1980, 1984, and 1988, white evangelicals appear to have voted at levels not far below those of other major groups in the electorate. In the midterm elections of 1982 and 1986, however, evangelicals returned to their old pattern of participating well below the national average.

If evangelicals continue to produce Republican majorities at anything approaching the size of 1984 and 1988, and *if* they vote at the level of their recent participation in presidential elec-

---

1. *The New York Times*, 8 November 1988 and 10 November 1988. Figures available at the time of writing for 1988 are not directly comparable with 1980 and 1984 because of a change in the question used in the *CBS-New York Times* survey to identify white evangelicals. The identification used in 1988, "white fundamentalist or evangelical Christian," may have produced a slightly higher Republican response than that employed in 1980 and 1984, "white born-again Christian." Some analysts, notably Jim Castelli in *A Plea for Common Sense* (San Francisco: Harper & Row, 1988), have doubted that evangelicals were heavily Democratic before 1980. But Gary W. Copeland and Jeffrey L. Brudney have found that as recently as 1980 evangelicals were registered 56 percent Democratic, 28 percent independent, and only 16 percent Republican ("Ronald Reagan and the Religious Vote," paper delivered at the 1988 meeting of the American Political Science Association).

tions, the Republican party will have taken an important step toward regaining the national majority status it lost at the beginning of the 1930s.

Even if such developments should occur, a number of complicating factors would make their political and ideological effects less than clear-cut. First, support from the evangelicals, while so far a net electoral plus for the Republicans, has already produced some negatives and could cause considerably more in future elections. The evangelicals, while a sizable group within the electorate, remain very much a minority. The Republicans will have to attract several other major groups, as well as retaining most of the traditional Republican base, to achieve their goal of becoming again the national majority party. Some of the participants in the coalitions that elected Reagan and Bush, including many traditional Republicans, are decidedly put off by both the tone of political utterances from some leaders of the religious right and by the content of some of the issues that have helped draw evangelicals toward the Republicans. If the Republican party were to appear to be dominated by its new evangelical recruits, as already seems to have happened in some parts of the country, and if the evangelicals were to press for strict loyalty to their social agenda, the electoral losses suffered by the Republicans among other supporters or potential supporters could in the long run more than offset the gains brought to them by the religious right.

Second, the evangelicals, while for the most part socially conservative—in fact, attracted to the Republicans by their social conservatism—have by no means given up all the other attitudes and dispositions that for many years kept them loyal to the Democrats. In the early 1980s, when the religious right first joined the Reagan coalition, its leaders accepted without much question the full conservative package on economic and foreign policy issues, which they regarded as of secondary importance. But as the evangelicals have begun to acquire political confidence, some have shown signs of doubting that there is a necessary connection between traditional morality and, say, supply-side economics or an aggressively interventionist foreign policy.

Older themes of economic populism and foreign policy nonin-
terventionism, even isolationism, have begun to reappear.

Nevertheless, the switch by the evangelicals in partisan
and ideological attachments, if it continues, will certainly pro-
foundly affect national politics. There are some, moderates as
well as liberals, who hold that the results of this change will be
extremely negative. The evangelicals' new political role, they
argue, will create a shrill and divisive social atmosphere, introduce elements of dogmatism and intolerance and even bigotry
into political life, and move the nation not merely in a conservative direction but toward outright social reaction. To determine how seriously one should take these predictions, it is necessary to arrive at some understanding of the social and
ideological and even theological nature of the religious right,
as well as of its political potential.

Fundamentalists and Evangelicals

I will first define the subject with which we are to deal, and say
something about how it is to be labeled. The general topic of
this book is the "fundamentalist phenomenon." But for political analysis, the older and more inclusive term, "evangelical,"
in many ways works better.

The term "evangelical" has been used at times to designate all Protestants or even all Christians. Some small Protestant denominations in the United States have called themselves
Evangelicals with a capital "E," and the established Protestant
church in Prussia, formed through a union of Lutherans and
Calvinist Reformers, took the name Evangelical. In the United
States, however, this term has generally been used to describe
those denominations and sects and independent churches that
descend from the pietist branch of the Reformation. Baptists
and Methodists were formerly the two major denominational
representatives of evangelicalism in the United States; evangelicalism has also been powerfully represented within the Presby-

terian and Lutheran denominations, and to a lesser extent among Episcopalians.

In a general way, evangelicals have been viewed as those Protestants who put particular emphasis on establishing a direct relationship between the individual and God, and on the conversion experience—the event of being "born again," which many evangelicals hold is a necessary prerequisite for salvation for all Christians, not simply for persons growing up outside the faith. Evangelicals concentrate on spiritual inspiration of the individual, rather than on church doctrine and the moral reform of society (like many Calvinists), or on ritual and church tradition (like many Lutherans and Episcopalians, as well as Catholics). Evangelicals generally became associated with the inerrancy side in the debate that developed among Protestants in the latter part of the nineteenth century over the degree of literal truth to be assigned to the Bible.

When several of the major Protestant denominations joined in 1908 to form the Federal Council of Churches, evangelicals were for the most part skeptical of this move toward church unity—engineered, as they saw it, by theological and social liberals who aimed to use the churches for social action, while glossing over doctrinal differences and shifting emphasis away from individual spiritual experience. The denominations that participated in the Federal Council of Churches and in its successor, the National Council of Churches, established in 1950, including the Methodists as well as the Presbyterians, Episcopalians, and some Lutherans, have come to be designated the "mainline" Protestant churches. Those who stayed outside these ecumenical bodies, including most Baptists and many Lutheran as well as many smaller sects, are generally termed "evangelicals." Many individual members and some ministers in the "mainline" denominations remain "evangelical" in their theological and cultural, and more recently political, outlooks.

During the 1920s, the label "fundamentalist," derived from a series of theological volumes, *The Fundamentals,* was applied to conservative evangelicals, at times by the conservatives themselves, but even more by their political and cultural opponents. In the 1930s and 1940s evangelicalism went into relative decline, and fundamentalism became a kind of national joke, lampooned in the funny papers and in popular plays and movies. When conservative evangelical Protestantism enjoyed a modest revival, led by Billy Graham and others, in the early 1950s, its participants generally avoided the fundamentalist label.

At the present time, some conservative evangelicals, such as Jerry Falwell, identify themselves as fundamentalists. But many others, including many who are doctrinally fully as conservative as the avowed fundamentalists, prefer the older term, "evangelical." Thus "fundamentalist" has become a label used by outsiders, usually pejoratively, to characterize a group, many of whose members do not use it themselves, and some of whom strongly resent it.

Such terms have, in some cases, come over time to be accepted, and proudly worn, by persons so labeled—Quakers and Methodists being well-known examples. But at present its connotation is mainly negative—particularly since it is now applied to practitioners of almost any kind of religious fanaticism, including such unpopular figures among Americans as the late Ayatollah Khomeini.

Fundamentalists, like other evangelicals, have numerous theological and cultural divisions among themselves. (The emphasis of evangelical Christianity on personal religious experience has seemed almost to guarantee the frequent breaking away of dissenting subgroups or individuals, some of whom found churches of their own.) The most important division among fundamentalists is between those, like Pat Robertson, who are "charismatics," believing in faith healing and other exercises of miraculous power by chosen individuals, and those, like Falwell, who are not. Many noncharismatic fundamentalists regard the religious claims of charismatics as socially dangerous and theologically preposterous.

For social or political analysis, neither evangelicals nor fundamentalists are easy to identify. They cannot be located simply by denominational designation, since they are found in many denominations, including some of the mainline denominations, and some belong to local churches (like Falwell's church in Lynchburg, Virginia) that are not affiliated with any organized denomination. In recent years, pollsters have tried to identify them by responses to questions dealing with such issues as belief in the inerrancy of the Bible, belief in the divinity of Jesus Christ, belief that Jesus was born of a virgin, commitment to bringing nonbelievers to Christianity, and the experience of being "born again." Some of these questions, however, would be answered affirmatively by many Christians whose other attitudes or behavior would not place them among those who are usually regarded as evangelicals or fundamentalists.

The two questions that most clearly separate evangelicals from nonevangelicals are those regarding the inerrancy of the Bible and the born-again experience. Those who answer both these questions affirmatively may fairly be considered evangelicals. White Protestants who meet this criteria make up about 20 percent of the total population of the United States.[2]

Many black Protestants are also evangelicals, but since their political and social experience has been so different, they are best regarded for political discussion as a separate group. Some Catholics meet the evangelical criteria, but come out of a quite different social tradition. Though some of them have recently established political ties with evangelical Protestants, they are more usefully considered politically with their fellow Catholics.

For many kinds of social and cultural analysis, it is worthwhile to divide white Protestant evangelicals into fundamentalists and nonfundamentalists. There is, however, no reliable statistical tool for distinguishing within evangelical ranks between fundamentalists and nonfundamentalists. Fundamental-

2. Gallup Organization, *Religion in America* (Princeton: Princeton Religion Center, 1982), pp. 31-32; and James Davidson Hunter, *American Evangelicalism: Conservative Religion and the Quandary of Modernity* (Princeton: Rutgers University Press, 1983), pp. 139-41.

ists are generally considered to make up about one-third of white evangelicals, or about seven percent of the total population, but this estimate is to some extent conjectural. The most that can be safely said is that there are more intense evangelicals, who may be called fundamentalists, and relatively moderate evangelicals.[3]

This distinction has some political significance, but fortunately it is not crucial. Whatever the cultural and social differences between fundamentalists and other evangelicals—and they are important—both groups seem to respond similarly to political stimuli. The religious new right, which became active as a political force around 1978, has won its most active adherents among fundamentalists (though a portion of fundamentalists have vigorously opposed it), but the issues that it has emphasized have also been among those drawing other evangelicals toward political conservatism and Republicanism. Obviously, the impact of the larger body on national politics, if it may be considered analytically as a distinguishable group, is more important than that of the more extreme fundamentalists only. In this paper, therefore, I will usually be dealing with the political behavior and potential impact of the full body of white evangelical Protestants.

Religious Personalism

Among interpreters of the role and sources of religion in human life, there is of course a distinction between those who believe, from their own experience or training, that religion relates to a transcendent force or being that actually operates (or is present)

3. Corwin Smidt, "Evangelicals within Contemporary American Politics: Differentiating between Fundamentalist and Non-Fundamentalist Evangelicals," *Western Political Quarterly* 41/3 (Sept. 1988): 606, categorizes as fundamentalists persons who use the label to identify themselves—a useful approach for some purposes, but for political analysis this approach suffers from the problem discussed above.

in the universe, and those who are convinced that no such force or being exists and that religion therefore must rise from purely natural causes. Both groups, however, except for those believers who reject all forms of scholarly or scientific evidence not derived directly from their sacred texts (which includes some fundamentalists), are agreed that religion has evolved over time. The believers view this evolution as God's gradual revelation of his nature through history, and the nonbelievers regard it as the working out of natural processes—the history of an illusion, as Freud would say.

In either case, primitive religions seem to fall into two main types: the religion of the priests, teaching solidarity with the tribe; and the religion of the shamans, exotic creatures attached only loosely to the tribe, providing release for spiritual aspirations of the individual which the priestly religion seems incapable of fulfilling, or, in the naturalist interpretation, simply letting off emotional steam for individuals frustrated by social discipline or intractable reality.[4]

The religions associated with more complex forms of civilization, such as Hinduism, Buddhism, Judaism, Christianity, and Islam, have to a great extent transcended these rival forms of primitive religion, blending them into deeper and more powerful insights regarding the inner nature of reality or transcendent being. But the religious tendency of the primitive tribal priests, which may be called legalism, and the religious tendency of the shamans, which may be called personalism, seem to persist as strains in virtually all religions, occurring as forms of emphasis only partially subsumed by the deeper insights of the more advanced religions. It may be that there is a kind of natural rhythm within the development of most religions, whatever their deeper truth or wisdom: a drift toward

4. The distinction between the functions of priests and shamans in primitive religion has been made by many sociologists and social theorists, including Max Weber, *The Sociology of Religion*, tr. Ephraim Fischoffs (Boston: Beacon Press, 1964), p. 30; Peter Farb, *Man's Rise to Civilization* (New York: Dutton, 1968), p. 182; Robert R. Wilson, *Prophecy and Society in Ancient Israel* (Philadelphia: Fortress Press, 1980), pp. 24-26.

legalism as the religion becomes embodied in institutions, and then a swing toward personalism as these institutions seem, to some at least, to smother the religion's original inspiration.

Personalism, like the primitive shamans, offers the individual an opportunity to establish direct contact with transcendence, undiluted and unhindered by the conventions of either civil society or prescribed ritual. Personalism in its most extreme form is pure mysticism. It is untranslatable into ordinary experience, and therefore unpreservable through time beyond the consciousness of the individual (space and time being among the conditions that personalism claims to transcend).

Some personalists, however, are moved to communicate their transcendent experience to others, and to preserve their insights, and the possibility of recurrence of such insights, for persons who will follow them in time. They therefore form institutions, even if at first no more than language, and the tendency toward legalism seems often to be resumed—though stoutly resisted by some who wish to stay as close as possible to the original personalist inspiration.

Personalism, offering direct experience of transcendence, seems totally authoritative within the life of the individual believer, and within the community that forms around the spiritual insights that it offers. When it begins to return through institutionalization to society and becomes involved with ordinary civil affairs, this sense of absolute moral authority is likely, for a time at least, to be transferred to the institutions that it creates. Individuals or sects who feel they have *known* God, known not through priestly intermediaries but directly, are likely to feel they know with certainty what God wants for the world, including the temporal society in which they happen to find themselves. Thus personalism, while intensely individualistic, may also become highly absolutist in its moral expression.

The Protestant Reformation was a complex and many-sided event in religious and social history. Among other things, it was a reassertion of the personalist side of Christianity. Pietism, the religion of Protestant sects like the Anabaptists and the

Quakers, and later the Methodists, carried this personalist revolt beyond where Lutheranism or Calvinism were prepared to go.

An inherent danger associated with personalism when it reenters society is anarchy—both social and religious anarchy. On the one hand, if the individual communicates directly with transcendence, why should he defer to any outside authority, civil or religious? On the other hand, how can the individual, or the larger society, be sure that what he is communicating with is not actually the force of evil that also inhabits the universe? The response of Protestantism and particularly of pietism, the most radical form of Protestantism, to these problems was absolute reliance on the authority of the Bible. If the authority of church tradition developed by Catholicism was to be overturned and ignored, it was necessary that the Bible, which also for other reasons was being given new emphasis by Protestantism, be regarded as the absolute arbiter between true and false inspiration. The foundation was laid for insistence by latter-day pietists that the Bible must be literally true in every particular—inerrant.

Evangelicals in Politics

American evangelicalism, including fundamentalism, carries on the tradition of pietism in the United States. (To speak of a *tradition* of pietism is itself to some degree anomalous, since personalism, of which pietism is a variant, by its nature challenges the authority of most tradition; but to continue over time it must be embodied in some kind of tradition, however loosely formed.) Evangelicalism has usually expressed the tendency of pietism to regard civil society as largely irrelevant to the spiritual welfare of the individual, if not inherently and irredeemably corrupt (contrasting in this respect with Calvinism, which regards civil society as a flawed instrument but nevertheless as a proper arena for realizing a part of God's purpose; and with Lutheranism, which has tended to view civil society as a necessary corrective to corruption within the individual). At the same time, when evangelicalism is drawn to participation in civil politics, it is likely to speak with the conviction of absolute moral authority.

The political expression of personalism, when it enters civil society, may be radical. Its aspiration to spiritual perfection for the individual may lead it, once it is persuaded that social involvement is in any way appropriate, to aim for social perfection as well. Such a direction may well place it on a collision course with established social authority, formed by pragmatic compromise among dominant social and economic interests. This happened in Germany in the sixteenth century, when radical pietists rose against the feudal nobility (to the horror of Martin Luther), creating a utopian republic in Münster in 1534, put down with much bloodshed. It happened in England in the seventeenth century, when pietists formed the radical cutting edge of the Puritan Revolution. And it is happening today among the small minority of radical pietists, such as the Sojourners group in Washington, who campaign for egalitarian populism and pacifism.

Pietism, however, may also take a conservative turn in politics. Several factors attract some pietists, often the majority, toward social conservatism. First, emphasis on belief in original sin, which is a usual though not invariable element in pietist theology, often persuades pietists that stern social authority, even authority exercised by pagans, is needed to deal with natural corruption. (The thirteenth chapter of Paul's epistle to the Romans is often cited in support of this belief.) Second, the ascetic behavior associated with pietism often leads, paradoxically, as John Wesley pointed out, to worldly success.[5] Many pietists, therefore, acquire an economic stake in maintenance of the existing order (and are tempted, as Wesley warned, to slip away from the faith that shaped their characters). Third, the leading opponents and critics of the established social order in the West since the French Revolution have often attacked not

---

5. Quoted in James Hastings Nichols, *Democracy and the Churches* (Philadelphia: Westminster Press, 1951), p. 72.

only traditional social authority or the existing economic system but also all institutions linked to a religious view of reality, pietist as well as legalist or hierarchical. Social and political radicalism has therefore been linked for many pietists with antagonism toward their most cherished associations and beliefs.

All of these factors have contributed to the recent shift of evangelicalism toward political conservatism. But there is another, perhaps even more basic, reason, not tied directly to religion.

Evangelicalism in the United States has maintained its greatest strength among those groups, predominantly rural but also substantially represented in some urban areas, that have remained most closely attached to what I would call traditional social structures—I am tempted to say structures embodying the predominant human tradition, but at least the tradition that at the level of the family and the community has been dominant at most times in the history of the West. This tradition has varied widely over time—so widely that many historians and sociologists would challenge its existence as a distinct form. I would suggest, without here trying to prove, that its general characteristics have normally included hierarchical order within the family and the community (though not necessarily at more spatially extended levels), dictation of different social and economic roles for men and women, maintenance of rigid though somewhat varied sexual taboos, intense local patriotism, mutuality among insiders, suspicion of outsiders, identification with the local natural environment, and resistance to change. This tradition also includes religion, in the sense of belief in a transcendent moral order that reinforces the authority of its internal order.

These characteristics have often drawn social traditionalism toward the legalist brand of religion. In some times and places, however, the legalist religion supported, or imposed, by the larger society has been allied with political forces—military empires, tax-gathering bureaucracies—that have seemed to threaten the local traditional social system. Among northern European peoples, in particular, aversion toward the political attachments of legalist religion helped attract many social traditionalists toward religious personalism.

In the United States, social traditionalism (family oriented, patriotic, culturally conservative) has in recent times felt itself under intense pressure from destabilizing forces rising from the dynamic economic, political, and cultural systems that have created and shaped the modern world. These varying forces of modernity have often been in combat with each other (capitalist industrializers against egalitarian collectivizers, both against bohemian aesthetes), but have held in common the tendency, whether or not intended, to undermine the traditional social system. Since evangelicalism happened to be the prevailing religious faith in some sectors of society where traditionalism has remained strong (in other sectors it has been Catholicism), evangelicalism has been enlisted in defense of traditional social structures.

Particularly in the South, there has also been the issue of race. Before the Civil War, southern pietists, most of whom were small farmers or mechanics, were probably less implicated in support of slavery than were practitioners of the more hierarchical forms of religion. Nevertheless, most white evangelicals adhered to strict social distinction between the races (most emphatically within their churches, leading to the founding of separate black evangelical denominations). After the abolition of slavery, white evangelicals, tending to come from lower-income groups, were the group most subject to direct economic competition with blacks. Early attempts by some southern populist leaders, like Tom Watson in Georgia, to form political alliances between economically deprived whites and blacks foundered on the rock of racial antagonism. White evangelicals, Watson among them, became among the most intransigent supporters of racial segregation.

When the national Democratic party in the 1960s became a major participant in the drive to dismantle the machinery of official racial segregation, many southern white evangelicals were shaken loose from their traditional loyalty to the Democrats—first to vote for Barry Goldwater in 1964, then for

George Wallace in 1968, and finally to normal support for Republican candidates in national elections. Some commentators have argued that racial prejudice is the major, almost the only, factor motivating the political shift among white evangelicals. Historical evidence and survey research do not, I think, support this claim, but certainly racial feeling has been a contributing cause.

Rise of the Religious Right

In the middle of the 1970s, all of these factors came together among evangelicals in a national society undergoing severe strain. At the national level, dissension over the Vietnam War and disgust caused by the Watergate scandals had left wounds in the social fabric. At more intimate levels of experience, increase in violent crime, spreading use of drugs, rising divorce, weakening of family ties, assault on traditional sexual distinctions, and virtually unchecked availability of pornography contributed to a general sense of social unease, especially among, though not limited to, social traditionalists. Evangelicals in particular, along with many conservative Catholics, associated these social developments with a series of Supreme Court decisions, beginning with the 1962 decision prohibiting organized prayer in the public schools, and reaching a kind of climax with the 1973 decision establishing, essentially, a constitutional right for a woman to have an abortion.

Popular television preachers like Jerry Falwell and Pat Robertson told their audiences that these judicial decisions grew from a conspiracy by secular humanists—persons hostile to any religious faith—to take over the national political system. Many evangelicals became convinced that if they were to turn back the tides of destructive cultural and social change, they would have to give up their traditional avoidance of politics and become active players in the political system.

The first major beneficiary of the changing attitude among

evangelicals toward politics was Jimmy Carter in 1976. The evangelicals' support for Carter, their co-religionist, not only enabled him to be the first Democratic presidential candidate since 1964 to sweep most of the South, but also brought him enough backing in the rural areas of northern states like Pennsylvania and Ohio to capture these states' crucial blocs of electoral votes. In a close national election, evangelicals could fairly claim to have supplied Carter with his margin of victory over Gerald Ford.

After taking office, Carter failed to support the evangelicals' social agenda and promoted some measures they regarded as hostile, such as the women's Equal Rights Amendment. Not insignificantly, he also did not appoint evangelical leaders to positions in his administration that some of them felt they had been encouraged to expect.

During the early 1970s, increasing numbers of white evangelical congregations, partly in response to court-ordered stripping of religious associations from the public schools, and partly as a result of racial desegregation, began setting up independent Christian academies in which students could be indoctrinated in traditional values. One result of this development was to relax the evangelicals' historic opposition against state financial aid to private schools. Another was to give the churches sponsoring schools a direct interest in resisting what they regarded as excessive government regulation of private education.

In 1978, the Carter administration tightened standards for tax exemptions for church-operated schools, requiring that the percentage of their student bodies coming from racial minorities be at least one-fifth of the percentage of such minorities in the local population. A group of the Christian academies reacted by forming a national association to look after their interests in Washington.

Meanwhile, a number of veteran champions of right-wing causes, such as Paul Weyrich, director of the Committee for the Survival of a Free Congress, and Howard Phillips, founder of the Conservative Caucus, a grass-roots conservative coalition, had begun scouting the aggrieved evangelicals as a potential mass base for a national militant conservative movement. Wey-rich and Phillips held a series of meetings with evangelical leaders, including Falwell, from which emerged agreement that the association representing Christian academies should be con-verted into a more broadly based national political organization promoting restoration of traditional moral values. In June, 1979, Falwell announced formation of the Moral Majority.

At first, the Moral Majority was not much more than a let-terhead organization. Groups like Christian Voice and the Re-ligious Roundtable soon rivaled it for influence within the re-ligious right. But the Moral Majority, partly because of its catchy title and partly because of Falwell's skills as a publicist, was adopted by the national media as a kind of surrogate for the en-tire movement.

The election of Ronald Reagan as president in 1980, and the Republicans' capture of control of the U.S. Senate for the first time in twenty-six years, was a political earthquake that called for explanation by the news media. Shift of white evan-gelicals from support of Carter in 1976 to a 60 percent margin for Reagan in 1980 was certainly part of the cause for the tri-umph of conservative Republicanism, and offered a ready handle for the media trying to interpret the election.

The religious right in general, and the Moral Majority in particular, were given sensational media attention. Some liber-als began to warn that know-nothing fundamentalists were on the verge of taking over the United States. "I am beginning to fear," said Patricia Harris, Secretary of Health and Human Serv-ices in the Carter administration, "that we could have an Aya-tollah Khomeini in this country, but he will not have a beard . . . he will have a television program."[6]

Assertive remarks by some of the television preachers and their political allies were quoted to fuel the alarm. Pat Robert-son bragged, "We have enough votes to run the country." Jim Bakker, formerly Robertson's protégé, and then his rival in re-

---

6. Quoted in Samuel S. Hill and Dennis E. Owens, *The New Religious Right in America* (Nashville: Abingdon Press, 1982), p. 78.

ligious broadcasting, chimed in: "Our goal is to influence all viable candidates on issues important to the church. We want answers. We want appointments in government." Paul Weyrich went even further than his clerical associates: "We're radicals working to overturn the present structure in this country— we're talking about Christianizing America."[7]

Reagan was careful not to repeat Carter's political error of seeming to turn against the evangelicals once he was in office. Though the legislative agenda of the religious right, calling for constitutional amendments to prohibit abortion and permit organized prayer in the public schools, achieved little headway, Reagan made what most evangelicals, at the grass-roots level if not among the leadership, regarded as good faith efforts. A number of key players in the religious right were given posts in the Reagan administration at secondary and tertiary levels. Appointments to the federal judiciary, though by no means drawn mainly from the ranks of right-wing fundamentalists, began to reflect more conservative social attitudes.

In the 1982 congressional elections, occurring toward the end of that year's deep economic recession, the Republicans lost 26 seats in the House of Representatives. The religious right was relatively inactive and seemed to have little success at dissuading economically pressed evangelicals from returning to their traditional support for the Democrats. Many national commentators concluded that the revolt of the evangelicals had been no more than a political blip.

In 1984, however, the religious right was more active than ever. Evangelical groups appeared better organized and helped the Republicans win an easy victory in the fight for new registrants. Jesse Jackson's candidacy for the Democratic nomination for president produced a large outpouring of new black registrants, most of whom voted for Walter Mondale in Novem-

7. See Francis Fitzgerald, "A Disciplined Charging Army," *New Yorker*, 18 May 1981, p. 60; James David Fairbanks, "The Evangelical Right: Beginning of Another Symbolic Crusade," paper delivered at the 1981 American Political Science Association meeting.

ber; but registration drives among white evangelicals helped the Republicans do even better. A study by the nonpartisan Committee for the Study of the American Electorate found that new registrants voted for Reagan over Mondale by a majority of more than two to one.[8] White evangelicals cast ballots for Reagan by a margin of four to one, and gave Republican candidates for the House of Representatives 65 percent of their vote.[9]

A study by James Guth showed, significantly, that while in 1980 41 percent of Southern Baptist ministers had considered themselves Democrats and only 29 percent Republicans, by 1984 this distribution had altered to 66 percent Republican and 25 percent Democrat.[10] Change in party identification among the evangelical laity came more slowly, but here too the Republicans were making progress. In 1980, evangelical voters, despite their strong support for Reagan, were 56 percent Democratic, 16 percent Republican, and 28 percent independent. By 1984, this balance had shifted to 40 percent Democratic, 23 percent Republican, and 37 percent independent.[11]

The Robertson Campaign

In the 1986 midterm elections, the Republicans made a net gain of eight governorships, many in states with large evangelical constituencies, but suffered a net loss of eight seats in the U.S. Senate, many also from states heavily populated by evangelicals. The Democrats recaptured majority control of the Senate. Elec-

8. See Curtis B. Gans, *Non-Voter Study '84-'85* (Washington: Committee for the Study of the Electorate, 1985).

9. Data supplied by *CBS-New York Times* election day survey, 1984.

10. James L. Guth, "The Christian Right Revisited: Partisan Realignment Among Southern Baptist Ministers," paper delivered at the 1985 meeting of the Midwest Political Science Association.

11. See Copeland and Brudney, "Ronald Reagan and the Religious Vote."

toral turnout was down steeply among most voter groups from 1984, but the decline was particularly sharp among evangelicals. Exit polls indicated that white evangelicals, who had made up about 17 percent of the total electorate in 1984, composed only 12 percent in 1986—a change which by itself probably cost the Republicans at least five Senate seats.[12]

Besides failing to halt the Democratic takeover of the Senate, the religious right suffered some notable losses in contests for the House of Representatives. Mark Siljander, a Republican representing the largely rural fourth congressional district in southwestern Michigan, had been the religious right's most outspoken supporter in Congress. Early in 1986, Siljander sent a taped message to evangelical ministers in his district urging: "We need to break the back of Satan and the lies that are coming our way." In the primary election he was defeated 55 to 45 percent by a more moderate Republican.[13]

In the Republican primaries in Indiana, two House candidates sponsored by the religious right defeated opponents backed by the regular Republican organization. Both lost to Democrats in November, one in a district that had previously been safely Republican.[14]

In North Carolina's fourth district, the one-term incumbent Republican Bill Cobey addressed fundraising letters to "Dear Christian friend," asking, "Will you help me so our voice will not be silenced and then replaced by someone who is not willing to take a strong stand for the principles outlined in the word of God?" He was defeated for re-election by Democrat David Price, a political scientist with a degree in divinity.[15]

Despite these setbacks, Pat Robertson in 1987 found sufficient evidence of evangelical surge in recent elections, and enough indicators that a large share of the electorate hold conservative social attitudes, to declare his own candidacy for the

12. Data supplied by *ABC-Washington Post* election day survey, 1986.
13. See Michael Barone and Grant Ujifusa, *The Almanac of American Politics, 1988* (Washington, D.C.: National Journal, 1987), p. 590.
14. Ibid., pp. 401, 407.
15. Ibid., p. 887.

Republican nomination for president.[16] Running on a platform pledging to restore the nation to traditional morality, Robertson scored startling successes in early tests in Michigan and Iowa.[17] The media again sounded the alarm that the religious right was threatening to capture the Republican party, if not to take over the country.

Robertson continued to do well in Republican party caucuses and county conventions, where participation was small and an effective organization mobilizing dedicated supporters, even if relatively few in numbers, could often carry the day. But once the race for the Republican nomination moved to states where national convention delegates are elected through primaries, Robertson was easily overwhelmed by the candidacy of George Bush. In the Super Tuesday primaries on March 8, held mainly in the South, where evangelicals are most numerous, Robertson was wiped out by the Bush avalanche. In every state holding a primary, Bush received more votes *among evangelicals* than Robertson, not to mention among nonevangelical Republicans, whose negative ratings of Robertson were exceptionally high.[18]

Robertson's accomplishment in 1988 should not be underestimated. While he did poorly in primaries, his ability to carry caucuses enabled his followers to take over or win powerful roles in party organizations in such states as Iowa, Texas, Michigan, Louisiana, Nevada, Washington, Oklahoma, Alaska, Hawaii, and Georgia. In several states where Bush won the primary, and state law required the delegation to back the primary victor at the national convention, the actual delegate slots were filled by Robertson supporters. In some nonprimary states like Washington, most delegates selected by party caucuses favored

16. Lee Sigelman and Stanley Presser, "Measuring Public Support for the New Christian Right," *Public Opinion Quarterly* 52/3 (Fall 1988): 325, argue that some interpretations of survey evidence have exaggerated the level of public support for positions on social issues taken by the religious right.

17. For a sympathetic account of Robertson's positions on the issues by a political scientist, see Hubert Morken, *Pat Robertson: Where He Stands* (Old Tappan, NJ: Fleming H. Revell, 1988).

18. *Public Opinion* 11/1 (May/June 1988): 24.

Robertson, but shifted to Bush at the convention following their candidate's recommendation.[19]

During the struggle for the nomination, many Robertson backers had the experience of being resisted in Republican caucuses, sometimes to the point of being physically excluded, by agents of established party organizations wearing Bush buttons. Some commentators predicted that support by the Robertsonites for Bush in the fall election would be no more than lukewarm, and that many of them, reacting to Robertson's defeat, would become disillusioned and drop out of politics.

In some states, leaders of the Robertson campaign were right-wing firebrands who appeared to be using Robertson's candidacy for their own purposes, and whose interest in achieving Republican unity seemed minimal. Nevertheless, ordinary Robertson delegates from Georgia and the state of Washington whom I interviewed at the Republican convention in New Orleans indicated almost without exception that they intended to pitch into the fight to elect Bush, and that, although most of them had no previous political experience, they planned to remain politically active.

Some polls during the summer showed as much as 40 percent of white evangelicals prepared to return to their Democratic origins, making Michael Dukakis, the Democratic presidential candidate, competitive in many southern states. But as the fall campaign got underway, white evangelicals were among the first to abandon early leanings toward Dukakis and shift to Bush. In the end, evangelicals voted almost as heavily for Bush in 1988 as they had for Reagan in 1984, helping Bush carry every southern state and pile up large majorities in the rural areas of northern states like Pennsylvania, Ohio, and Indiana.

Perhaps most significantly, Republican candidates made impressive breakthroughs in 1988 at the state and local levels in some of the southern states where evangelicals are most heavily concentrated. In North Carolina, Governor James Martin be-

19. See Bob Benenson, "Roberston's Cause Endures Despite His Defeat," *Congressional Quarterly*, 14 May 1988, pp. 1267-73.

came the second Republican in history to win a second term, and Republicans gained three seats in the state senate and ten in the house of representatives. In Texas, Republican candidates for the first time won statewide offices below the office of governor: three seats on the state supreme court and one on the state railroad commission (which sets levels of oil production). In Florida, Republicans for the first time were elected to the offices of state treasurer and secretary of state. In Georgia, Republicans gained one seat in the state senate and seven in the house.

Evangelicals in a Pluralist Society

What will be the future effects of the evangelicals' participation in politics? My own expectation is that evangelicals will continue to be a force in national politics, predominantly on the conservative side. They have come to enjoy the power that goes with political participation. They like being courted by national political leaders. They have found, as one of their leaders put it, that "politics can be fun." And they have an unfulfilled social agenda which they remain most determined to enact.

They may be less patient with George Bush in the White House than most of them were with Ronald Reagan. Bush, however, understands their importance to the Republican coalition, and will probably, like Reagan, give them a share in the fruits of victory—both in federal appointments and in the formation of social policy.

How politically effective the evangelicals will be in the future remains questionable. If they behave like a rigid political sect, they will turn off many voters, including many traditional Republicans. Early impressionistic reports indicate that in many places they are developing the usual tendency of most politicians, whatever their ideological origins, to subsume their particular programmatic goals to their party's interest in winning elections. It should be remembered that many of the regular Republican organizations the evangelicals are now entering, or challenging, are controlled, not by moderate or "Rockefeller" Republicans, but by devoted conservatives who themselves achieved dominance during the Reagan uprisings of 1976 or 1980 or as long ago as the Goldwater revolution of 1964.

Even if the evangelicals acquire some of the pragmatic attitudes that most political analysts believe are needed to enhance political effectiveness, their influence within the Republican party may be limited by their tendency to fragment, which in the past has usually been one of their characteristics in politics as well as in religion. In 1980 and 1984, they were remarkably united in support of Reagan (although in the early stages of the 1980 campaign, many evangelicals backed the presidential candidacies of former Governor John Connally of Texas or Representative Philip Crane of Illinois). But in 1988 they failed to come together on a single candidate for the Republican nomination for president. Some evangelical leaders supported Robertson, but Falwell and some others aligned themselves with Bush, and others backed Senator Bob Dole of Kansas or Representative Jack Kemp of New York.

Robertson's failure to rally a majority of evangelicals to his cause is instructive. When Robertson in the summer of 1986 scored a startling early success in the first round of the process through which Michigan Republicans were to select their national convention delegates, many commentators predicted that when the campaign turned to the south, where evangelicals are much more numerous than in Michigan, Robertson would sweep all before him and might even win the nomination. In reality, the southern strongholds of evangelicalism were the very places where Robertson's identification with the charismatic brand of religion, and his long-standing rivalries with other television preachers like Falwell and Bakker, could be expected to limit his appeal. A leader like Reagan, who projects sympathy for the values of the movement but has not risen through its ranks, actually has a better chance than one of its own leaders to get its united support. As matters turned out, Robertson ran behind Bush in every southern primary.

The Republicans may be able to assemble an enduring

national majority coalition sometime in the 1990s. If a stable conservative majority emerges, conservative evangelicals will be one of its most important constituencies. Certainly evangelical leaders, or politicians identified with their cause, will be rewarded with some role in the national government and some implementation of their social agenda, whether through legislation or judicial decisions. Persons who oppose the evangelicals' agenda will understandably be displeased if it is put into effect, even to a limited extent. But some tightening of moral regulation would probably be accepted without extreme protest by most liberals, just as most conservatives, however unhappily, accepted loosening of restraints in the 1960s and 1970s.

Among the middle-of-the-road majority within the concerned political community, the main source of worry about evangelicals holding access to political power is that some evangelical activists do not seem to grasp that the American polity, as it was designed by the founders, and as it has evolved, is not merely majoritarian, but also requires a considerable degree of consensus. The party that elects its candidate president, which in a nation as diverse as the United States must always represent a coalition, has won the right to direct administration of the executive branch and to nominate federal judges. But groups that do not form part of the majority in any given election, or even in a series of elections, must also be able to feel that their rights and interests will be respected. If the numerical majority seeks to run roughshod over the rights of minorities, the American system, as the authors of *The Federalist* papers long ago observed, simply will not work. Some utterances by some of the evangelical leaders and their allies—"We have enough votes to run the country," "We need to break the back of Satan," "We're radicals working to overthrow the present structure in this country"— suggest that they do not fully subscribe to this principle.

Fortunately, our constitutional and political systems are to a great extent self-corrective against incursions by extremist groups. The governmental system of checks-and-balances and the protections of individual rights established in the Constitution by the founders provide institutional safeguards for minorities. Beyond these formal defenses, the American political system has an inherent tendency to require that governmental authority be based not merely on majoritarian rule but also on widely extended public acceptance. In a pluralist society like the United States, no single group is able, by itself, to form a majority. A group that finds itself in a majority coalition after one election must expect to be part of the minority at some future time. Even during the course of a single administration, shifting alignments of interests may place a particular group in the majority on some issues but in the minority on others. Every group, therefore, has a vested interest in maintaining the principle of respect for minority rights and interests.

One of the qualities that distinguishes leaders of the current religious right from earlier political enterprises by evangelicals or fundamentalists is that some of them seem to have learned at least part of this lesson. At earlier times, fundamentalists were cut off from potential allies by their identifications with anti-Catholicism, anti-Semitism, and racism. These tendencies have not totally disappeared, particulary at the grassroots level, from the current evangelical movement. But evangelical leaders like Falwell and Robertson have taken pains to ally themselves with Catholics in opposition to abortion, and to cultivate friendly relations with Jews through support for Israel (for which they also have theological justifications, troubling to many Jews). Conservative evangelicals have never been in the forefront of the struggle to extend civil rights, but most of their leaders are now careful to avoid any connection with racism. Some of them, in fact, have taken Martin Luther King as a role model for expressing moral protest.

This change in social tactics by conservative evangelicals has had two effects: first, it has made them politically more formidable; and, second, it has drawn them more into the mainstream of American life. The first gives those who oppose the social agenda of the religious right additional cause for alarm. But the second reduces the danger that evangelicals will misuse whatever political power the electoral tides may bring their way.

6. The Fundamentalist Phenomenon: A Psychological Perspective

Mortimer Ostow

At this late date in human history, one would be surprised to discover a religious phenomenon that is, in its psychologic essence, new and unique. In probably all instances, beneath what current particularities stamp as novel, one can recognize one or more of a relatively limited number of old and familiar psychodynamic mechanisms. My assignment requires that I try to transcend definitions and descriptions of fundamentalism formulated by the fundamentalists themselves, in order to discern the psychologic mechanism constituting its underlying structure, and its motivations and consequences. If we succeed in this task, we may be able to recognize similar psychologic structures in other religious phenomena and movements from the past and present, in our own and other milieux, that could profitably be related to the subject of our concern.

Having been invited to provide a psychologic discussion of a religious subject, I am assuming that I shall be permitted to use psychologic language and adduce psychologic theories and concepts, without being suspected of trying to challenge, violate, undermine, or reduce religious propositions.

In order to fulfill my assignment, I require a data base. When I write a clinical paper, I rely upon observations that I make in my own practice. When I try to apply psychodynamic

99

principles to social and behavioral phenomena, I look in documents and in recorded history for the patterns I recognize from
clinical experience. These data are one step removed from clinical observation, but in many instances, psychoanalytic methods
permit some useful constructions.

Books written by fundamentalists, and books written
about fundamentalism, add up to a very sizable library. Careful
scrutiny, from the psychoanalytic point of view, of the data produced within the fundamentalist movements will doubtless
repay the effort. I have not had the opportunity to review more
than a few books, including history, sociology, criticism, and
popular exposition. From these and from reports in the press,
I believe I have put together a reasonable picture of at least the
gross contours of such movements, though many details and
subtleties I am sure elude me.

The central text of American Christian fundamentalism is,
of course, the Bible. Not a text produced by any unified, coherent
group of fundamentalists, the Bible has been used by various
groups in various ways. What is characteristic of fundamentalism
is not the text, but the way it is used, the significance and meaning that are assigned to it. That the book of Revelation and other
segments of the Bible suggestive of apocalyptic thinking play such
a central role in fundamentalist thinking is a matter of psychologic
interest, and I shall develop its implications somewhat later on.

Finally, I have treated only a few patients who could be
considered fundamentalists, and some of these few, many years
ago. I shall refer to them in the course of our argument.

What qualities characterize the fundamentalist community? Even the fundamentalist community in America alone is
far from homogeneous. It overlaps with but is not coextensive
with the evangelical movement. It overlaps with but is not coextensive with the dispensationalist movement. One of its most
visible and unfortunate qualities is its tendency to split into
quarreling subunits which contend with each other over their
differing positions on religious and social issues, and frequently
on the degree of accommodation that they are willing to extend
to the outside community and to the realities of modern life.

80724

According to Marsden, the "five points of fundamentalism" in the American Protestant community were derived from the declaration of "essential" doctrine adopted by the Presbyterian General Assembly in 1920, namely, the inerrancy of Scripture, the Virgin Birth of Christ, his substitutionary atonement, his bodily resurrection, and the authenticity of the miracles.[1] In subsequent use, premillennialism was substituted for the authenticity of the miracles. What do we learn from this statement? Fundamentalists commit themselves to belief in a specific way of looking at the world as it is described literally in an ancient document. The need to consider Scripture inerrant and to subscribe to a fixed and rigid creed suggests a reluctance to tolerate doubt, uncertainty, and ambiguity. The references to the death and resurrection of Jesus, and to premillennialism, suggest a belief in the inevitability of rebirth following death.

In a recent sociologic study of a community of fundamentalists, Ammerman records the following observations. More than half of the community became fundamentalist by conversion. Conversion offers escape from anxiety or depression induced by visible external stress or by inner crisis. Converts need and are offered special support that creates a feeling of fellowship. The members of the fundamentalist community cannot tolerate uncertainty. The world seems to them dangerously chaotic. To overcome the uncertainty created by multiple translations, interpretations, and commentaries, they restrict themselves to a single translation and insist that it is absolutely correct and unambiguous. The Bible makes the world predictable. It reveals the secrets of the future. They accept the prophecy in Revelation that the world is coming to an end and they alone will be "raptured," that is, saved, by virtue of their belief. They see the world outside their community as wicked, depraved, and doomed to apocalyptic destruction. Their community stands alone as an island of righteousness that, by virtue

1. George M. Marsden, *Fundamentalism and American Culture* (New York: Oxford University Press, 1980), p. 117.

80724

of their beliefs, in the end will be saved and rewarded. The members display a tendency to submit passively to authority.[2]

Obviously, Ammerman is describing the behavior of followers. The leaders are often contentious, so that the community fragments into contending subgroups. Optimism is cultivated as a way of denying anxiety and fending off depression, but also as proof of the efficacy of belief. (I am reminded of the vacuous smiles seen on the faces of cultic converts that so exasperate their parents and that betray their fear of dealing with the real world.) The fundamentalist community maintains strict separation from the outside world with its immorality, unbelief, and temptations. They are more afraid of, and more militant against, Christians who deviate than against pagans or atheists, because deviation casts doubt upon their convictions. Separateness and defiance of modernism are maintained especially vigorously. The outside world offers no hope. Central commitment to the church and the community by a large part of the membership encourages and reinforces fellowship, which seems to provide much of the gratification and pleasure that the members enjoy. Fundamentalists display a tendency to think in terms of polarities—righteous and wicked, God and Satan, darkness and light. The pastor is recognized as the leader of the community and is idealized. Singing, especially in unison, plays an important role in church services. Since the fundamentalists as a group have achieved political power by virtue of their numbers and increasing affluence, they have embarked upon a program to impose their vision of proper behavior and proper belief upon the rest of the community.

Richard Hofstadter develops at great length the anti-intellectualism of evangelicals (including the fundamentalists), the paranoid attitude of fundamentalists, their militance and oppositionalism, their devotion to a populist democracy, their intolerance of ambiguity, and what he calls their "phobia" of

2. Nancy T. Ammerman, *Bible Believers: Fundamentalists in the Modern World* (New Brunswick, NJ: Rutgers University Press, 1987), pp. 29-30.

sexuality, that is, their intolerance of any sexual language or behavior outside family channels.[3]

One of the characteristics that comes across in all descriptions of fundamentalism is zeal, which sometimes translates to constructive energy, sometimes to divisive militance.

Lazarus-Yaffeh enumerates a number of features that she finds common to contemporary fundamentalist groups in Judaism, Christianity, and Islam. They separate themselves from the surrounding modern society. They reject the political state and political democracy. They yearn for their version of a theocratic state. Fundamentalists resent and criticize institutionalized religion, traditional religious scholarship, and traditional religious leadership. Fundamentalists reject science in general and the theories of evolution in particular, because they contradict their Scripture, but do not hesitate to use technology to further their cause. Scripture plays a central and preeminent role among all fundamentalists. It is true on a literal level; other types of explanations are rejected. (Among Jews, literal meaning and practical authority are extended to the "Oral Law," the writings of the talmudists and subsequent religious authorities, especially as these are given in the generally respected codes.) Scripture becomes a textbook and forecast of contemporary history and a guide to the incipient messianic age. The emphasis on the literal validity of the Scripture generates a negative attitude toward traditional interpretation and toward recognition of the significance of the historical development of theology. Literalness demands a primitive theodicy in terms of reward and punishment and belief in the power of Satan. Miracles are credited in a literal way. Fundamentalism is basically apocalyptic and messianic. The messianism may be expectant or aggressive. Messianic expectation is associated with subservience to charismatic leaders. Women are expected to assume their "natural state" in society and family, and are to be segregated from men. Members of the other religions are the source of all evil and mis-

---

3. Richard Hofstadter, *Anti-intellectualism in American Life* (New York: Random House-Vintage, 1962), p. 116 et passim.

fortune. Fundamentalists do not tolerate others, except as converts, and conversion of others is highly desired.[4]

Can we find a psychodynamic mechanism that would account for this entire syndrome, without explaining too much, and without reducing complex phenomena to oversimplified schemata? I should like to propose that the destruction-rebirth pattern possesses just those characteristics. Students of religion will have no difficulty in recognizing expressions of this pattern. The mythology of every religion that I have heard of incorporates accounts of the death and rebirth of the gods, of semidivine entities, and, in some cases, even of human beings. The classical "Book of the Dead," of which I have seen the Egyptian and the Tibetan, describes the induction of the souls of the dead into a new life, in which those who have been lost are found, and those who have separated are reunited. The term "out of body" phenomenon (cf. 2 Cor. 12:2-3) has recently been given to an illusion reported by people who believe that they are in imminent danger of being destroyed. They see their bodies, in whatever position of mortal danger applies, from some point removed (usually above) where they, as the observer, are immune from this danger. In one way or other, very similarly to the processes described in the Book of the Dead, they are inducted into a blissful and exalted new life.

Of course, the most dramatic and best known of these phenomena is the apocalypse. Although apocalypses have assumed different forms in response to the particular circumstances for which they were created, basically they all report a revelation, a prophecy of events that will terminate the present era of human history. The world as we know it will be destroyed, but a remnant of humanity will be saved to repopulate the world as a new era of perfection, happiness, and immortality is begun. In the various apocalypses, we can recognize a number of recurrent stereotypes in addition to destruction and rebirth: the seer who provides the revelation; the messiah who delivers; a

---

4. H. Lazarus-Yaffeh, "Contemporary Fundamentalism in Judaism, Christianity, Islam," *Jerusalem Quarterly* 47 (Summer 1988): 27-39.

journey around the universe; a vehicle in which the journey is made.

One can interpret a number of other patterns of hoped-for salvation as derivatives of apocalypse: millenarianism in general, specifically what is called "premillenarianism" involves this apocalyptic pattern fairly directly. Following God's wrathful destruction of the earth and its population, the righteous remnant will be saved ("raptured" in current Christian fundamentalist terminology), and will survive, in fact, will be reborn into a millennium of idyllic tranquility. The various forms of millenarianism formulate the relation among the destruction, the millennial rebirth, and the end of time differently, but the basic patterns remain. A focus on the hope for salvation at the hands of a divine or semidivine deliverer or a deliverer dispatched by the deity, whether it follows a general destruction or just provides an escape from current misery, constitutes messianism. A focus on the aspiration for and expectation of an ideal society that will supersede the current imperfect society yields utopianism. The gnostic believes that after death his soul will leave its body and ascend to unite with the deity in his celestial domain. Again, rebirth follows death.

Mysticism deals basically with the mystic's aspiration to unite with the deity. To this end, he may become seriously involved with theosophic speculation, an activity in which he attempts to satisfy that aspiration. Or, he may invite the illusion of union or connection by inducing a state of ecstasy (again, "standing outside" the body). Or, he may, by theurgic maneuvers, attempt to win recognition, propinquity, or union with the deity. I should like to propose that the mystical enterprise too can be seen as a death-rebirth experience. The death component is not explicitly stated but is implied in the mystic's turning away from the world of reality. He rejects it and finds joy and renewal only in his quest for mystical union or communion. This statement sounds like reduction or oversimplification, but I believe that the pattern can easily be recognized in every account of mystical experience and in all mystical literature that I have seen. It is important to distinguish here between mysticism as a principal and highly invested activity of the mystic on the one hand, and his full complement of behavior on the other. The mystic elects on frequent and extended occasions to disengage from the real and material world, but the rest of the time he may apply himself to it with earnestness and success. His disengagement is facultative rather than obligatory, and recurrent rather than continuous. For most mystics, mysticism is a part-time activity. But even mundane experience may be imbued with sacred significance. Kadushin uses the term "normal mysticism" to designate the attribution of supernatural significance to the ordinary experiences of daily life.[5]

These comments have been intended to introduce the proposition that the fundamentalist phenomenon too can be comprehended in the death- or destruction-rebirth framework. Specifically, for the Christian American fundamentalist, the experience of conversion is openly called a rebirth. The individual becomes a "reborn Christian." On that level, the antecedent death consists of rejection of the world of painful reality. By credo the fundamentalist Christian finds salvation, that is, rebirth, by identifying first with the Christ in his Crucifixion, and then in his Resurrection. The premillennialist among the fundamentalists literally projects himself into the premillennial scheme and anticipates experiencing the death and rebirth of the world. The focus here is on the experience of rebirth, in the conversion itself, and in induction into the tight fraternal, utopian society that fundamentalists attempt to create. As in the case of mysticism, the destructive component is expressed in the hostile rejection of society, on which they turn their backs.

Can we find the death-rebirth mechanism in the descriptions of fundamentalism that we have considered? With respect to the "five points of fundamentalism," the fundamentalist takes Scripture as the divinely given revelation, the text of the prophecy corresponding to the secret revelation of the apocalyptic and gnostic scriptures. If this text's veracity is challenged, the

---

5. Max Kadushin, *The Rabbinic Mind* (New York: Jewish Theological Seminary of America, 1952), pp. 194ff.

basis for the entire religious system is jeopardized. A worldview or outlook that depends upon a specific revelation cannot tolerate a questioning of its validity. The other four of the five points all deal with the death-rebirth sequence, namely, Christ's substitutionary atonement, his miraculous birth and resurrection, and the millennial promise.

Ammerman's description of the fundamentalist community also complies with that framework. More than half the community, she observed, became fundamentalist by experiencing conversion.[6] The invitation to convert is itself an invitation to a rebirth, by means of which care and anxiety and depression are put behind one. The conversion program of the group serves to enlarge and strengthen its utopian community. The uncertainty of life, the possibility of misadventure, illness, and death, are seemingly replaced by certainty and reassurance, offered by the guidelines of an inerrant scripture, equivalent to the secret revelation of classical apocalypse. The belief in the promise of "rapture" permits the fundamentalist to anticipate apocalyptic destruction without fear for himself. The world outside this group, which will not be saved, becomes the target of God's apocalyptic, destructive anger. The tendency to submit that Ammerman describes applies to the followers, who anticipate the premillennial tribulation and rapture passively. By contrast, some leaders consider an activist approach to the outside world, differing in degree and kind of position that they are ready to mobilize against it. Ammerman describes a pervasive optimism which seems to serve the need to deny continuing concern with the heavy burden of reality that has been pushed aside.[7]

A *zealous separateness* from the outside world seems to be the most consistent and striking characteristic of the fundamentalist community. The nonfundamentalist world is avoided for two reasons. First, that is the world that the fundamentalist has abandoned because he could not live comfortably with its uncertainty, its competitiveness, its frustrations, and its disappoint-

---

6. Ammerman, *Bible Believers*, pp. 29-30.
7. Ibid., p. 74.

ments. Second, that world and its less than complete commitment to the Christian religion, as the Christian fundamentalist
sees it, with its modern reinterpretations of the Bible, variant
translations, and relativistic doctrines, threaten the absolute system in which he believes. The outside world is the world of evil
that will be destroyed in the imminent apocalypse. The fellowship cultivated by the community strives to approach a utopian
ideal, an anticipation of millennial fraternal love even in a premillennial society. Ammerman observes that the fundamentalists think in terms of polarities.[8] The readiness of the fundamentalist to think in polar terms and the polar distinctions implicit
in apocalyptic thinking—good versus evil, God versus Satan,
light versus darkness—reinforce that individual's receptiveness
to apocalypse as the goal of life. The idealization of the pastor
that Ammerman describes follows from the projection upon
him of the fundamentalist's messianic expectation. Singing,
Ammerman says, plays an important part in the church service.[9]
Mystical accounts of the worship of God by his retinue of min-
istering angels commonly describe group singing. Communal
singing tends to unify groups and to encourage mutual identification of the members with each other. It strengthens the communal fellowship that replaces the contact with the outside
world. The eagerness of fundamentalist groups to impose their
version of morality upon the rest of the population flies in the
face of their declared indifference to it, but does correctly reflect the degree of their anger. The prophet who prophesies destruction may be suspected of wishing it, and the apocalyptic
prophet sounds furious.

Hofstadter confirms the militance of fundamentalists; their
devotion to populist democracy which I have associated with their
utopianism; their Machiavellian outlook which reflects the polar
destructiveness of apocalyptic; and their intolerance of ambiguity
which expresses their fear of chance and fate. He also speaks of
a paranoid tendency, which I interpret as the projection outward

8. Ibid., p. 82
9. Ibid., p. 130.

of their overt hostility. Despite the fact that it is they who wish to circumscribe the lives of their fellow citizens with their own extremist views of morality, they see themselves as victims rather than perpetrators. He emphasizes their anti-intellectualism.[10] Intellectuality obviously challenges belief when that belief is supported only by tradition. It questions the divine origin of texts. It requires the constant adaptation of religion to newly discovered facts: about cosmogony, about history, about the origin of humanity. One cannot adhere unquestioningly to the inerrancy and literal veracity of the Bible, if one takes seriously the accumulating knowledge of the universe and mankind.

A patient of mine converted to fundamentalism in late adolescence. Although he was peaceable and genial in his daily encounters with others, his childhood behavior and his adult dream life were marked by apocalyptic destruction, images of the destruction of the world followed in some cases by the expectation of rebirth. Politically he followed belligerent leaders, hoping to be led into a utopia which never arrived.

The fact that American Christian fundamentalism took origin in revivalistic and evangelical milieux highlights the centrality of utopian fellowship and communal modes of achieving union or communion with the divinity. The recruitment of as many outsiders as possible into the community strengthens it in its confrontation with the world.

These qualities clearly characterize some similar groups that do not claim religious orientation and sponsorship, as well as those that do. Associating fundamentalism with the death-rebirth mechanism makes it possible for us to understand, to a certain extent, why it appears to be an attractive modus vivendi to many people. The death-rebirth mechanism assumes a prominent role not only in the several religious and parareligious systems that I have mentioned above. It also plays a central though usually invisible role in the lives of almost all of us, but becomes clearly visible in much of serious mental illness. Here are two dreams reported by a woman at the onset of her schizophrenic psychosis.

10. Richard Hofstadter, *Anti-intellectualism*, passim.

"One was a painting of a city that seemed dead—a ghost city. It was painted in black and white and no human or animal figure appeared. All at once the doors of the houses opened and gaily dressed people came out, including my husband and me."

In the second dream, the patient was driving very fast in an automobile with her husband. She was afraid of a crash. Suddenly she was resting on a peaceful green meadow.

The first dream starts with the image of a world which is dead, lacking in life and color. Suddenly life and color return. The second starts with her closeness to her husband. Things escape control, and a crash presumably kills everyone. However, she awakens on a green meadow, which meant to her rebirth.[11] Such dreams and fantasies are also encountered among a group of patients who are diagnosed as having borderline personality disorder. These are individuals characterized by unusual emotional lability, impulsivity, and a talent for self-defeating and self-destructive behavior. Patients who are depressed may not report the threat of destruction in the dream text, since such patients find themselves in a desperate mental state already. The dream usually shows their attempt to escape by some form of rebirth. However, until they are ready to recover, the rebirth fails. Those of us who are not mentally ill experience these death and rebirth dreams and fantasies at critical moments in our lives.

The death-rebirth sequences reported by patients closely resemble those that we encounter in religious and parareligious scriptures and behavior. In both instances, we find angry and threatening prophets, wise seers and guides, saving messiahs, revelatory texts, instructive journeys, vehicular travel, and safe enclosures. The destructive component may assume any of a number of forms. Commonly, in both individual and group fantasy, it takes the form of a battle or a war, in process or threatened. In psychosis, while the dream or delusion may ex-

---

11. For a detailed description of this case, see M. Ostow, *Drugs in Psychoanalysis and Psychotherapy* (New York: Basic Books, 1962), pp. 227ff.

press destruction and death in imagery, and while the outcome in behavior may be murder or suicide, in the pathogenesis of the psychosis itself, the fury takes the form of an obligatory rejection of the world of reality in favor of the world of psychosis. As I noted above, in the Book of the Dead, the destructive phase of the sequence is represented by the death itself. In the "out of body" phenomena, it is the threatened death and the despair associated with it. From the point of view of psychosexual development, destructive dreams, fantasies, and play characterize especially the Oedipal child (age 3-6), who imagines that he must defend the world against the destructive villain, who, in the case of the boy, usually stands for his father.

In individual psychology or psychopathology, the rebirth components of the death-rebirth mechanism also assume a variety of forms. People who have experienced the "out of body" phenomenon sometimes describe images that seem to be literal descriptions of the experience of being born: proceeding through a long tunnel toward light at the end. Similar images are encountered at times in dream representation of rebirth. Rebirth may be expressed in dreams as joining the mother or both parents. That union may be symbolized by travel or movement to a hospitable container, a claustrum. The latter—and sometimes the vehicle itself—usually assumes a rectangular configuration, reminiscent of the child's crib or cradle, or the parent's bed; though at times it is spherical. (The divine figure is sealed within the maternal rectangular claustrum visualized by the prophet Ezekiel [Ezek. 1], who, by his mystical experience, is called to his prophetic duty.)[12] The image is repeated in Revelation to validate the prophecy of that prophet. It is this image that forms the basis of what has become known as *merkavah mysticism,* the mysticism of the divine chariot. Induction into a community of equals as a mode of rebirth occurs occasionally, but less fre-

---

12. See Jacob A. Arlow, "The Consecration of the Prophet," *The Psychoanalytic Quarterly* 23 (1951): 374-97. Reprinted in *Judaism and Psychoanalysis,* ed. Mortimer Ostow (New York: Ktav, 1982), pp. 45-72.

quently in the dreams of the mentally ill. Among the population not considered mentally ill, it forms the basis for utopianism and religious fundamentalism.

Which of these images of rebirth is offered may, I suspect, relate to the psychosexual and psychosocial maturity of
the subject. Clinical experience suggests the following interpretations. The straightforward image of emergence through
a narrow opening into the light probably expresses a rebirth
fantasy for an individual functioning at that moment at the
most regressed level. The movement by a vehicle to a rectangular or spherical claustrum expresses the fantasy of an individual functioning at the level of a child who feels utterly
dependent upon his parents. Rebirth expressed as victory
over a deadly opponent characterizes the Oedipal phase. Rebirth imagined as union with a group expresses the fantasy of
an individual functioning on a still higher level, the level of
latency, that is, from about the sixth to the tenth year, when
the child becomes ready to associate with peers to form the
earliest social groups.

It seems that the death-rebirth mechanism functions as a
primitive device for coping with extreme degrees of distress,
whether imposed from the outside or developing internally.
Though it becomes manifest to the psychiatrist most strikingly
in serious mental illness, it may be activated in one form or other
in any of us who are confronted with a significant degree of
stress. It is a common though regressive response to serious
threat or disaster.

The attachment of the fundamentalist to his community
and its fraternal members reminds the psychoanalyst of the
phenomenon called *separation-individuation,* first described in
detail by Margaret Mahler. The first years of a child's psychological development are concerned with establishing a sense of
separateness from the mother and pleasure in recognizing one's
own individuality. Like all developmental steps, this one is
fragile, and in the absence of a certain degree of wholesome-
ness in the child, the parent, and the parent-child relationship,
the process may be arrested or, if negotiated, may easily reverse

from time to time when the stresses that need to be confronted in individual life seem overwhelming.[13]

Fundamentalists think in terms of black-and-white polarities, finding the intermediate shades of gray inconceivable. They do not tolerate uncertainty or ambiguity. They disparage those outside their own group. They feel protected against separation and death, and they believe that their loyalty to leaders and group guarantees that protection. They look for authority and submit to it. They believe in the rigid relation between behavior and consequent reward and punishment.

These qualities all suggest the attitudes of the "undifferentiated" child who fears to acknowledge the inevitability of separation, disappointment, and pain; in short, reality. In regressing from participation in the differentiated, hierarchical group of settled adult society to participation in the fraternal, utopian, egalitarian group similar to the groups formed by latency (age 6 to 11) children, the fundamentalist is also regressing to the state of mind of the child who resists differentiation from its mother. The messiah and the group itself represent the returning mother.

We can generalize with some degree of confidence that the illusory rebirth of the apocalyptic mechanism is always a regression. The aggressive response to despair is real and dangerous, but the rebirth expected is illusory and usually fails to protect against the destructiveness of the previous phase, except to the extent that the hope that it inspires sustains morale and thereby reinforces resolution and courage.

What triggers the expression of the death-rebirth mechanism, and how does it work? The death-rebirth mechanism is invoked on the occasion of critical deviation from mental equilibrium. It is seen during the period of spontaneous attempts to restore equilibrium in the lives of all of us. It is also seen on the occasion of the incipience or exacerbation of the major ill-

13. Margaret Mahler (with Fred Pine and Annie Bergmann), *The Psychological Birth of the Human Infant: Symbiosis and Individuation* (New York: Basic Books 1975).

nesses, schizophrenia and depression, or on the occasion of episodes of acute exacerbation of borderline disorders. When it no longer appears, the individual's self-reparative efforts have come to a halt. The relative prominence of the destruction versus the rebirth phase of the prototypical apocalyptic pattern reflects the relative prominence of destructive versus constructive efforts, of depressive versus euthymic or euphoric tendencies. These are not merely academic distinctions; they can be used to help with the selection and monitoring of the actions of the major classes of medication used in the treatment of psychotic illness. In a most general and approximate way, one can anticipate that in the presence of a predominance of destructive imagery in the dreams and fantasies of the mentally ill, an antidepression drug is called for, and in the presence of the predominance of rebirth images, a tranquilizing drug is appropriate.

Actually, the straightforward and simple death-rebirth sequence does not always occur. Sometimes we see more than two phases, rather, a struggle between the two tendencies, one of which seems to dominate and often to terminate the dream. For example, the dream may start with an image of destruction, which is then countered by an image of a reconstructive process, and the latter may fail or abort, so that the destructive process resumes. From such observations, we must infer that the destructive-rebirth mechanism is invoked for the purpose of correcting a tendency that has gone too far.

We are describing, then, a regulatory mechanism. Under normal circumstances, it corrects incipient deviations from psychic energy equilibrium effectively and quickly, so that the regular mood swings of daily life do not escape control and induce mental illness. To the extent that the regulatory mechanism fails, mental disequilibrium occurs. The restorative efforts are reflected in dreams and fantasies where they are fairly transparent, and in overt behavior in which they are not so clear. It is these restorative efforts that are often represented in apocalyptic form. It follows that effective treatment can shift the quantitative balance between destructive and constructive tendencies, restoring equilibrium values so that the apocalyptic pattern tends to drop out.

From the point of view of individual mental illness, we can expect a pattern of death-rebirth imagery specific for each state of disequilibrium. When the energy levels rise too high and are not appropriately corrected, the apocalypse is dominated by the rebirth fantasy, as, for example, in the first two dreams presented above, and the mental deviation induced is mania or a "high" form of schizophrenia. The corrective efforts that are made are reflected in temporary though often violent interruptions in the movement toward good fortune. The patient becomes detached from reality, and his loss of reality is expressed by the illusion or delusion of world destruction. The rebirth fantasy finds expression in various delusions. When energy levels fall too low, the accompanying apocalyptic productions exhibit a predominance of destructive tendencies, and the deviation we see is depression or a "low" form of schizophrenia. Corrective efforts are usually represented in the apocalyptic productions as interruptions of the destructive processes and threats, but they do not succeed. In behavior, the destructive fantasies may find expression in suicide or other self-destructive actions.

A phenomenon that is interesting and important is the reinforcement of efforts to escape depression. The efforts may be reinforced spontaneously, as a result of intrapsychic or even physical changes. They may be reinforced by the administration of antidepression medication. They may be reinforced by changes in the environment that promise relief from great external pressure. To the extent that these reparative efforts succeed in restoring the equilibrium, the patient improves clinically. However, too often the attempt succeeds only in remobilizing the aspiration for relief accompanied by anger, giving rise to destructive impulses directed either toward the self or outward. This state of inadequate repair of depression then becomes dangerous. It may focus its destructive energies by means of apocalyptic illusion and undertake destruction in the hope that reconstruction will follow—usually a vain hope.

In sum, we see that the apocalyptic fantasy or any of its derivatives may be invoked on the occasion of mental disequilibrium as part of an effort to correct it. Subjectively the invocation of that fantasy is accompanied by hope, and we may say, with some justification, that from the subjective point of view, the purpose of apocalypse is to inspire hope in the hopeless. When it miscarries, it can cause death and destruction.

After this extensive excursion from our concern, let us try to apply some of these conclusions to fundamentalism. As we have noted, fundamentalism reflects features of apocalypse and several of its derivatives. It seems to me that the essential and characteristic dynamic of fundamentalism is the achievement of the illusion of rebirth in the comforting and reassuring effect of belonging to a fraternal group of like-minded, nonthreatening individuals. The larger community in which most of us live is a community of competition and rivalry, a community of opportunity for great success but also for equally great failure. Its social welfare program barely protects us against starvation and against dying as a result of inadequate medical care, and to depend on such programs is to lower one's status in the society. Along with opportunity comes risk. Even in the most protective of societies, we are each subject to the vagaries of chance, as it affects our physical or mental state and our economic and social positions, and as it affects the entire society or world in which we live. At most times in many places one finds a portion of the population averse to the risks that the society entails, and who therefore are attracted to risk-reducing measures and illusions. Against the risks of illness and death, some cultivate magical protective practices—the fads, the quackery, the frauds of pseudomedicine, or belief in magical religious cures. Against the risks of competition, such individuals prefer subgroups of society in which it is generally agreed that universal love shall prevail and individual ambition will be suppressed. And against all risks, the belief in a divine Providence whose favor can be won by specific religious acts and abstentions can create an illusion of protection.

Fundamentalists, it seems to me, protect themselves against

danger both by their conviction that proper behavior and worship will secure for them the protection of Providence and by moving from the larger world of chance and hazard to the smaller world of fraternity. It is not surprising that American Protestant fundamentalism should have appeared within the context of evangelicalism, a movement devoted to the recruitment of as many people as possible into the denominational community of the recruiter. Nor is it surprising that Ammerman found that half the members of the community that she studied had become members by conversion.[14] The new, fraternal community is formed by secession from and rejection of the larger community. This rejection is effected by virtue of a good deal of anger, which appears as the individual realizes his discomfort and his need to escape to a safe haven. The affiliation with the new group constitutes the realization of the rebirth fantasy. The premillennial doctrine tells us just how the fundamentalist feels about the world outside his fraternal community.

Social Psychology of Apocalypse

While current formulations of individual psychology and psychopathology are problematic enough, extension of these formulations into the realm of social psychology creates even more formidable hazards, but let us try to stay close to observable data and restrict ourselves to a small number of reasonable formulations.

The first question to ask is whether apocalypse as a determinant applies to group as well as individual behavior. The Nazi phenomenon and particularly the Shoah (Holocaust) clearly represent an apocalypse acted out. The Jews and other minorities were designated as the satanic enemy with which there could be no coexistence, and they had to be destroyed to make way for the emergence of the purified and revitalized German

14. Ammerman, *Bible Believers*, pp. 29-30.

people. We can recognize in history other campaigns of destruction, aimed not to overcome a truly dangerous enemy or an untrustworthy one, but solely to destroy a segment of the population that serves as a scapegoat.

Second, does the genre of apocalypse serve a regulatory function for the community as it does for the individual? The answer to this question is more difficult to determine.

It is oversimplifying to assert merely that the noncompetitive group is more comfortable than the competitive one. I believe that there is an important, real psychological difference between the utopian, egalitarian, fraternal group on the one hand, and the wider, competitive, multistatus group on the other. On the one hand, the fraternal group appeals to individuals functioning on a less mature level. It promises unconditional love and protection, and demands only that the individual member adhere to uniform rules of conduct and cooperate with the others on an equal basis. On the other hand, the conventional community, while it offers some degree of protection, rewards courage and enterprise and risk taking, and penalizes timidity. To the individual who is anxious and discontent in the wider community, entry into the fraternal group, or transformation of the conventional into a fraternal community, provides not only relief but often a sense of renewal and rebirth. Most of us have experienced the electrifying effect of patriotic fervor elicited on occasion when national or group unity is called for, to the accompaniment of patriotic music and stirring patriotic orations. Less dramatically, most of us have experienced a kind of mild exaltation while joining a group of fellows in unison singing—as, for example, at a religious service. The adolescent peer community, with its uniform dress code and idiosyncratic language, adolescent athletic teams and adolescent gangs, provides a similar experience, though on a constant rather than episodic level.

On some religious occasions, members of the fraternal group wish to incorporate all of mankind into a homogeneous religious community. "Peace on earth and good will toward men." There seem to be no enemies—only potential companions. On most other occasions, however, the cohering group sees itself as distinct from and set against antagonists or hostile forces; for example, the enemy of the country, rival teams, other ethnic groups, traditional religious congregations. A nationalist, regressive transition into a patriotic commune can provide intranational harmony, for example, during war time. But when the fraternity is more limited and takes neighboring groups as its natural enemy, it threatens to become a divisive force, promoting ethnic or religious or class conflict.

I believe that Hofstadter, in speaking of a "thorough-going . . . fear of normal sex and deviation" among fundamentalists, is exaggerating.[15] From what I have read, sex life is considered appropriate in marriage. Fundamentalists are not celibate. They do fear the intragroup rivalry that extramarital sexual attraction and behavior entails, and they condemn these with zeal. Other similar groups, without religious sponsorship, prevent such rivalry by making all women available to all men. One of my patients could not tolerate heterosexual contact, and though attracted to men, he avoided homosexual intimacy purely out of religious principles. With him the avoidance of competitive heterosexuality took the form of neurotic inhibition. In contrast, another patient subscribed to religious proscription of premarital sexual behavior, but nevertheless could not abstain from it and was overcome with remorse on occasions when he lost control and indulged. In the case of this man, conscious self-control was the method of preventing heterosexual rivalry.

It is difficult to know what influences on society induce disequilibria analogous to those that occur among individuals. Is there a social phenomenon homologous with the automatic correction of excessive energizing that we encounter in "high" schizophrenics? Do self-confident, powerful societies become disabled by internally arising inhibitions that create apocalyptic fantasies and fears? If that indeed does occur, it is not an easily recognized phenomenon. We must conclude that although

15. Richard Hofstadter, *Anti-intellectualism*, p. 119n.

apocalyptic fantasies may determine the forms of behavior for both some individuals and some societies, the two are not exactly similar.

We are familiar with demoralized populations, suffering privation or oppression or frustration, hoping for years for messianic rescue. This situation reminds us of the depressed individual, though he has no hope. His dreams invariably end in defeat and anxiety. In this respect, society and the individual are not exactly analogous.

We are also familiar with situations in which an oppressed people, patient and long-suffering, is granted some relief and then becomes aggressively demanding. That phenomenon, known as the "revolution of rising expectations," corresponds to the phenomenon of angry but inadequate correction of the depressive state in individual psychology that I described above. We find great variation in the degree of aggressiveness exhibited by the several fundamentalist communities, and even by the same community at different times. The depressed, distressed community, if it can cultivate hope, may encourage some vague messianic expectation, an anticipation of rescue by supernatural influence. The situation may be compared to the individual depressed patient, usually unable even to mobilize hope. Hopelessness is characteristic of melancholic depression. With the slightest hint of encouragement, a lightening of political oppression, the community may organize itself into a fundamentalist, egalitarian fraternity that fosters the belief that salvation can be forced, and apocalyptic "end time" can be pushed ahead, by means of personal and group religious dedication, submission, and self-abnegation. From the fundamentalists' intolerance of uncertainty and risk, we must infer timidity and fearfulness as characteristic of the average follower. We certainly see this timidity and fearfulness in depressed populations, as well as in the individual depressed patient. With the formation of the fraternal community, the members borrow courage from each other and from the leader. Or, if not courage, at the very least they acquire some degree of self-respect. If events promote self-confidence through a military victory, for example, or a significant increase in the size or strength of the community, political recognition, or the respect of outsiders, the fundamentalist community becomes more self-confident, assertive, and ultimately belligerent and threatening. The members now become fierce and aggressive. Again, the situation can be compared with the vicissitudes of the individual depressed patient. When recovery starts, whether spontaneous or induced by psychiatric drug treatment, he becomes more angry, hostile, and combative. It is in this state of mind that the fundamentalist community becomes a threat to its neighbors, whether of the same religious denomination or political or ethnic group, or to outsiders. As their strength grows, they progress from political activism to terrorism to military adventurism.

But the apocalyptic frame of mind is highly ambivalent. Death and rebirth succeed each other, excessive excursion in one direction being corrected by an excess in the opposite direction. In individual psychopathology we see such alternation clearly in dreams, and even in abrupt shifts between homicidal and suicidal tendencies. In the militant fundamentalist community, this ambivalence finds expression in undertaking adventures that seem to its members destined to succeed, but that to the outside observer, uninfected by group madness, are visibly destined to end in defeat. He sees foolhardiness rather than courage. Contemporary and historical examples come easily to mind. If the individual depressed patient, by virtue of inner spontaneous therapeutic powers, or by proper treatment, recovers completely from his depression, then the interim hostility subsides and he can resume reasonable and appropriate behavior. Similarly, if, the fundamentalist society does achieve a complete victory, self-destructive tendencies and outside forces notwithstanding, the community loses its need for militant unity and separatist zeal, and may settle down to a pacific, postbelligerent state of mind. In short, we see that it is misleading to define the fundamentalist community as though it were static and unchanging. Its qualities vary as its strength and position in the wider community progress and regress.

We must also wonder how the fantasies of individuals and

the myths of society influence each other in their origin and evolution. This too is a problematic area. Some of my initial explorations suggest that a leader with activist apocalyptic fantasies offers them to a group. Those of its members who harbor similar fantasies seize upon the leader's fantasies, because they validate their own and seemingly convert illusion to reality. This phenomenon creates a central group of committed members who have a strong interest in following and supporting the leader. When this central committed group exceeds a critical size, it attracts others as members, not out of conviction, but simply out of a desire not to be left behind.

What induces individuals to retreat from the conventional world into a fundamentalist fraternity? In a most general way, we can say that reality is always painful, disappointing, and frustrating. Things never seem to work out the way we wish. Some of us are able to maintain the hope that things will improve. Others cannot maintain that hope and become discouraged. The difference seems to be one of temperament, perhaps inborn, perhaps influenced by early experience. We try to protect ourselves against this pain, each in our own way. Some of us develop illusions, some develop symptoms, some succumb to depression. The apocalyptic mechanism permits us to see the disappointing world as destroyed, and ourselves ready to be elevated by one rebirth mechanism or other. The mechanism, though general, can easily be demonstrated in the lives of many individuals.

But the next question is more difficult, namely, how is it that, from time to time, a number of individuals within a given community all seem to be ready to cooperate in fostering the same illusory defense against reality? When a common misfortune affects a large number of people in the same community, one can understand that a common solution, real or unreal, might appeal to most of them. However, in many historical instances of millenarian campaigns, utopian aspirations, messianic movements, or separatist religious fervor such as fundamentalism, the nature of the misfortune eludes us. All we know is that group humiliation and shame seem to be especially potent precipitants. Some discontent prevails across the community. We may not know whether it is of common quality and common origin, or whether it originates differently in each individual. It is of the nature of the human organism that all of a number of disparate forms of distress may be defended against by a small number of mechanisms. In other words, a common defense may be invoked to overcome distress of different origins and kinds.

The Role of Leadership

Ammerman observes that fundamentalists tend to feel obligated to obey authority, even authority outside their religious group.[16] It seems easy to understand that a community that encourages individual subjection to the will of the group and submission to divinely ordained fate, that encourages optimistic expectation of providential protection, that maintains egalitarian modes of relating to each other, that expects messianic salvation, will feel obligated to submit to authority in general and to religious authority in particular. Therefore such communities will easily fall prey to unscrupulous individuals who possess the capacity to suggest divine inspiration. I refer here to what are called charismatic leaders.

Charismatic leadership requires study in its own right. Many but not all of such leaders are unscrupulous. Some are sincere and earnest, and others are ambivalent. The qualities that they exhibit and that give them credibility include: a truly unusual capacity of some kind, for example, a remarkable memory, an unusual appearance or voice; an ability to project the image of a reliable and caring parent; and a readiness to make outrageous and illogical statements, thereby sanctioning their followers' rejection of reality. In any case, a promising leader will be welcomed and followed and obeyed even to the

16. Ammerman, *Bible Believers*, p. 56.

detriment of the individual follower and the community. The Jonestown incident comes to mind.

Summary

Fundamentalism may be described as a derivative of apocalyptic thinking, in which the destructive phase consists of condemnation and rejection of the outside world and the rebirth phase consists of reorganization into an egalitarian, populist, fraternal community inspired by a charismatic leader.

Individual or group discontent, probably not always the same from time to time and place to place, frequently challenges self-love and self-esteem. The discontent initiates a tendency to seek relief by invoking an illusion that the real present can be overcome, rejected, destroyed, and replaced by a reborn world. A population of individuals, not mentally ill, who share such feelings of discontent, may with the encouragement of a charismatic leader reorganize so as to eliminate competition and rivalry and to unite against the outside world. The new fraternal organization provides a feeling of individual and group strength, overcoming weakness and shame that prevail under normal circumstances. As their actual strength grows, by recruitment, by learned techniques of terrorism, or by military buildup, their separation gives way to a hostile attempt to impose their beliefs and community organization onto the rest of the world. The characteristics of the fundamentalist community vary with its strength and its phase of destruction. It must be seen as a dynamic rather than a static entity.

Those of us who are not fundamentalists have no quarrel with their zealous separatism, so long as they do not threaten us or threaten to destroy the community in which we live and which they have rejected.

To hope that we shall ever succeed in eliminating the stimuli to apocalyptic thinking, to attenuate the harshness of the reality in which we all live, and to overcome significantly and permanently challenges to one's self-love and self-esteem, is itself an exercise in utopian and messianic thinking.

See also:

Barr, James. *Beyond Fundamentalism.* Philadelphia: Westminster Press, 1984.

Berger, Peter L. *The Sacred Canopy: Elements of a Sociological Theory of Religion.* Garden City, NY: Doubleday-Anchor, 1969.

Cohn, Norman. *The Pursuit of the Millennium.* New York: Oxford University Press, 1961.

Kimball, William R. *The Rapture: A Question of Timing.* Grand Rapids: Baker Book House, 1985.

Lewis, Sinclair. *Elmer Gantry.* New York: New American Library, 1927.

Lindsey, Hal. *The Late Great Planet Earth.* Grand Rapids: Zondervan Publishing House, 1970.

———. *Satan Is Alive and Well on Planet Earth.* Grand Rapids: Zondervan Publishing House, 1972.

———. *The Liberation of Planet Earth.* Grand Rapids: Zondervan Publishing House, 1974.

Mojtabai, A. G. *Blessed Assurance: At Home with the Bomb in Amarillo, Texas.* Boston: Houghton Mifflin, 1986.

Szasz, Ferenc Morton. *Three Fundamentalist Leaders: The Roles of William Bell Riley, John Roach Straton, and William Jennings Bryan in the Fundamentalist-Modernist Controversy.* Ann Arbor: University Microfilms, 1969.

7. Fundamentalism and the American Polity

Richard John Neuhaus

Many, perhaps most, Americans who are not fundamentalists view fundamentalism as a threat to the American polity.[1] In the last decade especially, the emergence of fundamentalism in the form of the religious right has been perceived as a dangerous disruption of the established procedures by which we order our public life.[2] Admittedly, the deeper reality is a widespread anxiety about particularist religion in "the public square."

In 1984, when John Cardinal O'Connor came to New York, there was a series of dinner meetings to introduce him to a number of area leaders. One dinner was held with media leaders during a period of public controversy over the Cardinal's challenging of Geraldine Ferraro, then the vice-presidential candidate, on her version of Catholic teaching regarding abortion. In the course of the conversation, one of the most influential news executives in the country explained to the Car-

1. Current data on attitudes towards religion and public life are usefully brought together in the Williamsburg Charter Survey. See summary and comment on the survey in "Trying to Make Sense of the Americans—A Survey on Religion and Public Life," *The Religion and Society Report*/Special Report, April 1988.

2. For a more complete analysis of this phenomenon and reactions to it, see Richard Neuhaus, *The Naked Public Square* (Grand Rapids: Eerdmans, 1984).

126

dinal that, when John F. Kennedy was elected in 1960, he and his colleagues concluded that Roman Catholics really "belonged" in America. He continued, "But I must frankly say, Archbishop, that since you've come to this city some of us are beginning to ask that question again, whether you Catholics really understand how we do things here."

The understanding of "how we do things here" is even more deeply disturbed by publicly assertive fundamentalism. Membership in the "we" is, in the main, undefined, but there is no doubt that the fundamentalists are "them." I have participated in symposia on fundamentalism that included no presentations by fundamentalists. Quite clearly, and quite typically, "we" gather to talk about "them." This situation reflects an assumption in some circles that fundamentalists are the "threatening others" who are beyond the pale of civil discourse. Needless to say, most, but by no means all, fundamentalists return the compliment by deeming us to be beyond the pale of their discourse.

In most academic settings, "fundamentalism" is a pejorative of deepest hue. The same is true in the establishment news media; witness the routine references to "Islamic fundamentalism." Despite the fact that fundamentalism is a peculiarly Christian belief system of American origin, the term is applied to militant Muslims and others who threaten our conventional ways of thinking and acting. Fundamentalism has become, in short, a synonym for fanaticism. That many fundamentalists are fanatical cannot be denied. We would be well advised, however, to consider whether there is not an element of the fanatical in much of the reaction to fundamentalism. One recalls that "fanaticism" is derived from *fanum*, meaning temple. The fanatic is one who lives in a *fanum* without windows, in a space of sacred ideas and attitudes that may not be questioned. History has many ironies in the fire, and one irony may be that assertive fundamentalism is poking windows through the *fanum*, whether religious or secular, in which America's elites live, and within which we define "how we do things here."

In addressing "Religious Fundamentalism and the American Polity" one must take into account, then, the commonly expressed anxiety that publicly assertive fundamentalism violates the American polity. A few years ago many bumpers sported the sticker, "The Moral Majority Is Neither." They are not moral because they violate our civil religion's dogma of tolerance. And, far from being a majority, they are a rabid minority who would "impose their values" on the rest of us. Or so the indictment reads. In the history of discussion about the American polity, the appropriate word for this kind of threat to the polity is *faction,* and one of the most authoritative voices on that subject is the voice of James Madison.

The most quoted of Madison's words on faction and factionalism appeared in the *New York Packet* on Friday, November 23, 1787. Madison wrote: "The influence of factious leaders may kindle a flame within their particular States, but will be unable to spread a general conflagration through the other States. A religious sect may degenerate into a political faction in a part of the Confederacy; but the variety of sects dispersed over the entire face of it must secure the national councils against any danger from that source."[3] The security of the republic, Madison argues, rests in the multiplicity of factions that constitute countervailing forces, resulting in a reasonably stable equilibrium.

Although *The Federalist No. 10* is frequently cited in connection with the dangers of religious factionalism, it is worth noting that in it, religion is mentioned almost in passing. The quotation above continues in this way: "A rage for paper money, for an abolition of debts, for an equal division of property, or for any other improper or wicked project, will be less apt to pervade the whole body of the Union than a particular member of it; in the same proportion as such a malady is more likely to taint a particular county or district, than an entire State."[4] Earlier Madison had stated that "the most common and durable source of factions has been the various and unequal distribution of

3. *The New York Packet,* 23 November 1787.
4. James Madison, *The Federalist No. 10.*

property." Long before Marx's critique of capitalism, Madison well knew that the various interests divide the people "into different classes." Such interests, he believed, "grow up of necessity in civilized nations," and it is "the principal task of modern legislation" to regulate these interests to the common good. Far from being the chief source of factionalism, religion was viewed by Madison as a necessary but insufficient force for the restraint of factionalism. When factionalism arises, Madison wrote, "neither moral nor religious motives can be relied on as an adequate control."

While Madison was not primarily concerned about religious factions, *The Federalist No. 10* is regularly invoked in discussions of the subject and therefore a closer look into its argument would seem to be in order. What exactly did Madison mean by a faction? He answers the question with satisfying directness: "By a faction, I understand a number of citizens, whether amounting to a majority or minority of the whole, who are united and actuated by some common impulse of passion, or of interest, adverse to the rights of other citizens, or to the permanent and aggregate interests of the community." While satisfyingly direct, that definition is not very satisfying on other grounds. In historical retrospect, it may seem pitiably naive. It would not be long before the formation of political parties, for instance, would regularize the factionalism that the founders viewed as such a peril to their republic in formation.

The observation is easily made that a faction is any party whose purposes I do not share. Most of us like to believe we occupy the high moral ground above faction and partisanship. Our purpose is the common cause, theirs is factionalism. The conventional charge against fundamentalism, when it goes public, is precisely that it is a force "adverse to the rights of other citizens [and to] the permanent and aggregate interests of the community."

For those who live in the established world of conventional wisdom, it is difficult to understand how fundamentalists turn that charge around. Their claim is that it is the minority of the societal elites (the "secular humanists") who exercise an influence adverse to their rights and to the interests of the community. Involved here is a dispute over rights and over the common good (if we may assume that it is in the interest of the community to pursue the good). The hope is that this presently confused and raucous dispute may be reconstituted as a civil argument, with the result that we may arrive at something like a public philosophy for our continuing experiment in democratic governance. There is no denying that this seems a forlorn hope at present, while our society is engaged in a war of symbols and ideas, a veritable *Kulturkampf* over the definition of the American enterprise.

This *Kulturkampf* was dramatically evidenced in the 1988 presidential campaign. There were innumerable laments about the low level of the debate between the candidates and their failure to "address the real issues." It is true that the dependence upon televised "sound bites" did little to elevate the level of public discourse. But I suggest it is a great mistake to think the candidates did not address the real issues. Mr. Bush's focus on the pledge of allegiance, the American Civil Liberties Union, and crime in the cities was not a distraction from the real issues. These *are* the real issues for millions of Americans. That they were presented in "code words" should not be viewed as sinister. In our public discourse, debased by politicians and news media alike, "code words" are the price paid in response to the demand for brevity. At a deeper level, any viable social order does, in fact, have a code. That is, it is possessed of a set of often unarticulated assumptions, anxieties, and aspirations. The successful politician is able to read the societal code, and knows the words that actuate popular support.

(The supposedly sinister aspect of "code words" arises when the subject touches on race in connection with, for example, crime. In the 1988 campaign, Democrats did not hesitate to accuse their opponents of exploiting "racism." But the grossly disproportionate number of criminal acts perpetrated by elements of the "black underclass" is no longer a dirty little secret, except perhaps in sectors of an aging civil rights leadership. That this reality was not addressed as sensitively and constructively as it should have been may well be the case. The claim that it should not be addressed at all is to ask the American people, both black and white, to pretend not to know what they know all too well.)[5]

The 1988 presidential campaign has everything to do with Madison's understanding of faction. The claims and counterclaims with respect to whether Mr. Dukakis was outside the "mainstream" of American life were another way of arguing about what Mr. Madison called "the permanent and aggregate interests of the community." To put it quite simply, the Republican strategy was to portray the party of liberalism as a faction. At the same time, the ACLU and Planned Parenthood took full-page ads deploring the Republican party's captivity to the faction that is politicized fundamentalism. And so, two centuries later, we are, in important respects, right back with *The Federalist No. 10*.

In our continuing *Kulturkampf*, the opprobrium attached to "faction" has great political potency. Both our political parties stand accused of factiousness, and each says to the other "You're one too." It is not a very edifying spectacle. To adjudicate the dispute in terms of distributing political power, we have popular elections. But elections cannot settle the underlying and more important conflicts. Perhaps those conflicts cannot be settled at all, but we can, through reasoned and open-minded inquiry, at least achieve a better understanding of what has brought us to our present pass.

Among fundamentalist voters, support for Mr. Bush was well above 70 percent. Much the same was true among conservative Roman Catholics, Lutherans, Orthodox Jews, and that large cohort of Christians who call themselves evangelicals. Despite the positions adopted by their institutional leaders, we should also not underestimate the conservative constituency of the mainline/old-line churches of liberal Protestantism. Robert

---

5. See William Julius Wilson, *The Truly Disadvantaged: The Inner City, the Underclass, and Public Policy* (Chicago, 1987). Wilson, a black sociologist at the University of Chicago, offers one of the most thorough accounts for data describing the plight of the black underclass.

Wuthnow of Princeton has made the suggestive proposal that
we are witnessing the development of "two civil religions" in our
culture, and that each is religiously legitimized by realignments
within our religious communities.[6] Wade Clark Roof and William McKinney have persuasively argued that those religious
groups that were once viewed as marginal—and are still viewed
as marginal by our societal elites—are becoming the new religious mainline.[7]

I expect that such a long-term realignment is indeed underway, and that it was powerfully precipitated by the fundamentalist insurgency beginning in the 1970s. At the beginning of this decade we spoke about the "new religious right."
Then, when it was no longer so new, we called it simply the "religious right." With its continuing political ascendancy, and
much slower cultural ascendancy, it now lays claim to being the
mainstream that reflects "the permanent and aggregate interests of the community."

And yet there is a marked ambivalence in fundamentalism's claim that by successfully reading the societal code it has
become part, maybe the leading part, of the mainstream. Fundamentalism was forged in the fires of oppositional controversy.
It was energized by an intense minority consciousness, by re-
sentment, by a determination to wield the sword of the Lord
against the infidel. There is an understandable uneasiness
among fundamentalists about whether their seeming political
potency has not in fact turned fundamentalism into a gelding
that has been co-opted by the political "system." According to
many writers, co-optation is precisely what the American polity
is designed to do, and historically has done so well. But the
anxious question remains, Who is co-opting whom? Those who
see fundamentalism and its agenda in terms of a dangerous faction are not comforted to learn that what they fear has now been

6. Robert Wuthnow, *The Restructuring of American Religion: Society and
Faith Since World War II* (Princeton: Princeton University Press, 1988).
7. Wade Clark Roof and William McKinney, *American Mainline Religion:
Its Changing Shape and Future* (Princeton: Rutgers University Press, 1987).

incorporated into the system. At the same time, fundamentalists who have drawn strength from thinking of themselves as a faction are troubled by the suspicion that, in exchange for respectability and apparent power, they are selling their birthright of doing battle for the Lord.

Fundamentalists who fear that they are being corrupted by success are greatly overestimating their achievements in the public arena during the past decade. Some fundamentalists may be in the process of being corrupted by the *desire* for success, but that is a somewhat different matter. The fundamentalist insurgency in American public life is still generally viewed—and is certainly viewed by society's elites—as a faction, with all the negative connotations that Madison attached to that term. For the foreseeable future fundamentalism will be motored, as it has been motored in the past, by a reaction to the societal elites' reaction to it.

The Federalist No. 10 is instructive in understanding that reaction and counterreaction. "There are two methods," Madison wrote, "of curing the mischiefs of faction: the one, by removing its causes; the other, by controlling its effects."[8] He continues: "There are again two methods of removing the causes of faction: the one, by destroying the liberty which is essential to its existence; the other, by giving to every citizen the same opinions, the same passions, and the same interests."[9]

After discussing the various ways in which the causes of factions might conceivably be removed, Madison reaches a firm conclusion: "The inference to which we are brought is, that the *causes* of faction cannot be removed, and that relief is only to be sought in the means of controlling its *effects*."[10] With that conclusion in mind, it is important to understand how Madison was brought to it. It is important because, in responding to fundamentalism and other troubling movements, American society has attempted to do what Madison says cannot be done, namely,

8. James Madison, *The Federalist No. 10.*
9. Ibid.
10. Ibid.

to remove the causes of faction. This is how many fundamentalists perceive the matter, and I believe their perception has considerable merit.

The first way to remove the cause of factions, said Madison, is to destroy the liberty which is essential to its existence. Madison had no doubt that this would be done; his argument is that it should not be done. "It could never be more truly said than of the first remedy, that it was worse than the disease. Liberty is to faction what air is to fire, an aliment without which it instantly expires. But it could not be less folly to abolish liberty, which is essential to political life, because it nourishes faction, than it would be to wish the annihilation of air, which is essential to animal life, because it imparts to fire its destructive agency."[11]

The second way to remove the cause of factions is to make everybody alike. "The second expedient," Madison argued, "is as impracticable as the first would be unwise." Here we encounter Madison's previously cited words about the unequal distribution of property and other distinctions and differences that "grow up of necessity in civilized nations." Of course, a strenuous effort could be made to level and homogenize the society by force, but in Madison's view the result would almost certainly be greater injustice and a nation no longer civilized.

Those who view publicly assertive fundamentalism as a faction in Madison's sense of the term might well consider whether both expedients rejected by Madison (denial of liberty and enforced homogenization) have not been employed in the past and are not being employed at present. It might well be argued that a third expedient has also been employed, that of dismissive derision. Since the 1925 Scopes trial, most Americans have been educated to believe that fundamentalism is a dead or dying belief system that hopelessly backward rustics who have opted out of the modern world cling to desperately. Since the insurgency of the late 1970s, such dismissive derision is highly implausible, although it is still practiced by those who

11. Ibid.

desperately cling to the hope that the modern world, at least in America, is not turning out the way it does indeed seem to be turning out. But the fundamentalism that we can no longer ignore or dismiss can still be contained, many believe, if we remove its causes by the denial of liberty and enforced homogenization.[12]

These two expedients are closely, indeed causally, related. Enforced homogenization requires the denial of liberty. A number of examples of the two expedients at work, and how they are related to one another, might be cited. Perhaps the most obvious illustration is in the field of education. Whether one approves of it or not, the "common school movement" of the nineteenth century, aimed at mandatory education under government auspices, resulted in the most ambitious program of social homogenization in America history.[13] Of course, the original impetus of that movement was directed toward making "good Americans" of the "unwashed immigrant hordes," mainly Roman Catholics. But today, most of the conflicts with the existing scheme of government education arise in connection with fundamentalist and evangelical Christians.

From Horace Mann through John Dewey, the movement was expressly understood to have a religious purpose—to replace particularist beliefs that offended the "enlightened" mind with a belief system more acceptable to those who were in a position to define acceptability. Horace Mann offered his supposedly nonsectarian version of Unitarianism, while Dewey more straightforwardly proposed "the religion of humanism"

12. For a closer discussion of denial and self-delusion in attitudes toward fundamentalism, see Richard Neuhaus, "What the Fundamentalists Want," in Richard Neuhaus and Michael Cromartie, eds., *Piety and Politics* (Washington: University Press of America, 1987).

13. For the best account of the social, including religious, ambitions of the movement, see Charles Gleen, *The Myth of the Common School* (Boston: University of Massachusetts Press, 1988). On the myth of the effectiveness of "the little red school house" see Diane Ravitch, *The Great School Wars: A History of the New York Public Schools* (New York: Basic Books, 1974). For the current state of the discussion about what might be done to remedy the situation, see Richard John Neuhaus, ed., *Democracy and the Renewal of Public Education* (Grand Rapids: Eerdmans, 1987).

to take the place of untenable "supernatural" religions and provide a "common faith" for American democracy. For both the strategy was to use persuasion, example, cultural intimidation, and state power in order to make "them" like "us."

In the half century since John Dewey, government schooling has largely lost any sense of religious mission. Dominated by formidable institutions such as the National Education Association, the public school has indeed moved toward a denial of any religious interest at all. It came to be accepted doctrine that "the separation of church and state" means that the schools must be neutral, if not indifferent, toward religion. More than that, the new orthodoxy prescribed, for a time, that the schools must not only be religion-neutral, they must also be value-neutral. In recent years—and for reasons that include much more than the fundamentalist insurgency—there has been an earnest, almost fevered, return to interest in values. This has inevitably reopened the religion question, since for the great majority of Americans values and religion are inescapably, if confusedly, connected.[14] And John Dewey's formula for the homogenization project will not work for the simple reason that John Dewey's common faith is in fact not common at all.

Thus were we brought to current complaints by fundamentalists in particular (but not by fundamentalists alone) that the public schools are teaching the "functional" religion of secular humanism. That complaint has found some significant support among both social scientists and jurists.[15] Here the public schools find themselves in a bind. Whether they claim to be value-neutral, or whether they claim to be deeply devoted to values (yet determinedly indifferent to the religious grounding of those values), they are accused of inculcating a de facto religion. Fundamentalists who, among others, make that accusa-

14. For an analysis of relevant research data on the connections between religion and values in American life, see Richard Neuhaus, ed., *Unsecular America* (Grand Rapids: Eerdmans, 1987).

15. See James Davison Hunter, "America's Fourth Faith: A Sociological Perspective on Secular Humanism," *This World*, Fall 1987, pp. 101-10; and Brevard Hand, "Humanism a Religion?" *This World*, Spring 1987, pp. 110-14.

tion are also somewhat ambivalent when it comes to what to do about it. Should the complete package of values-cum-religion be reintroduced in the government classroom, or should Christians who care about transmitting the complete package educate their children in their own schools and homes? This question touches on prayer in public schools, an issue which so agitates fundamentalist America.

It is almost impossible to overestimate the degree to which the removal of prayer from the classrooms of state schools in the early 1960s triggered the beginnings of the fundamentalist insurgency. Some fundamentalists want their own children to pray in school. Others want to educate their children in their own way but nonetheless believe that the well-being of the entire nation is enhanced by the daily prayers of millions of children in all the schools. Questions related to religion and public education will continue to be agitating. A renewed interest in teaching about religion will unavoidably raise the question of where or how to draw the line between teaching _about_ religion and teaching religion. The acknowledgment in the classroom of some transcendent authority (i.e., "God" for most Americans) will continue to be pressed, in the form of voluntary prayer, a moment of silence, or simply the pledge of allegiance with its reference to "one nation under God." It is possible that, through a combination of teaching about religion and some minimal and very generalized ritual, the homogenization project in public education may be revived. In that event, one of the two ways described (and rejected) by Madison for removing the cause of faction might be given a new life.

No revival of the homogenization project, however, is likely to satisfy parents, including fundamentalist parents, who believe that all of education should be imbued with the teaching and spirit of religious faith. And this brings us to the other way that Madison says we might try, wrongly, to remove the cause of faction, namely, by the denial of freedom. For well over a century, Roman Catholics have protested what they view as an abridgement of their religious freedom by the public school's monopoly of government funding. In the last twenty years, that argument has been advanced also by Missouri Synod Lutherans, Orthodox Jews, and, among others, many fundamentalists. Efforts to increase the measure of parental choice, both within and outside the government school systems, continue to grow. Despite the powerful resistance of most sectors of the education industry and their unions, it seems probable that proposals for vouchers, tax credits, and other devices will gain further ground in the years ahead.

And yet many fundamentalists are not primarily concerned, or concerned at all, with the question of funding. They want greater choice in how their children are educated in the public schools or they want to teach their children at home. They believe, with considerable justice, that these legitimate concerns are frustrated by a denial of freedom.[16] We see, regularly, cases in which fundamentalist parents protest books that are either included in or excluded from the public classroom. Such cases are routinely protested, in turn, by civil libertarians and the education industry, and especially by textbook publishers who have a deep interest in protecting their marketing practices.

These interventions by fundamentalists are condemned as "censorship," which, we are told, has no place in education. But, of course, to censor *(censere)* is to assess or supervise. In this sense, all of education is, by definition, an exercise in censorship. The question is: who will do the censoring, and whether it will be done in a reflective manner or left to the willy-nilly outcome of contending prejudices. Excluding parents from this process is probably very bad educational policy. Certainly it is a denial of their freedom. And, if they are excluded on the grounds of their being religiously motivated, it is a denial of that free exercise of religion which is the right protected by the religion clause of the First Amendment.

Other disputes, also frequently in the courts, raise the question of freedom being denied in the pursuit of educational

16. For an overview of legal cases arising from such real or alleged denials of freedom, see William Ball, "What's Not Wrong with the Williamsburg Charter," *This World,* Winter 1989.

alternatives. Many state education bureaucracies do not stop short of harassment in their efforts to discourage home schooling, an alternative elected by growing numbers of parents. Fundamentalists and others who operate their own schools are regularly confronted by state demands for certification and inspection which, they believe, would severely dilute and compromise the purposes for which such schools are founded.

It is commonly charged that such schools are designed to be refuges from a pluralistic society, and especially from children of another race. As the literature cited in the notes appended to this paper makes abundantly clear, such charges are not supported by the empirical evidence. No one doubts that, in terms of basic knowledge and skills required to play a constructive role in society, it is generally true that these voluntary schools do a much better job than their public school counterparts unless—and this is a very significant "unless"—one wishes to make the argument that socialization in the public school system is itself a requirement of citizenship. That argument is indeed made by those who accentuate the "pluralistic" nature of our society. In response to that argument, one must ask whether it is not precisely genuine pluralism that the proponents of the homogenization project are rejecting. Real pluralism, one might contend, requires granting the largest possible measure of diversity, including diversity in the education that parents choose for their children.

I have focused only on education to illustrate the ways in which, as a society, we have responded to the putative faction of fundamentalism by doing the two things that Madison says we should not do. The first is to deny liberty and the second is to impose sameness, and each entails the other. If, for the sake of argument, we allow that fundamentalism threatens "the mischiefs of faction," how ought we to respond to this phenomenon? Madison answers that we should focus on "controlling its effects." This is to be done by a republican policy that encourages great variety through a broadly dispersed population. Recall again Madison's rather sanguine prognosis: "The influence of factious leaders may kindle a flame within their particular States, but will be unable to spread a general conflagration through the other States. A religious sect may degenerate into a political faction in a part of the Confederacy; but the variety of sects dispersed over the entire face of it must secure the national council against any danger from that source."[17]

Those who worry about the mischiefs of faction cannot be so sanguine today, for our situation is dramatically different from the United States of two centuries ago. The "megastructures" of our society—government, mass communications, corporations, unions, the education industry—would no doubt have alarmed James Madison. The expansion of government's sway in particular has undermined the genuine pluralism that Madison thought to be security against the mischiefs of faction. The differences that were once permitted to flourish beyond the notice of government are increasingly drawn into the arena of public dispute and state adjudication. Years before the emergence of the religious right, Leo Pfeffer (then with the American Jewish Congress) understood this dynamic. "Matters which have long been considered private," he wrote, "are increasingly becoming the concern of government." He added, " The thirst for power is a potent force even in a democracy, and the state will be tempted and will yield to the temptation of seeking to exercise dominion over religion for no other reason than because it is there."[18]

Even if one accepts the sharp "we" versus "them" polarity mentioned at the beginning of this essay, it should be obvious that our options are limited in responding to the putative faction of fundamentalism. We should not deny their freedom, we cannot impose our preferred sameness upon them, and we can no longer depend upon the dispersed and countervailing forces that gave Madison such confidence.

What then is to be done? We should, I believe, rethink from the bottom up what we mean by "pluralism." While we cannot dismantle the megastructures of contemporary life, we

17. James Madison, *The Federalist No. 10.*
18. Quoted in Neuhaus, *Piety and Politics*, p. 16.

can work much harder to let the full diversity of our society find expression in those megastructures, notably in communications and education.

In education, this means rethinking the two-part religion clause of the First Amendment, and once again giving priority to the "free exercise" provision which the "no establishment" provision is designed to serve.[19]

A more promising future also depends, however, on our overcoming the "we" versus "them" polarity. Those who call themselves fundamentalists—and it is well to remember that there are worlds within worlds of fundamentalism—are fellow citizens with us in this American experiment. There is a minority among them that challenges the American polity in principle. But that minority in practice, and the overwhelming majority in principle, affirm the American polity as a worthy— many of them say a providentially given—way of ordering civil life. Their affirmation of the polity is evident in their eagerness to be full participants in it. If some of them want to dominate the polity, there is nothing unusual about that. What "faction" in American life does not include an element driven by the desire for power?

Candor requires those of us who are included in the "we" to acknowledge that "they" are viewed as a mischievous faction in large part because they disturb our domination of the polity. To be sure, all the sins that mark the human condition are manifest also among fundamentalists, and there are no doubt a few in which they excel. We can entertain ourselves by cataloguing their sins and our supposed virtues, but that serves no purpose other than self-righteousness, smugness, and the desire to continue business as usual with, as the news executive told Cardinal O'Connor, "the way we do things here." We may not like it, but business as usual has been disrupted, and, I expect, permanently disrupted, by the changing role of religion in American public life.

The fundamentalists are among those who are demand-

19. For a fuller explanation of this argument, see Richard Neuhaus, "Genuine Pluralism and the Pfefferian Inversion," *This World*, Winter 1989.

ing changes in business as usual, but the changes the fundamentalists want are not really all that radical. The theme of their
agenda is, as they frequently say, to "restore traditional moral
and spiritual values to American public life." That includes
prayer and Bible reading in public schools, the common practice until the last quarter century. They want the legal protection for unborn children that was in place until twenty years
ago. They want greater restrictions against pornography, resistance to radical feminist and gay rights legislation, a more
ample definition of religious freedom in education and elsewhere, a secure defense, and strong American support for
Israel. All of these policies are eminently debatable within the
principles and procedures of the American polity. Our fellow
citizens who are also fundamentalists simply want to be full participants in the debate. Like every other group in American life,
they will usually debate poorly and they will sometimes debate
unfairly, but neither competence nor virtue nor religion (as Article VI of the Constitution makes clear) is a test for admission
to America's public square.

The boast of authentic liberalism is that it is inclusive, responsive, and respectful of diversity. That boast has often been
justified. Whether it is justified now is very much open to question. It is not fundamentalism that is on trial today. We who
cherish the essentially liberal polity of this American experiment are being tried by the challenge of fundamentalism. In
the process, both the "we" and the "them" will be changed. So
far we have not done very well. But then, the challenge is still
relatively new. If we have the imagination for it, there is reason
to hope that the challenge will result in the strengthening of a
polity that serves, in the words of Mr. Madison, "the rights of
Citizens" and the "permanent and aggregate interests of the
community."

James M. Dunn

Richard Neuhaus and I discuss fundamentalism from vastly different perspectives. First, if one hears only the Texas twang, I might be seen as the fundamentalist whose absence from the program Neuhaus laments. Born and bred a Southern Baptist, born again long before it was fashionable, I am a tract-carrying member of the Southern Baptist Convention. I can speak fundamentalese. But then, from another angle, I am an existential expert on fundamentalism, a certified victim. One can afford a certain dispassionate distance if one has not been targeted for extinction. I am reminded of the difference between the sources for a traditional breakfast of ham and eggs: the chicken only makes a contribution, but for the pig, it's a real sacrifice.[1]

Despite disparate points of departure, I can appreciate the contributions of the Neuhaus paper. There are, however, some presuppositions that must be challenged and aspects of the argument for a kinder, gentler approach toward religiopolitical

1. See Jim Asker, "Baptists Will Tackle 'Inerrancy' Question," *The Houston Post*, 12 June 1982, p. 6AA: "Another showdown could come on a rumored effort to deny denominational funding to the Baptist Joint Committee on Public Affairs, which is headed by the Rev. James Dunn, a Texan and Southern Baptist who has blasted Reagan's prayer amendment. 'I think there will be something done to silence him,' says Patterson."

fundamentalism that must be questioned. At the very least, the discussion about the relationship of American fundamentalism to polity is just beginning.

Positive Contributions

First, Neuhaus's principal appeal for "civil argument" and inclusion of fundamentalism in "civil discourse" is essential to "reasoned and open-minded inquiry" and "a better understanding" of the society. One who would insist upon religious liberty and not mere toleration will pursue "genuine pluralism," however great the pain of that pursuit. "Granting the largest possible measure of diversity" is a worthy goal even if it is not appreciated and shared as a goal by all the diverse groups who benefit from it.

Since Roger Williams made plain that the Puritans were interested in religious freedom only for those who agreed with them, Americans have insisted that everyone has the right to be wrong. The calls for a "Christian nation" and "re-Christianizing America" evidence fundamental error. Regarding the American polity, the New Christian Right is not wrongly fundamental. It is fundamentally wrong. Saying that, one assumes the burden of exposing error and trying to persuade. This demands the discourse that Richard Neuhaus properly called for.

Next, the suggestion that overwhelming numbers of theologically conservative Christians have been slighted or completely ignored is correct. But religiously conservative Christians and Jews may not be politically right wing, and they are most often not fundamentalists. These people have resented and resisted the stereotypes so glibly linking them with political fundamentalists. Nor are the political activists a persecuted minority to be coddled. In fact, the fundamentalist/right-wing Republican partnership is the strongest alliance of religion with power since the Puritans.

Bill Moyers repeatedly reveals the vitality, rich diversity, and complexity of the conservative Christianity he knows so well. Martin Marty respects and identifies with healthy, respectable, mainstream Christianity and the traditional values espoused by the massive theological middle. Jimmy Carter exemplifies the intellectual integrity of a socially responsible Christianity that is theologically fundamental.

For one with a Southern Baptist history and education, it is almost amusing to note that "those once viewed as marginal" are "becoming the new religious mainline." We have been the mainline for many years and are just now being discovered by intensely parochially educated Easterners.

Neuhaus correctly points out that the education establishment, religious leaders, and public servants are once again focusing on values and teaching about religion in the public schools. Individuals need not agree with every particular of historical analysis to work together in the present situation for openness to religion and value-oriented public education.

Groups as diverse as the National Conference of Christians and Jews and the Christian Legal Society, the National Council of Churches and the National Association of Evangelicals have joined with ten other religious and educational groups in a 1988 statement on "Religion in the Public School Curriculum."[2] It is interesting to note that value-laden preparation for teachers comes now from a wide range of sources including John Dewey's old haunt, the Teachers College, Columbia University.[3]

Finally, Neuhaus is correct when he points out that Madison's discussion of factions in *The Federalist No. 10* is "not primarily concerned about religious factions" and that "our situation is dramatically different from the United States of two centuries ago." Madison would, indeed, be spinning in his crypt if he could

2. The brochure "Religion in the Public School Curriculum: Questions and Answers" can be obtained by writing the Baptist Joint Committee on Public Affairs, 200 Maryland Avenue, N.E., Washington, D.C. 20002. For further information write the fourteen national organizations listed on the document.
3. See an excellent example in a Columbia University Publication, Frances S. Bolin and Judith McConnell Falk, eds., *Teacher Renewal* (New York: Teachers College Press, 1987).

see the 3,000 religious groups, the complexity of government, the instant communication, the slick persuasions of television, and the appalling ignorance of the average citizen today.

Troubling Presuppositions

First, one must question a basic premise. Is there actually "a widespread anxiety about particularist religion in 'the public square?'" Like Speakers' Corner in Hyde Park, the public square allows almost any expression. One watches Billy Graham and dozens of other religious particularists on television. Senator Robert Byrd goes on about the beauty and power of the King James Version of the Bible on the floor of the U.S. Senate. Any weekly issue of the *New York Times Review of Books* deals with Judaism, Christianity, and Islam in a wide range of offerings. Equal Access legislation allows students to meet for religious activities before and after the school day. Released-time religious education is part of the school day for children across the United States, constitutionally accepted and conveniently provided by churches and synagogues. One is distressed not by specificity of religious witness, but rather by the dogmatic insistence upon being the sole possessor of truth, followed by demonstrable dishonesty. This is what troubles many about the political activity of fundamentalists.[4] One engaged in the day-to-day struggle is acutely aware of the end-justifies-the-means tactics of the radical right.

Second, why would anyone be eager to defend a government-prescribed religious ritual? Mandated "voluntary" school prayer makes no sense at all for people who are convinced that the public schools have been taken over by "secular humanists." What sort of prayer is inculcated in a homogenized, religiously

4. Instances abound: e.g., the unfounded story that Jerry Falwell told in 1980 about President Carter's approving of homosexuality, followed by Falwell's unwillingness to admit his distortion of truth. See also Oliver S. Thomas, "The Civil Rights Restoration Act," *Liberty*, July/August 1988, pp. 13-14.

neutral setting? Those who want *no* organized group prayer at all for the captive audience of vulnerable, impressionable children will continue to join those who want only the specific prayers of particular religion in opposing some watered-down, lowest-common-denominator exercise that cannot be called prayer and has no place in public school. "Prayer and Bible reading in public schools" were definitely *not* "the common practice until the last quarter century."[5] Never mentioned are the contributions of segregation academies to racial divisiveness, prejudice, and bigotry. Also ignored has been the fact that many schools that had prayers were also segregated.

Next, one cannot accept the argument by assertion that "no one doubts that, in terms of basic knowledge and skills required to play a constructive role in society, it is generally true that these voluntary schools do a much better job than their public school counterparts." I doubt that claim for private, parochial, and home schools on many grounds. The elite may indeed be able to afford an educational opportunity beyond the reach of poor children, with doors closed to the handicapped and students with discipline problems. These schools may offer personalized attention and other advantages, but they can by no stretch of the imagination be compared to public schools. The same testing and evaluation to which public schools are properly subjected is not required of nonpublic schools.[6] The American polity is the context in which Americans have chosen, and repeatedly affirmed, the common school. No amount of

5. Professor Richard Dierenfield of Macalester College in Minnesota conducted a survey of public school administrators in 1961. He reported that nationwide, only 33.16 percent of the public schools had Bible reading and prayer *prior* to the Supreme Court decisions. These numbers were clustered overwhelmingly in the Northeast and in the South. In the Midwest the number was 6.4 percent, and in the West it was only 2.4 percent. Dierenfield published a book about his findings in 1962.

6. For more analysis of fundamentalist schools, see the work of Alan Peshkin, professor of education at the University of Illinois, and contact Albert Shanker (American Federation of Teachers, 555 New Jersey Avenue, N.W., Washington, D.C. 20001) for his "Public Funds for Private Purposes? A Glimpse into Fundamentalist Schools."

right-wing ranting appears likely to turn this nation away from its dedication to universal public education.

More seriously, the notion that the "no establishment" clause of the First Amendment is simply "designed to serve" the "free exercise" clause smacks of revisionism. The two clauses affirm and complement one another even while held in creative tension. The historical backdrop of repressive religion, the manifold witness of those present at the Amendment's creation, even the specific wording, argue for the two-way street: limitations on both government and organized religion.

Edwin Gaustad highlights the interrelationship of the two religion clauses. "With a breathtaking economy of words, the Constitution now provided a double guarantee: first, that Congress shall do nothing to favor, promote, or endow religion; second, that Congress shall take no step that would impede, obstruct, or penalize religion. Neither hindering nor helping, government would simply leave religion alone."[7]

Unfinished Discussion

One must defend and extend the public discourse opportunity for all citizens, even those bound together by a shared zeal that is unsettling and by religious beliefs which, if possible, they would enact into law. It is not necessary, however, to provide any sort of balanced forum for views seen to be utterly without merit, to tiptoe around hard analysis because public policy suggestions have religious roots, to rewrite history or reinterpret the Constitution to make way for the public mood of the moment. Neither does one have to suffer unethical, dishonest methods, demagoguery, and intimidation because values are being upheld, religion is being freely exercised, and the motivation for this political activity is purely and spiritually motivated. It is quite

7. Edwin Scott Gaustad, *Religion, the Constitution, and the Founding Fathers* (Rome, GA: Shorter College, 1987), p. 11.

different to condemn the methodology and the tactics of a political group and to deny them the right to their beliefs. The cynical use of code words and symbols in the recent presidential election did not address the issues; it simply tapped the emotions around those issues without exploring the problems and alternatives. But that debate will continue for a long time. Further, it is not necessary—overtly or explicitly—to argue from religious premise in order to be guided by biblical warrants in shaping public policy. William W. Van Alstyne reaffirms the need for a level playing field in the American polity:

> The notion of the Public Square is itself a strong metaphor of the civil commonwealth. The Public Square is always *civil, e.g.,* it is not the State. And it does not profane religion by misappropriating from establishments of religion. It is, rather, the place where a polity's citizens meet on terms of common need and mutual regard under civil auspices. And the public square is not "naked" in being a civil place, *i.e.,* it need not be aluminumized, austere, unaesthetic, or cold. But it is laid out uninsinuatingly, and it is always conducted appropriately, without disregard or implied distinction among all citizens; it is conducted with the carefulness of equal and mutual civil regard.[8]

Finally, it seems clear that the tensions regarding the nature of freedom will continue. In this presentation and response is an element of that old philosophical question of freedom: are we obligated to extend freedom to those who would deny freedom to others? We certainly should try to understand them, learn from them, share any good gift they have to offer, sympathize with their needs, and be sensitive to them as persons made in the image of God. Yet, the one "freedom" a democracy cannot tolerate is tyranny.

When my wife, Marilyn, and I have visitors in Washington, one of our favorite places to take them is the Jefferson Memorial. It is just beyond the usual walk on the Mall. You would be surprised how many frequent visitors to Washington

---

8. William W. Van Alstyne, "What Is 'An Establishment of Religion'?" *North Carolina Law Review* 65 (1987): 915.

have never been there. My favorite words in the Jefferson
Memorial are the ones around the top of the dome. "I have
sworn on the altar of God eternal hostility to every form of tyranny over the mind of man." Not a bad rule of thumb for measuring the American polity.

9. The Burgeoning of Islamic Fundamentalism: Toward an Understanding of the Phenomenon

Riffat Hassan

This paper has been written from the perspective of a Muslim who has been much involved in Jewish-Christian-Muslim inter-religious dialogue in the last decade and who has striven earnestly, through personal interaction as well as through research, to break through the complex web of ignorance and fear which makes dialogue among Jews, Christians, and Muslims so difficult. For me, engaging in interreligious dialogue with other Muslims and with "the People of the Book" (i.e., Jews and Christians) is not merely an interesting pastime. It is a life commitment which is deeply rooted in my faith in God, who is described in the opening statement of the Qur'an as *Rabb al-'alamin:* creator and sustainer of all the peoples. That God has willed not only diversity of peoples but also of religions is pointed out in a number of Qur'anic passages. A few examples are given below:

> To each is a goal to which God turns him; then strive together (as in a race) toward all that is good. Wheresoever ye are, God will bring you together. For God hath power over all things.[1]
>
> To each among you have we prescribed a law and an open way. If God had so willed, He would have made you a single People,

1. Surah 2: *Al-Baqarah:* 148; *The Holy Qur'an,* translated by A. Yusuf Ali (Brentwood: Amana Corp., 1983), p. 60.

but (his plan is) to test you in what He hath given you: so strive
as in a race in all virtues. The goal of you all is to God; it is He
that will show you the truth of the matters in which ye dispute.[2]

And (know that) all mankind were once but one single community, and only later did they begin to hold divergent views.
And had it not been for a decree that had already gone forth
from thy Sustainer, all their differences would indeed have been
settled (from the outset).[3]

The God who has decreed diversity has also decreed dialogue in order that we may discover our common roots and journey together toward our common goal. The paths we follow may
not be the same, but the agony of the quest, the passion of seeking, is the same. There is much in the Qur'an which relates particularly to the relationship of "the People of the Book"—Jews,
Christians, Muslims—to God and to each other. I believe that if
we could understand what the Qur'an is telling us, we would be
able to overcome many difficulties which impede our dialogue.
But much work has to be done—by Muslims, Jews, and Christians—separately and together, before we can comprehend and
transcend all that separates us as human beings and as believers
in the same loving, merciful, dialogue-oriented God.

One area which requires particular attention in the context of Jewish-Christian-Muslim interreligious dialogues is that
of terminology. While it is a precondition of interreligious dialogue that each partner defines herself or himself,[4] it has been

2. Surah 5: *Al-Ma'idah:* 51; *The Holy Qur'an,* p. 258.

3. Surah 10: *Yunus:* 19; *The Message of the Qur'an,* trans. Muhammad Asad
(Gibraltar: Dar Al-Andalus, 1980), p. 292.

4. This is the "fifth commandment" in "The Dialogue Decalogue"
(Ground-rules for Interreligious Dialogue) by Leonard Swidler, *Journal of Ecumenical Studies* 20 (Winter 1983): 2. The "commandment" reads: "Each participant must define himself. Only the Jew, for example, can define from the inside what it means to be a Jew. The rest can only describe what it looks like from
the outside. Moreover, because dialogue is a dynamic medium, as each participant learns, he will change and hence continually deepen, expand, and modify his self-definition as a Jew—being careful to remain in constant dialogue
with fellow Jews. Thus it is mandatory that each dialogue partner define what
it means to be an authentic member of his own tradition."

the common experience of Muslims who participate in inter-religious dialogue in the West that such dialogues are dominated by Christian concepts and categories, and Muslims are required to "dialogue" in terms which are not only alien to their religious ethos but may even be hostile to it. One such term which is in great fashion today is "fundamentalism." Both in the media and in academic circles, there is much talk about "Islamic fundamentalism" and "Muslim fundamentalists," and scholars of Islam are constantly being asked to explain "the burgeoning of Islamic fundamentalism" in the contemporary world. As a person engaged in the study and teaching of religion, I certainly think that the phenomenon commonly referred to as "fundamentalism," which is of intense interest to many people in the present-day world, needs to be understood. But I have serious objections to the use of terms such as "fundamentalism" and "fundamentalists" with reference to Islam or Muslims.

Before I endeavor to explain why I object to the use of these specific terms, it is important to point out that these currently fashionable terms have been preceded by many other terms which have also been objectionable to Muslims engaging in interreligious dialogue with Jews and Christians. For instance, Muslims are all too often asked by Christians, "What is the Islamic concept of salvation or redemption?" Since "salvation" and "redemption" have no particular meaning in the Islamic tradition, which does not accept the Christian idea of salvation or redemption, the asking of such questions points to either an ignorance of Islam—a common problem—or an assumption that concepts which are important in the Christian tradition must necessarily be so in the Jewish and Islamic traditions, and that Jews and Muslims who dialogue with Christians should somehow be able and willing to find a content for these concepts from within their own distinctive—and different—religious beliefs and experience. Many Muslims, including myself, who, through a long history of being colonized not only politically but also intellectually by the Christian West, have internalized the vocabulary of our erstwhile colonizers, try—sometimes for years—to respond to such questions, not facing the fact that in many cases they stem not only from an ignorance of Islam but also from an attitude of religious imperialism. But there comes a time when we have to recognize that we cannot give authentic answers to in-authentic questions. There comes a time when, in faithfulness to our own basic integrity as Muslims, we have to refuse to answer such questions.

Religious imperialism, like other forms of imperialism, exhibits itself in a variety of ways. One way is to elevate one's own conceptions of reality or truth above those of the "other," having first assumed the right to define the "other" in one's own terms. For instance, it is not uncommon in Jewish-Christian-Muslim "dialogues" about the nature of God for a Christian to say to Jews and Muslims: "Your God is the God of justice, our God is the God of love." Since it is obvious that the speaker has assumed that "love" is better than "justice," such a statement reflects an attitude of religious triumphalism, even though, if pushed theologically, no one who professes to be a monotheist is likely to proclaim that there are two Gods—one of justice and the other of love. If God is one—and this is what Jews and Muslims as well as Christians affirm—then the reference in the statement is not to two Gods but to two understandings of the one God.

Here a number of critical questions arise. What is the meaning of saying, "Our God is the God of love" or "Your God is the God of justice"? How does the Christian who uses "love" and "justice" as antithetical terms understand these terms? While most Christians who use the formula "God is love" seldom elaborate on what is meant by "love"—whether it is a feeling, thought, or action—they generally tend to define "justice" narrowly in terms of what they believe to be the essence of the Mosaic law of "an eye for an eye," namely, the law of retribution. Rarely, if ever, are Jews or Muslims asked by Christians to tell them how they would define this "justice" which has been designated to be the primary characteristic of "their" God. If they were asked to do so, Jews may have the opportunity to

state that the Mosaic law is a limiting principle which emphasizes that "no more than" an eye may be taken for an eye, and
Muslims may be able to point out that in the Qur'an, "justice"
embraces both *'adl* and *ihsan*. While *'adl* requires that special
merit be considered in matters of rewards and special circumstances be considered in the matter of punishments, *ihsan* requires that compassionate action be performed to make up the
loss or deficiency suffered by those who are disadvantaged in
society.[5]

It is important for Westerners to realize that Muslims feel
angry and bitter when American mass media present the complex situations and issues which confront them in such oversimplified terms that the "truth" is seriously distorted if not lost
altogether. They obviously feel much worse when they come
across the same tendency to oversimplify even in assemblies of
so-called dialogue-oriented Westerners. If interreligious dialogue between Westerners and Muslims is to be an authentic
encounter, that which the latter perceive or conceive to be a
multilayered, multifaceted religious reality or truth cannot be
reduced to a simple formula by the former. Representing one's
own religious beliefs in simplistic terms is dangerous enough.
Representing the religious beliefs of the "other" in such a way,
and then comparing them unfavorably with one's own, make
interreligious dialogue a tool of religious polemics or politics
and not a journey of faith.

In the last decade, the West has had a sudden explosion
of interest in Islam. This was due, largely if not wholly, to events
such as the Arab oil embargo of 1973 and the Iranian revolution of 1979, which shocked many Westerners into realizing that
Islam—which they had long assumed to be dying, if not dead—
was in the process of being "revived." Muslims living in the
West, particularly those of us who participated in interreligious
dialogue, were asked continually to explain the nature, mean-

---

5. For a more detailed description of *'adl* and *ihsan*, see Riffat Hassan,
"On Human Rights and the Qur'anic Perspective," in Arlene Swidler, ed.,
Human Rights in Religious Traditions (New York: Pilgrim Press, 1982), pp. 56-58.

ing, and implications of "Islamic revival." Both elated and confounded by the West's unprecedented interest in Islam, we spent countless hours trying to do that, not realizing that while to many Christians terms such as "Christian revival" and "Christian renewal" are very significant, the term "Islamic revival" is a Western invention which has no corresponding reality in the life of Muslims in general. Something of great importance has, indeed, been going on in the Muslim world in recent times, but it is not the "revival" of Islam. Islam has never ceased to be a living reality to the vast majority of Muslims in the world, and it continues to give form and meaning to every aspect of their lives, even at a time when secularism has spread far and wide. In retrospect, it seems to me that our efforts to make Islam and Muslims more comprehensible to the West would have been better directed if, instead of answering questions which exist mostly in the minds of Westerners, we had endeavored to explain why Muslim societies are in such a state of ferment today and why certain issues appear to be so critical to contemporary Muslims.

Perhaps, if we had not been willing to answer questions on "Islamic revival" ten years ago, we would not be asked—in what seems like a replay of an old scenario—to answer questions on "Islamic fundamentalism" today. Many of the questions that Muslims are asked about "Islamic fundamentalism" are not very different from the ones they were asked about "Islamic revival" a decade ago. In fact, as many Muslims see it, in the West generally there is no clear-cut separation between "Islamic revival" and "Islamic fundamentalism." However, the obvious anxiety which many "liberal" and "dialogue-oriented" Westerners have felt in recent times on account of the so-called rise of fundamentalism, not only in the Islamic but also in the Jewish and Christian traditions, introduces a new element into the old scenario. Whereas, in the last decade, Muslims were on call to explain "Islamic revival" to their Jewish and Christian dialogue partners, now many Jewish-Christian-Islamic conferences are being organized where all three—Jews, Christians, and Muslims—are asked to "dialogue" about the emergence of "fundamentalism" in their respective traditions. Some months ago, I was invited to such a conference, and as I began to gather my thoughts to write a paper on "Islamic fundamentalism," I was struck by the realization that I was about to do exactly what I had done ten years ago. In other words, I was about to accept the West's understanding of what it refers to as "Islamic fundamentalism" and respond to it as a Muslim, instead of telling my Western dialogue partners what "fundamentalism" means to the majority of Muslims in the world. My reflections on this subject led me to see that it was not only highly inappropriate to use expressions such as "Islamic fundamentalism" and "Muslim fundamentalists" as they are generally used in the West, but also highly dangerous.

Even a summary review of the way in which the West in general, and American media in particular, use the term "fundamentalism" with reference to Islam shows that this term is the equivalent of emotionally loaded terms such as "extremism," "fanaticism," and even "terrorism." For instance, when most Americans read an expression which has appeared countless times in daily newspapers, namely, "the fundamentalist Shiites of South Lebanon," they assume that the Shiites in question—about whom they probably know very little, if anything—are extremists, fanatics, or even terrorists. Thus the term "fundamentalist," when used by the West with reference to Muslim leaders or groups, clearly embodies a negative value judgment and evokes a powerful image of persons who are irrational, immoderate, and violent. While the term "fundamentalist" may be relatively new, the image is that of a ferocious-looking Arab, wearing a flowing white robe, riding a white charger, and flashing a saber. This image has a long history and derives from the Christian West's age-old perceptions of the Prophet of Islam and of Islam. For instance, Dante, the great poet of medieval Christianity, perceived the Prophet Muhammad as a "bloody" figure who "divided" the world of Christendom, and assigned him to all but the lowest level of hell for his grievous "sin." His description of the Prophet Muhammad is not easily forgotten:

A wine tun when a stave or cant-bar starts
does not split open as wide as one I saw
split from his chin to the mouth with which man farts.

Between his legs all of his red guts hung
with the heart, the lungs, the liver, the gall-bladder,
and the shriveled sac that passes shit to the bung.

I stood and stared at him from the stone shelf;
he noticed me and opening his own breast
with both hands cried: "See how I rip myself!"

See how mahomet's mangled and split open![6]

Alas, many Westerners who know virtually nothing about Islam still identify it with "Holy War," which, it is important to note, is not an accurate or adequate rendering of the Qur'anic concept of *jihad*.[7] It is, rather, a Christian term associated with the Crusades. Even those Westerners who know that one of the primary meanings of the very word "Islam" is "peace" seldom focus on the centrality of the concept of peace to the Islamic worldview.[8] Images of Muslims as barbarous and backward, frenzied and fanatic, volatile and violent, continue to pervade Western consciousness.

The terms "fundamentalism" and "fundamentalists" have been used extensively in the 1980s to epitomize the negative images of Islam and Muslims prevalent in the West, although they have been used also for expressing value judgments about other religious traditions, groups, or persons. As Patrick J. Ryan has observed:

> Labeling various people fundamentalists has become stock-in-trade in political and journalistic discourse in recent years. As

6. Dante Alighieri, *The Inferno*, trans. John Ciardi (New York: Mentor, 1954), p. 236.

7. A classic on the subject of *jihad* is Moulavi Cheragh Ali, *A Critical Exposition of the Popular Jihad* (Karachi: Karimsons, 1977).

8. For a detailed discussion on the concept of peace in Islam, see Riffat Hassan, "Peace Education: A Muslim Perspective," in Haim Gordon and Leonard Grob, eds., *Education for Peace: Testimonies from World Religions* (Maryknoll, NY: Orbis Books, 1987), pp. 90-108.

long ago as the fall of 1980, the major American newspapers contained advertisements deploring the rising tide of religious fundamentalism on the political shores at home and abroad. The avowedly secularist signatories of these advertisements, citing specific examples of what they meant by religious fundamentalism, named such diverse figures as the Rev. Jerry Falwell, the Ayatollah Ruhollah Khomeini and Pope John Paul II. The term fundamentalism has been employed in the press in recent months, as well, to categorize the Sikh revolutionary separatist in India, Jarnail Singh Bhindranwale, who was killed in the Indian Army assault on the Golden Temple of Amritsar early in June 1984.[9]

Many, if not most, who use the terms "fundamentalism" and "fundamentalist" as if they were generic categories with universal applicability do not know or have forgotten the particular Christian context in which these terms arose. The term "fundamentalism," which *The Shorter Oxford English Dictionary* dates to 1923,[10] emerged in the wake of the publication between 1905 and 1915 of twelve theological tracts entitled *The Fundamentals: A Testimony to the Truth*.[11] These writings by biblical literalists denounced the adoption by other Protestant theologians of a scientific-critical approach to the study of the Bible.[12] As George Marsden has pointed out: "'Fundamentalism' is a subspecies of evangelicalism. The term originated in America in 1920 and refers to evangelicals who consider it their chief Christian duty to combat uncompromisingly 'modernist' theology and certain secularizing cultural trends. Organized militancy is the feature that most clearly distinguishes fundamentalists from other evangelicals."[13]

9. Patrick J. Ryan, "Islamic Fundamentalism: A Questionable Category," *America*, 29 December 1984, p. 437.

10. Ibid.

11. Ibid.

12. Ibid.

13. George M. Marsden, "Evangelical and Fundamental Christianity," in Mircea Eliade, ed., *The Encyclopedia of Religion* (New York: Macmillan, 1987), 5:190-91.

The fact that the terms "fundamentalism" and "fundamentalist" do not "quite apply" to Islam or Muslims is, of course, recognized by Christians, as well as Jewish and Muslim scholars. For instance, Fredrick M. Denny, a Christian scholar of Islam, states:

> The term "fundamentalism" was coined early in this century in an American conservative Protestant framework to characterize a Scripture-based doctrine embracing five key points (the virgin birth of Jesus, his physical Resurrection, the infallibility of the Scriptures, the substitutional Atonement, and the physical Second coming of Christ). The only point with which Muslims agree concerns the infallibility of Scripture—in the Islamic case, of course, the Qur'ran. In recent years it has become popular to refer to conservative militant Muslims as fundamentalists. The name *does not quite apply,* when taken at its original meaning.[14]

Bernard Lewis, a Jewish scholar of Islam, states:

> It is now common usage to apply the term "fundamentalist" to a number of Islamic radical and militant groups. The use of this term is established and must be accepted, *but it remains unfortunate and can be misleading.* Fundamentalist is a Christian term. It seems to have come into use in the early years of this century, and denoted certain Protestant churches and organizations, more particularly those which maintain the literal divine origin and inerrancy of the Bible. In this they oppose the liberal and modernist approach to the Qur'an, and all Muslims, in their attitude to the text of the Qur'an, are in principle at least fundamentalists.[15]

Seyyed Hossein Nasr, a Muslim scholar of Islam, states:

> As far as fundamentalism is concerned, use of the term by journalists and even scholars to refer to a wide variety of phenomena in the Islamic world and currents in Islamic thought *is most unfortunate and misleading* because the term is drawn from the Christian context, where it has quite a different connotation.

14. Frederick M. Denny, *Islam and the Muslim Community* (New York: Harper & Row, 1987), p. 117; italics mine.
15. Bernard Lewis, *The Political Language of Islam* (Chicago: University of Chicago Press, 1988), pp. 117 n. 3; italics mine.

Fundamentalism in Christian religious circles, especially in the United States, refers to conservative forms of Protestantism, usually antimodernist, with a rather narrow and literal interpretation of the Bible and a strong emphasis upon traditional Christian ethics. . . . The use of the term fundamentalism and the classification of a widely diverse set of phenomena and tendencies under such a name are misleading features of many of the current studies on Islam, and help to hide the more profound realities involved, including the essential fact that much of what is called fundamentalist Islam is anti-traditional and opposed to both the spirit and the letter of the Islamic tradition, as understood and practiced since the descent of the Qur'anic revelation.[16]

Why, when so many well-known scholars of Islam agree that the use of the term "fundamentalism" in the context of Islam is "unfortunate" and "misleading," should it continue to be used? According to Bernard Lewis, "The use of the term is established and must be accepted." If the logic of this statement is accepted, however, then how can one argue for the abolition, say, of sexist language or of racist language, which have also been long established in many places and cultures?

It seems quite obvious that the usage of the terms "fundamentalism" and "fundamentalist" even by outstanding Muslim scholars of Islam shows the extent to which the religious imperialism of the Christian West has penetrated the psyche of those whom it has colonized. Fazlur Rahman, one of the finest critics of modern Islam, was aware of this phenomenon even though he chose to accept its terminology, for he observed: "The colonial phenomenon is not something only of the past; it appears to be continuing indefinitely. Political and military imperialism was bad enough, but more heinous is the ethical, cultural, and intellectual arrogance of the West. In the past, all ascendant civilizations have had their moments of self-righteousness, but probably no civilization before that of the

16. Seyyed Hossein Nasr, "Present Tendencies, Future Trends," in Marjorie Kelly, ed., *Islam: The Religious and Political Life of a World Community* (New York: Praeger, 1984), pp. 279-80; italics mine.

modern West has felt itself to be so universally and comprehensively valid that the mere questioning of some of its values can be tantamount to barbaric backwardness."[17]

While many Westerners, as well as Easterners under the influence of the West, have come to apply the terms "fundamentalism" or "fundamentalist" to all kinds of phenomena or persons, there is no logical or theological reason why any person— non-Christian or even Christian—needs to accept this usage as necessary or as mandated by heaven. In fact, the usage of highly emotive words such as "fundamentalism" or "fundamentalist" outside their proper historical setting is strongly to be discouraged, for it brings about, not enlightenment, but multiple forms of confusion and discrimination. The feminist movement has been insistent that sexist language be discarded because it leads not only to bias and injustice in this or that specific matter pertaining to man-woman discourse or relationship but also to the formation of what Mary Daly describes as "a universe of sexist suppositions."[18] Likewise, it is essential—in my judgment— to eliminate terms such as "fundamentalism" and "fundamentalist" from the discourse of interreligious dialogue since they not only smack of religious and cultural imperialism, but also create a negatively charged atmosphere in which authentic dialogue cannot take place.

That no term corresponding to what fundamentalism or fundamentalist means in the West has "traditionally existed in various Islamic languages"[19] demonstrates that such concepts are not integral or organic to the Islamic worldview, but are "outsider" categories which have been grafted "onto an Islamic development."[20] Though the Arabic term *usul* is used to refer to a fundamental or a principle, the term "fundamentalism"

17. Fazlur Rahman, "Roots of Islamic Neo-Fundamentalism," in Philip H. Stoddard, David C. Cuthell, and Margaret W. Sullivan, eds., *Change in the Muslim World* (Syracuse: Syracuse University Press, 1981), p. 34.

18. Mary Daly, *Beyond God the Father: Toward a Philosophy of Women's Liberation* (Boston: Beacon Press, 1973), p. 5.

19. Seyyed Hossein Nasr, "Present Tendencies, Future Trends," p. 280.

20. Patrick J. Ryan, "Islamic Fundamentalism," p. 437.

had no relevance for Muslims until it began to be applied to their tradition by Westerners or Western-conditioned Muslims. Muslims who know the English language and interpret the term "fundamentalism" literally, that is, as relating to fundamentals, would have little or no problem referring to themselves as fundamentalist since they do, with few exceptions, believe in the fundamentals of Islam set forth in the Qur'an in passages such as Surah 2: *Al-Baqarah:* 177:

> It is not righteousness that ye turn your faces towards East or West; but it is righteousness—to believe in God and the Last Day, and the Angels, and the Book, and the Messengers; to spend your substance, out of love for Him, for your kin, for orphans, for the needy, for the wayfarer, for those who ask, and for the ransom of slaves; to be steadfast in prayer, and practice regular charity; and fulfil the contracts which ye have made; and to be firm and patient, in pain (or suffering) and adversity, and throughout all period of panic, such are the people of truth, the God-fearing.[21]

From the perspective of many Muslims, therefore, a discussion on "Islamic fundamentalism" should be about the fundamentals of Islam, and the answer to the question "Is Islamic fundamentalism good or bad?" should be based on an objective evaluation of the fundamentals of Islam. In other words, if these fundamentals are deemed to be "good," then Islamic fundamentalism should be regarded as good; if these are deemed to be "bad," then Islamic fundamentalism should be regarded as bad. In the West generally, however, the very term "Islamic fundamentalism" triggers off a host of negative associations, many of them deriving from age-old stereotypes of Islam and the remaining deriving from ideas and images attached to fundamentalism by Western Christians. Prominent among these associations is the perception that fundamentalist Muslims are ultra-zealous, narrow-minded persons who tend to interpret the Qur'an literally and to implement its teachings by force, if necessary. These Muslims are seen as "backward" because they

21. *The Holy Qur'an,* pp. 69-70.

are out of step with modernity not only in the way in which they read sacred texts but also in the way in which they disregard the separation of the religious from the secular (or "Church" and "State" to use "Christian" terms).

Here an important difference between the Western and the Muslim understandings of the term "fundamentalism" needs to be clarified and emphasized. One of the major assumptions underlying the negative perceptions of fundamentalism in the West is that fundamentalism is in stark opposition to "modernism." Support for this assumption may be found in *The Shorter Oxford English Dictionary*, which defines fundamentalism as "Strict adherence to traditional orthodox tenets (e.g. the literal inerrancy of Scripture) held to be fundamental to the Christian faith *opposed to liberalism and modernism.*"[22] However, a review of Muslim thought in the modern period shows that instead of being in opposition to each other, the terms "fundamentalist," "modernist," and "liberal" are oftentimes applied to the same thinker. In the last three hundred years one can find a number of Muslim thinkers who were acutely conscious of the stagnation and decadence on Muslim societies in general and sought to re-infuse the dynamism of original Islam in them through application of "modern," "liberal" ideas. One of the most outstanding of these thinkers is Muhammad Iqbal (1877-1938), who has been a source of creative energy and inspiration to millions of Muslims in the twentieth century. Iqbal was a fundamentalist in that he strongly advocated a return to the Qur'an, which he regarded as the embodiment of what is fundamental in Islam, but he was also a "modernist" and a "liberal" in that he protested passionately against blind acceptance of a fossilized religious tradition and urged Muslims to understand the dynamic, evolutionary outlook of the Qur'an and to apply it to their own societies through a process of reasoning (represented by *'Ijma'* or collective thinking and *ijtihad* or individual

---

22. W. Little, H. W. Fowler, and J. Coulson, eds., rev. C. T. Onions, *The Shorter Oxford English Dictionary* (Oxford: Clarendon Press, 1964), p. 762; italics mine.

thinking). How fundamentalism, modernism, and liberalism, as Muslims understand these terms, came together in the writings of Iqbal may be seen from the following excerpts:

> I know the Ulama of Islam claim finality for the popular school of Muslim Law.[23]
>
> For fear of . . . disintegration, the conservative thinkers of Islam focussed all their efforts on the one point of preserving a uniform social life for the people by a jealous exclusion of all innovations in the law of Shari'at as expounded by the early doctors of Islam. Their leading idea was social order, and there is no doubt that they were partly right, because organization does to a certain extent counteract the forces of decay. But they did not see, and our modern Ulama do not see, that the ultimate fate of a people does not depend so much on organization as on the worth of power of individual men. In an over-organized society the individual is altogether crushed out of existence.[24]
>
> The closing of the door of Ijtihad is pure fiction suggested partly by the crystallization of legal thought in Islam, and partly by that intellectual laziness which, especially in a period of spiritual decay, turns great thinkers into idols. If some of the later doctors have upheld this fiction, modern Islam is not bound by the voluntary surrender of intellectual independence.[25]
>
> Since things have changed and the world of Islam is today confronted and affected by new forces set free by the extraordinary development of human thought in all its directions, I see no reason why this attitude (of the Ulama) should be maintained any longer. Did the founders of our schools ever claim finality for their reasoning and interpretations? Never. The claim of the present generation of Muslim liberals to re-interpret the foundational legal principles, in the light of their own experience and altered conditions of modern life, is in my opinion, perfectly justified. The teaching of the Qur'an that life is a process of pro-

---

23. Muhammad Iqbal, *The Reconstruction of Religious Thought in Islam* (Lahore: Shaikh Muhammad Ashraf, 1971), p. 168.

24. Ibid., p. 151.

25. Ibid., p. 178.

gressive creation necessitates that each generation, guided but unhampered by the work of its predecessors, should be permitted to solve its own problems.[26]

Contemporary Muslims are very interested in developing a hermeneutics of reinterpreting the Qur'an in such a way that the fundamentals of Islam which have universal applicability are separated from historical and cultural accretions which have impeded the growth of Muslim societies, keeping them shackled to a dead past rather than enabling them to move into a living present. Of pioneer significance in this regard is the work of Fazlur Rahman (1919-1988), who describes his own methodology as follows:

> This process of interpretation proposed here consists of a double movement, from the present situation to Qur'anic times, then back to the present. The Qur'an is the divine response, through the Prophet's mind to the moral-social situation of the Prophet's Arabia, particularly to the problems of the commercial Meccan society of his day . . . and for the most part consists of moral, religious, and social pronouncements that respond to specific problems confronted in concrete historical situations. Sometimes the Qur'an simply gives an answer to a question or a problem, but usually these answers are stated in terms of an explicit or semi-explicit "ratio legis," while there are also certain laws enunciated from time to time. But, even where simple answers are given, it is possible to understand their reasons and hence deduce general laws by studying the background materials, which for the most part have been fairly intelligibly presented by the commentators. The first of the two movements mentioned above, then, consists of two steps. First, one must understand the import or meaning of a given statement by studying the historical situation or problem to which it was the answer. Of course, before coming to the study of the macrosituation in terms of society, religion, customs, and institutions, indeed, of life as a whole in Arabia on the eve of Islam and particulary in and around Mecca—not excluding the Perso-Byzantine Wars—will

26. Ibid., p. 168.

have to be made. The first step of the first movement, then, consists of understanding the meaning of the Qur'an as a whole as well as in terms of the specific tenets that constitute responses to specific answers and enunciate them as statements of general moral-social objectives that can be "distilled" from specific texts in light of the sociohistorical background and the often-stated "rationes legis." Indeed, the first step—the understanding of the meaning of the specific texts—itself implies the second step and will lead to it. Throughout this process due regard must be paid to the tenor of the teaching of the Qur'an as a whole so that each given meaning understood, each law enunciated, and each objective formulated will cohere with the rest. The Qur'an as a whole does inculcate a definite attitude toward life and does have a concrete weltanschauung; it also claims that its teaching has "no inner contradiction" but coheres as a whole. Whereas the first movement has been from the specifics of the Qur'an to the eliciting and systematizing of its general principles, values, and long-range objectives, the second is to be from this general view to the specific view that is to be formulated and realized *now*. That is, the general has to be embodied in the present concrete sociohistorical context. This once again requires the careful study of the present situation and the analysis of its various component elements so we can assess the current situation and change the present to whatever extent necessary, and so we can determine priorities afresh in order to implement the Qur'anic values afresh. To the extent that we achieve both moments of this double movement successfully, the Qur'an imperatives will become alive and effective once again. While the first task is primarily the work of the historian, in the performance of the second the instrumentality of the social scientist is obviously indispensable, but the actual "effective orientation" and "ethical engineering" are the work of the ethicist. . . . This second moment will also act as a corrective of the results of the first, that is, of understanding and interpretation. For if the results of understanding fail in application now, then either there has been a failure to assess the present situation correctly or a failure in understanding the Qur'an. For it is not possible that something that could be and actually was realized in the specific texture of the past, cannot, allowing for the difference in the specifics of the present situation, be realized in the present context—where "allowing for the difference in the specifics of the present situation" includes both changing the rules of the past in conformity with the altered situation of the present (provided this changing does not violate the general principles and values derived from the past) and changing the present situation, where necessary, so it is brought into conformity with these general principles and values. Both tasks imply intellectual *jihad*, the second implying also a moral jihad or endeavor in addition to the intellectual. . . . The intellectual endeavor or jihad, including the intellectual elements of both moments—past and present—is technically called *ijtihad*, which means "the effort to understand the meaning of a relevant text or precedent in the past, containing a rule, and to alter that rule by extending or restricting or otherwise modifying it in such a manner that a new situation can be subsumed under it by a new situation."[27]

As the foregoing extracts from the writings of Muhammad Iqbal and Fazlur Rahman show, a return to the fundamentals of Islam is seen by modern Muslim thinkers as the surest, if not the sole, hope of gaining liberation from internal and external bondage and impediments to physical, intellectual, and spiritual evolution. This fact, important as it is in understanding what has been happening in the world of Islam in recent centuries, has received scant attention in the West, which continues to assume that the term "fundamentalism" can have no meaning other than the one assigned to it by them. This situation is lamentable enough. It is made worse by the fact that Western media in general apply the term "fundamentalism/fundamentalist" so loosely to Islam/Muslims that it ceases to be meaningful even within the parameters of the popular Western understanding of this term. For instance, in an article entitled "Syria's Assad: His Power and His Plan," in *The New York Times Sunday Magazine* (19 February 1984), Stanley Reed showed surprise that Assad could side with Ayatollah Khomeini when the latter's "Islamic fundamentalism" was similar to that of Assad's domes-

---

27. Fazlur Rahman, *Islam and Modernity: Transformation of an Intellectual Tradition* (Chicago: University of Chicago Press, 1982), pp. 5-8.

tic enemies, the Muslim Brotherhood.[28] In a penetrating article entitled "Islamic Fundamentalism: A Questionable Category," Patrick J. Ryan shows how the term "Islamic Fundamentalism" applies neither to Ayatollah Khomeini nor to the Muslim Brothers "at least if fundamentalism means orthodoxy reducible to a commitment to literal interpretation of Scripture."[29] In any case, the question arises: can Muslims as diverse as Ayatollah Khomeini and Muslim Brothers all be called by one name?

No phenomenon can be properly understood if it is not named correctly, for as the wise Confucius said: "If names be not correct, language is not in accordance with the truth of things. If language is not in accordance with the truth of things, affairs cannot be carried on to success."[30] One major reason why Islam and Muslims have been so little understood in the West is that they have always been seen through the colored lens of Western concepts and presuppositions. Though it is natural to compare that which we do not know to that which we do know (or think we know), or to try to understand the "other" in our own terms, it is dangerous to assume that one's perceptions of the "other" (especially if the "other" is considered an "adversary") in fact define the reality of the "other." Many Western scholars of Islam got off on the wrong track when, thinking that Islam centered upon the person of Muhammad as Christianity centered upon the person of Christ, they called Islam "Muhammadism."[31] Trying to rectify the damage done by earlier "Orientalists," Wilfred Cantwell Smith, despite his erudition and sensitivity, fell into another trap when he said that, not Muhammad

28. See Patrick J. Ryan, "Islamic Fundamentalism," p. 437.

29. Ibid.

30. Confucius, quoted by Huston Smith in *The Religions of Man* (New York: Harper & Row, 1958), p. 161.

31. That an Islamicist of the caliber of H. A. R. Gibb should have named his book, which has been widely used as a textbook, *Mohammadanism: An Historical Survey*, 2nd ed. (New York: Oxford University Press, 1962), seems amazing to Muslims.

but the Qur'an was to Islam what Jesus was to Christianity,[32] for in the final analysis, a book cannot be compared to a person. Now, those Western writers or journalists who are trying to figure out what "Islamic fundamentalism" is are, once again, on a wild goose chase. If they are genuinely interested in learning about and understanding the significant events, trends, and developments in the Islamic world, they will have to acquire knowledge of Islam and Muslim "from within" as it were. As an insightful Westerner remarks: "It is time for the Western press to learn more about the inner workings of the Islamic world, time to stop analyzing Islamic faith in Christian or Western secularized categories. One-fifth of the world's population is Muslim; before it is too late, the West must take it seriously."[33]

My personal experience of both intensive and extensive dialogue with a large number of Westerners in a variety of settings has shown me that, generally speaking, few of them—especially in the United States—know much about Islam or have any sense of the living reality of Muslims. They tend, therefore, to think of both Islam and Muslims in simplistic or reductionist terms. In this context, there is a certain aptness about the following remark by a Muslim graduate student about the Christian organizer of the Christian-Muslim dialogue group in which both participated: "He is really a well-meaning person, but the problem is that he believes Islam is a religion one can know all about over the weekend!" That such an attitude should exist even amongst those Westerners who are striving most sincerely to dialogue with Muslims makes the whole situation extremely depressing.

The seriousness of the crises which exist in our time in the Middle East alone, where adherents of the three Abrahamic faith traditions—Jews, Christians, Muslims—face each other in complex conflict, demands that all three make a determined ef-

32. See, for instance, Wilfred Cantwell Smith's article "Is the Qur'an the Word of God?" in *Religious Diversity: Essays by Wilfred Cantwell Smith*, ed. Willard G. Oxtoby (New York: Harper & Row, 1976), p. 24.

33. Patrick J. Ryan, "Islamic Fundamentalism," p. 440.

fort to subject to the most rigorous scrutiny the facile labels which we attach all too easily to each other, especially in times of trial and difficulty. These labels are not only misleading, confused, and confusing, but can also be dangerous. For instance, it is a common Western tendency to label Muslim leaders and groups perceived to be "anti-Western" (which becomes synonymous with "antimodern") as "fundamentalist." This label is meant to discredit these leaders or groups in the West. However, ironically enough, oftentimes it tends to serve an opposite purpose in the societies in which these leaders or groups are located. It is no secret that this is a time of great ferment in the Islamic world, and in every Muslim society numerous factions are vying for attention and allegiance. Some of these are so marginalized that they may even be considered to be "un-Islamic" in their orientation or agenda by the majority of people in that society. If once the label of fundamentalist is attached to them, however, they become associated in the minds of a number of Muslims with the fundamentals of Islam and thus acquire a sort of religious legitimization. Knowing what benefits accrue to them in their own societies once they have been labeled "fundamentalists" by the West, some unscrupulous Muslims deliberately appropriate the label which provides them not only with some social and political respectability but also the opportunity to act out the Western description of fundamentalism. Thus, there is a real danger that the loose application by many Westerners of a loaded term such as "fundamentalist" to a variety of Muslims, could, in fact, lead to the emergence of Muslims who fit the Western model of "fundamentalism."

10. The Reemergence of Fundamentalism in the Catholic Church

Patrick M. Arnold, S.J.

The recent fundamentalistic Zeitgeist sweeping the world's major religions has not left the Roman Catholic Church unaffected, though perhaps its presence is not so apparent as in other religious traditions. Though the term "Catholic fundamentalism" is recent,[1] the phenomenon that the phrase tries to name is not at all new to the Church but is only the latest version of a tendency which has regularly infected Catholicism. Earlier outbreaks of this chronic fundamentalism caused, in the distant past, such excesses as crusades and inquisitions, and as recently as this century, the relatively less extreme antimodernist Integralist movement. In many ways modern Catholic fundamentalism is essentially an outgrowth of the Integralist movement which stymied scriptural and theological research, as well as liturgical reform, for half a century.[2] Since twentieth-century Catholic fundamentalism is relatively milder than more ancient versions of the tendency, it is possible that the Church may have developed successful coping mechanisms which tend to limit the

1. See Peter Hebblethwaite, "A Roman Catholic Fundamentalism," *Times Literary Supplement*, 5-11 August 1988, p. 866.
2. See John Coleman, "Counting Catholic Noses: Recent Survey Results," *Church*, Spring 1988, pp. 3-11; idem, "Who Are the Catholic Fundamentalists?" *Commonweal*, Jan. 27, 1989.

severity of any given outbreak. Nevertheless, I would suggest that modern Catholic fundamentalism still poses a significant threat to the ability of a healthy and vital Catholic tradition to bring its distinctive gifts to the men and women of the world. For this reason alone, it deserves the concern and careful attention of a wide audience.

What is "fundamentalism"? Unfortunately, a workable definition continues to elude scholarship. On the one hand, many scholars would define the term precisely and narrowly—namely, as applicable only to the conservative Protestantism which produced the modern English term in the early twentieth century.[3] On the other hand, a scholar such as Robert Bellah uses the term in a fashion which completely divorces it from any connection with religion so that it means simply intolerance of any kind.[4] At the opposite extreme, some secular humanists would use the word tendentiously to describe "religion" itself.[5] Ironically, this latter usage by self-professed enemies of religion often matches closely many fundamentalists' insistence that the word only describes that which is truly "fundamental" or "orthodox" in their religious tradition.[6] Without doubt, however, the word is now in widespread popular use as a generic term suggesting religious extremism or fanaticism. While many academics eschew using such a term so loosely, especially when it has been made popular by the media, I believe that the widespread use of the word "fundamentalism" as a term attempting to describe a worldwide phenomenon featuring extreme fanaticism within several religious traditions fairly reflects an impor-

3. See Martin Marty, "Modern Fundamentalism," *America*, 27 September 1988, pp. 133-35; and Nancy Ammerman, *Bible Believers* (New Brunswick, NJ: Rutgers University Press, 1987).

4. See John Coleman, "Catholic Integralism as a Fundamentalism," in L. Kaplan, ed., *Varieties of Fundamentalism* (N.p.: forthcoming).

5. See Paul Kurtz, "The Growing of Fundamentalism Worldwide," in *Neo-Fundamentalism: The Humanist Response* (New York: Prometheus, 1988), pp. 7-26.

6. See Frank Morriss, "'Fundamentalist' Is the Latest Epithet Hurled against Orthodox Catholics," *The Wanderer*, 21 May 1987, pp. 4-8.

tant modern experience and is not to be dismissed lightly. Therefore, I will use the term generically throughout this essay to describe a religious tendency or phenomenon, and not necessarily any group which may label itself "fundamentalist."

I would define modern fundamentalism as an aggressive and marginalized religious movement which, in reaction to the perceived threat of modernity, seeks to return its home religion and nation to traditional orthodox principles, values, and texts through the co-option of the central executive and legislative power of both the religion itself and the modern national state. This definition implies that fundamentalism is much more than a purely religious movement; rather, it involves social and political forces as well. It describes in a relatively fair manner a number of tendencies or movements which are well underway in Christianity, Islam, Judaism, Hinduism, and other religious traditions. Yet the definition is insufficient from the perspective of the normative tradition in each religion which would regard such a phenomenon as aberrant and even alarming. Moreover, precisely the consistent practice of fundamentalists in claiming the term "orthodox" requires a response from mainline, traditional religionists. Contrary to the claims of both fundamentalists *and* their secular humanist enemies, fundamentalism is not normative religion, but rather a deviation from it.

Catholic Fundamentalism as a Religious Disease

Speaking as a committed Catholic priest and theologian, I would argue that the modern reappearance of fundamentalism in the Catholic Church requires a forceful response which would indicate precisely in which ways the new Integralism represents an extreme deviation from the best of the Catholic tradition and a return to the worst failings in Catholic history. In doing so, it is necessary to abandon a dispassionate or disinterested approach which would merely attempt to describe the phenomenon. Precisely the virtual claim of Catholic fundamentalists that they hold a patent on the word "Catholic" requires a responsive judgment that they indeed do not. It is in this context that I would therefore describe Catholic fundamentalism as a psychosocial disease affecting the conservative wing of our religious community.

It is crucial here to note that I do not equate fundamentalism with conservatism, which is a valuable and necessary component of any vital religion. In Catholic faith, for example, conservatism cherishes the traditional symbols, myths, rituals, kerygma, dogma, and spirituality which make Catholicism a religious treasury for humanity. As a result, genuine Catholic conservatism resists the fashionable adoption of practices which are merely trendy, or ideologies which have a shelf life shorter than many canned goods.

True conservatives in the Church also recognize consciously that they are only *part* of the whole, members of a body. As such, they do not pursue their conserving function in autonomous isolation but respect the Church's need to change, to adapt, and to learn from the modern world even while attempting to speak to it. The genuine conservative spirit of Roman Catholicism is patient and even humorous, qualities captured in the expression, "in our Church, we think in terms of centuries." It is precisely this sensitivity to the genuine Catholic tradition and modus operandi which may yet prove to be the most powerful bulwark against the innovative Catholic fundamentalists of the 1980s who insist on styling themselves the "neo-orthodox."

True religious conservatism functions in a manner comparable to the human body's immune system in recognizing and eliminating harmful foreign threats to the health of the whole. By contrast, fundamentalism resembles a disease of the immune system known as arthritis, a condition in which the immune system mistakenly targets parts of the body itself for attack and destruction. Arthritis is a particularly apt metaphor for fundamentalism precisely because this painful autoimmune disease turns its greatest crippling fury primarily on its own body, impeding the healthy functioning of its members.

Psychological and Mythical Beginnings

Where does Catholic fundamentalism originate? I would suggest, following the assumption that social aberrations are rooted in individual pathology,[7] that the best procedure for studying the tendency is to begin within the psychological and mythical lives of individuals, who in turn join small groups which ultimately affect the entire community. Fundamentalism seems to originate in a distinctive emotional or psychological complex in which individuals feel personally threatened by the modern weakening of institutions which would once have shielded them from making painful moral or value choices.[8] It is well known that the Roman Catholic Church once provided an ideal climate for such authoritarian personalities: clear rules with precise evaluations of sinfulness governed every conceivable moral and religious option. The Catholic myths that supported such individuals provided a seemingly secure spiritual haven: all authority seemed to stream from heaven above directly to the Pope in Rome. It subsequently flowed hierarchically to the bishops and eventually to the local priest's pulpit or confessional. Catholic philosophy and theology claimed to provide definite answers, indeed, truth itself. Catholic liturgy beautifully expressed eternal verities and otherworldly realities. In this mythical world, the vulnerable individual seemed to live a safe spiritual and intellectual life, defended from the vagaries of moral choices and the vicissitudes of worldly change.

Vatican II and the Collapse of a Catholic Myth

Events in the 1960s were to challenge strongly this confident Catholic ethos. The sweeping liturgical, theological, and spir-

7. See Carl Jung, *Man and His Symbols* (New York: Dell, 1964), p. 93.
8. See Mortimer Ostow's insightful study of the fundamentalist personality in chapter 6 above.

itual reforms fashioned by the Second Vatican Council brought many refreshing changes, but not without a time of questioning, uncertainty, and even excess. This period of transition evidently drove many authoritarian Catholics to a state of crisis. The liturgy had become plain to the point of blandness. Worse, the same Church which had explicitly condemned and persecuted Modernism several generations earlier now seemed to have adopted many of its most salient propositions. The Church seemed increasingly to resemble liberal Protestantism. Compounding the conservatives' confusion was the sense that liberal Catholics were flaunting their new-found freedoms and even taunting loyal conservatives. It should not go unstated that revenge for these excesses would play a major role in motivating fundamentalist activities of the next decade.

During the 1970s, many angry and fearful Catholics increasingly banded together in movements such as Catholics United for the Faith (CUF), Opus Dei, and Communion and Liberation, in order to bring pressure upon Church authorities to stifle the threatening changes which they saw around them.[9] These pressures effectively reenergized the dormant Integralist movement. Yet when most of the bishops resisted this pressure and forged ahead in the spirit of *aggiornamento*, the Catholic right-wing media shifted tactics, drumming up public criticism and letter-writing campaigns directed against members of the hierarchy itself, even including Pope Paul VI, who is still vilified by many reactionaries for his leadership of Vatican II.[10] The fundamentalist tendency to fratricidal warfare reached its most extreme point in French Archbishop Marcel Lefebvre's "Fraternity of Pius X" movement, which condemned the entire post–Vatican II Church and eventually precipitated the first formal schism within Catholicism in a century.[11]

9. See M. Timothy Iglesias, "CUF and Dissent: A Case Study of Religious Conservatism," *America*, 11 April 1987, pp. 303-7.

10. See Malachi Martin, *The Jesuits: The Society of Jesus and the Betrayal of the Roman Catholic Church* (New York: Simon & Schuster, 1987).

11. See William Dinges, "Lefebvre Abandons Ship," *Commonweal*, 12 August 1988, pp. 420-21.

The great majority of Catholic fundamentalists, however, were unwilling to bring themselves to such an openly schismatic state. Throughout the decade, they conducted instead an unrelenting vendetta against so-called "heretical" theologians, "dissenting" priests and nuns, and the "cowardly" bishops who refused to silence the liberals. The majority of Catholics tended to regard these groups and their newspapers (e.g., *The Wanderer, Twin Circle, The Remnant*) as irritating but essentially harmless extremists. Within a decade, several developments were to change this complacent attitude markedly.

Several years after the succession of John Paul II to the papacy, it became unmistakably clear that this pontiff deliberately intended to form a conservative administration of the Church on moral, doctrinal, and disciplinary matters. Yet among his conservative curial appointees were various high- and low-level officials who held ideological views sympathetic to those of the Catholic reactionaries. This development afforded the fundamentalists several encouraging strategic opportunities. First, they could now begin to shed their extremist image and appeal to the ultimate ecclesiastical authority—the papacy—in support for their views. In the American Church, this allowed reactionary Catholics to create a scenario in which they could present themselves as authentic Catholics unswervingly loyal to the Roman Pontiff, while depicting liberal American theologians and clergy as disobedient and disloyal to the personally popular Pope. Even more important, the fundamentalists now found sympathetic Roman curial officials who encouraged their plans to crack down on favorite liberal targets. As a result, fundamentalist "truth squads" began to stalk selected teachers, priests, and even bishops in order to report unorthodox thinking to Rome.

Eventually, this strategy resulted in a number of investigations and reprimands directed at such famous figures as theologians Hans Küng, Edward Schillebeeckx, Leonardo Boff, and Charles Curran, bishops Raymond Hunthausen and Pedro Casaldaliga, and a host of less famous—but more vulnerable—

laypeople, nuns, and priests. It became clear that the fundamentalists had found a successful modus operandi: identification of irritating liberal or moderate targets, hostile criticism of these individuals in fundamentalist media organs, which in turn directed mass letter-writing campaigns to such sympathetic curial ears as Cardinals Ratzinger and Hamer, who eventually initiated proceedings against the targets.

Yet perhaps even more energizing to the Catholic reactionaries than their ecclesiastical victories was the simultaneous widespread popular appeal and political success in the early 1980s of Protestant fundamentalist values and rhetoric. The door to direct partisan involvement in American politics had finally cracked open. In the United States, Catholic fundamentalists first had involved themselves directly in politics as a part of the "right-to-life" movement in reaction to the 1973 Supreme Court decision legalizing abortion. Throughout the following decade, they began to find common cause with their Protestant counterparts on an expanding variety of sexual, social, and political issues. Yet the power of this growing fundamentalist coalition did not burst fully into consciousness until 1980 with the election of its chosen candidate, Ronald Reagan. Suddenly, the political arena offered a tempting opportunity to enact the fundamentalist agenda through legislative pressure and executive fiat.

During the 1980s, American Catholic fundamentalism began to call itself variously "neo-orthodoxy" or the "Catholic Restoration Movement." Its agenda, originally concerned with liturgical practice and sexual morality, eventually merged into virtual identity with the platform of the right wing of the Republican party. Though it heatedly denies political involvement, recent issues of the fundamentalist flagship newspaper *The Wanderer,* for example, devote as much space to columns defending South Africa or promoting the deployment of the Strategic Defense Initiative as lambasting the critics of Humanae Vitae or vilifying liberal bishops. In promoting his plan to purge the American Catholic hierarchy and educational system of liberals, one stalwart reactionary, Dr. James Hitchcock, went so far as to claim the charismatic Reagan as a model of neo-orthodox Catholic success.[12]

Unfortunately, a decade of Catholic fundamentalist success has crippled the rest of the Church in at least three significant ways. First, many progressive theologians and bishops are frankly intimidated and unwilling to risk their careers on behalf of causes which raise fundamentalist hackles: academic freedom, women's rights in the Church, acceptance of gay Catholics, and support for the Third World liberation Church, among others. With notable exceptions, the ability of Church thinkers to propose and discuss creative answers to the increasingly baffling scientific, ecological, psychological, and social problems which the world faces has been noticeably hampered by the chilling effect of the new fundamentalist inquisition.

Second, in terms of the Church's image in the outside world, the fundamentalists threaten the mood of hope and outreach once symbolized by the outstretched arms of John XXIII. Increasingly, they promote an image to the world symbolized by the wagging finger, the closed door, and a self-righteous, "read my lips" mentality which cannot say no often or loud enough.

Finally, fundamentalism increasingly exacerbates old Church wounds: the Roman Vatican vs. the American bishops, the separation of laity and clergy, the role of women in the Church, disputes among theologians, and so forth. These problems always exist, but fundamentalists possess a seemingly inerrant instinct to irritate precisely the most sensitive and vulnerable areas on the Church's body. Rather than explore and even celebrate the enormous unity which all Catholics share as a way of healing the wounds, the fundamentalists' unbudging insistence that Catholicism entails complete obedience to their peculiar notions of doctrinal truth and moral probity provokes

---

12. James Hitchcock, "Suggestions for Reorienting Catholicism," *Fellowship of Catholic Scholars Newsletter,* 8-12 December 1985.

resistance and dispute. For the neo-orthodox, the Church finally is not a family, a community, or a body; it is an ideology.

The Symptoms of Fundamentalism in the Church

Jesus once said, "Beware of false prophets, who come to you dressed as sheep while underneath they are savage wolves. You will recognize them by the fruit they bear" (Matt. 7:15-16). It is always the task of theologians to test modern ideas and movements to see if they represent the genuine presence of the Holy Spirit; indeed, this responsibility is a genuinely conservative one. It is therefore appropriate to ask whether the practices and tenets of modern Catholic fundamentalism agree with Scripture and the tradition of the Church. If we adopt the discernment method suggested by Jesus, we may ask, "What fruit has militant neo-orthodoxy borne?" And if fear, dissension, vengefulness are the fruits of Catholic fundamentalism, how does an ordinary believer recognize the diseased tree before it bears such a harvest? I would propose four warning signs, each at odds with the mind of Christ and the best of Catholic tradition, which may reveal an aberrant fundamentalism.

1. Fear and Desperation

The first symptom of Catholic fundamentalism is its desperate fear of, and outright hostility to, modern values and thought, which are capsulized in the term "secular humanism" and regarded as an ideological conspiracy of liberal academicians, artist, politicians, and media figures intent upon eradicating from Western society the last vestiges of the Judeo-Christian ethic. The most recent predecessor to contemporary Catholic fundamentalism, Integralism, coined the word "modernism" as a new form of heresy, against which Catholic priests were to swear oaths as recently as the 1970s.

There is much in modern thought and value which *is* inimical to Christianity—but this is hardly a new problem (cf. John 17:13-19). Throughout its history the Christian Church has shown remarkable creativity in accepting modern scientific and philosophical insights and even fashioning out of them new theologies which express the Christian experience in fresh language and concepts. For the neo-orthodox, however, the validity of this enterprise apparently ended in the last century, so that Thomistic scholasticism represents the last valid philosophical system capable of expressing Christian truths. For the first time in its history, apparently, the Catholic Church has nothing to learn from contemporary people, nor, indeed, anything new to say to them.

What is most frightful to Catholic fundamentalists is their perception that the evils of modern thought have penetrated even the heart and mind of the Church. They claim that only their beleaguered prophetic remnant retains the last vestiges of Catholic truth, while bishops and liberals of all kinds lead most of the faithful into the modernist heresy. The ultimate secular humanist bête noir in the Church, however, is the Jesuit Order, excoriated in ex-Jesuit Malachi Martin's work, *The Jesuits: The Society of Jesus and the Betrayal of the Roman Catholic Church*. For some fundamentalists, the alleged existence of the secular humanist conspiracy inside the Church justifies their call for severe crackdown measures against the liberals.[13] Yet for others, this mass apostasy from God is nothing less than an apocalyptic sign.

Like its Protestant counterpart, Catholic fundamentalism occasionally manifests its despair over modernity in apocalyptic, esoteric sects which deliver eschatological announcements and claim to possess secret information regarding the end times.[14] Interestingly, Catholic millennial anxiety centers mainly around alleged apparitions of the Blessed Virgin Mary which announce imminent divine punishment for the sinfulness of the

---

13. See James Hitchcock, "Suggestions."
14. See Yves Dupont, *Catholic Prophecy: The Coming Chastisement* (Rockford: Tan Books, 1973).

world. One magazine, the virulently anticommunist *Fatima Crusader*, regularly threatens Catholics with the end of the world if they fail to increase their devotions to the Blessed Mother. While this strain of Marian apocalypticism predicts an end to the world when Our Lady can no longer restrain the wrathful arm of her Son, other Catholic reactionaries proclaim an imminent end to the entire apostate Catholic Church. This motif is strong in the aforementioned work of Malachi Martin and may be seen in a work such as Anne Roche Muggeridge's *The Desolate City: Revolution in the Roman Catholic Church.*[15]

While many observers dismiss such apocalyptic anxieties as paranoia, it is interesting to consider what social stresses the fundamentalists' doomsaying might represent. I would point out that, in contrast to many fundamentalistic sects that are rooted in the lower classes, most Catholic fundamentalists originate in upper socioeconomic classes, represent patriarchal interests, and descend from the Anglo-European cultural heritage. I would suggest that what they perceive as the threatened "end of the world" or the "desolation of the Church" in fact represents the social reality of the decline in the power and prestige of "Eurocentrism" and patriarchy in the Catholic Church as indigenous and Third World peoples and women begin to achieve positions of cultural acceptance and leadership in the Church. Though their actual numbers are relatively small—10 percent is probably a generous figure—the Catholic fundamentalists happen to possess by virtue of their class a disproportionately large political and economic influence which it would be unwise to dismiss.

Though the neo-orthodox wring their hands with anxiety over the Church, bemoaning its "confusion" over doctrinal and moral matters, it must be noted that a number of studies and surveys belie the notion that the Catholic Church, in the United States, at least, is experiencing decline and dissolution. Quite the contrary; recent studies report a high level of American

15. Anne Roche Muggeridge, *The Desolate City: Revolution in the Roman Catholic Church* (San Francisco: Harper & Row, 1986).

Catholic participation and satisfaction in their Church.[16] These surveys tend to confirm our impression that the elitist fundamentalists are clearly out of touch with the reality of the average Catholic's feelings and concerns.

2. Selective Textual Absolutism

A second symptom of fundamentalism, which many mistakenly believe to be its *only* feature, is the belief in the absolute inerrancy and infallibility of traditional religious texts. This characteristic is in many ways a function of fundamentalist anxiety about a modernity which purveys morally and spiritually bankrupt values and teachings. By contrast, the traditional text is believed to have been given during an ancient and holy time, a golden age of truth. It is important to note how thoroughly fundamentalism is wedded to, if not possessed by, the nostalgic myth of the Golden Age, which removes memories of real terrors and mistakes from the past as thoroughly as it denies the grace and possibilities of the present.

Catholic fundamentalism often goes unrecognized simply because it seizes primarily upon *papal* moral and doctrinal pronouncements as sources of absolute truth, and not *biblical* teachings as in Protestantism. This is not to say that Catholic reactionaries do not use the Bible fundamentalistically; in fact, certain passages are frequently used as proof texts. Yet this is almost always done in a way which supports papal authority in general, or a specific teaching in particular.

In reaction to the perceived "confusion" which plagues the Church in moral and doctrinal matters, papal fundamentalists point to magisterial pronouncements and encyclicals as clear and infallible teachings which present the authentic Catholic position on a given matter. Theological nuances and subtleties, or ethical distinctions and variations, whether they proceed from elements

16. See George Gallup and Jim Castelli, *The American Catholic People* (Garden City, NY: Doubleday, 1987); and John Coleman, "Counting Catholic Noses."

of the magisterium itself or from academic theologians, are regarded not as refinements or dialogical alternatives, but as proof of disobedience and evidence of disloyal dissent.

Papal fundamentalism represents a deviation from orthodoxy in several respects. First, Catholic tradition has been exceedingly careful to limit statements issued ex cathedra and hence to be regarded as infallible; only one such teaching, for example, has been so defined in the twentieth century—the Assumption of the Blessed Virgin Mary. The tendency to regard every papal pronouncement univocally is a theological aberration which has been termed "creeping infallibility." Second, papal fundamentalism so stresses centralized authoritarian power that the legitimate role of individual bishops is severely eclipsed. Finally, no moral teachings have ever been defined as infallible, nor indeed can they be; ethical doctrine cannot be couched in language specific enough to cover all human possibilities and still be meaningful.

More germane to our discussion of modern fundamentalism than such theological debate is the concrete determination of just which papal teachings the highly selective Catholic neo-orthodox regard as infallible. Just as Protestant fundamentalism strains at gnats regarding, for example, scattered biblical injunctions against homosexuality while swallowing whole camels of Christ's teachings on the evils of money, so its Catholic counterpart prefers a "canon within a canon" on papal teachings. Sexual and authority issues are given the most severe individualistic interpretation. I have been assured by several Integralists that failure to assent to each and every one of these teachings even privately excludes one automatically from the Catholic faith. Yet papal teachings on social issues such as war, human rights, workers' rights, and economic justice are treated with the widest possible latitude for discussion and interpretation. Lay theologian Michael Novak, who represents the capitalist American Enterprise Institute, has criticized moral theologian Charles Curran's "dissent" from papal sexual teaching while simultaneously conducting an extensive media campaign designed to undermine support for the American Catholic bishops' pastoral letters on nuclear warfare and the American economy.[17]

3. Right-Wing Political Alliances

The moral selectiveness of papal fundamentalists regarding progressive Catholic teaching on social issues masks a third, and in many ways most revealing, symptom of religious aberration: the penchant for alliances with right-wing, reactionary, and even repressive political regimes. As Ian Lustick observed in his study of the *Gush Emunim* in Israel,[18] modern fundamentalists, failing at measures to stymie change within their own religious institutions, usually seek to enforce their agenda through the legal and political machinery of the modern state. While these attempts have produced explosive results in certain Islamic, Sikh, and Jewish communities (whence "fundamentalism" became a popular media term), the relatively subtle Catholic right-wing infestation of American politics is no less important in view of the power of its host.

What began after *Roe* vs. *Wade* as a laudable attempt by pro-life Catholics to seek legislative redress for the growing problem of abortion-on-demand has since degenerated into a merely partisan political movement. Their eagerness to move from the extreme fringe to the center of political and religious discussion left them vulnerable to cynical political exploitation. During and since the 1980 and 1984 presidential elections, many Catholic fundamentalists have allowed themselves to be thoroughly co-opted by the right wing of the Republican Party for the purposes of moral legitimation and votes, with little or no return for their considerable investment of religious energy.

Other Catholics seem to exploit their religious heritage in

17. Michael Novak, "Dissent Should Be Intramural," *St. Louis Post-Dispatch,* 27 September 1986, p. 10.
18. Ian Lustick, *For the Land and the Lord: Jewish Fundamentalism in Israel* (New York: Council on Foreign Relations, 1988), pp. 4-8.

support of the Republican political agenda. A sampling of their favorite causes reveals how far they have strayed from a genuinely religious issue like abortion: Phyllis Schlafly's Eagle Forum now plunks for Star Wars; journalists Pat Buchanan, John McLaughlin, and Robert Novak push for increased military expenditures; Congressmen Dannemeyer and Dornan exploit fears of disease at the expense of the civil rights of AIDS patients; and Henry Hyde apologizes for the Iran-Contra scandal as Lt. Col. Oliver North salutes God and country. Last year, Fr. Virgil Blum, founder of the Catholic League for Religious and Civil Rights, even claimed that it was a Catholic duty to support the nomination of Judge Robert Bork to the U.S. Supreme Court.

Especially galling to the American neo-orthodox is the worldwide Church's support for a liberation theology which would promote justice for oppressed peoples in Latin America and Africa. Integralist response has ranged from academic critiques of liberation theology[19] to personal attacks in the popular Catholic press on the religious sincerity of liberation theologians,[20] and from wild charges in Protestant fundamentalist papers relating alleged plots by Marxist Catholic bishops[21] to alleged secretive financial support for the Nicaraguan *contras* funneled through the CIA and Oliver North by organizations such as the Puebla Institute and the Sword of the Spirit.[22] This hostility to liberation theology is only the latest outgrowth of a fanatical Catholic anticommunism which has used alleged statements of the Blessed Virgin Mary at Fatima as a basis for a highly politicized Christian faith.[23]

19. See Michael Novak, *Will It Liberate: Questions about Liberation Theology* (Mahwah, NJ: Paulist Press, 1986).

20. See James Hitchcock, "People of Faith Clinging Too Long to Sandinistas," *St. Louis Review*, 14 March 1986.

21. See Fr. Enrique Rueda, "Catholic Church Tolerance of Communism," *Family Protection Scoreboard: Special Edition Liberation Theology* (Costa Mesa: NCAN/Scoreboard, 1989), p. 20.

22. Russ Bellant, "Secretive Puebla Institute Has Ties to CIA, Contras, Conservative Bishops," *National Catholic Reporter,* 18 November 1988, pp. 8-20.

23. See Walter Sampson, "Fatima," *Convert Action Information Bulletin* 27 (1987): 47-49.

From a political point of view, the intention of the fundamentalist Catholics in opposing liberation theology is rather obvious: to sabotage the efforts of the Catholic Church on behalf of peace and social justice issues. The strategy is threefold: first, to equate morality primarily with individual sexual ethical standards so that virtue is thought to concern only activities in the bedroom, not the boardroom. Second, in the political sphere, fundamentalists obviously seek to protect Catholic upper-class, corporate, and international interests by undermining orthodox moral teachings regarding labor, fair distribution of wealth, human rights, and so forth. Finally, the effect of these tactics is to sow such dissension and discord as to intimidate the Church in its attempt to include peace and justice issues as part of the larger moral agenda.

4. The Attack on Coreligionists

The fourth symptom of fundamentalism, indeed its classic hallmark, is precisely its ability to create crippling antagonisms within its own religious community. Ultimately, fundamentalist rage is focused on coreligionists who appear to have adapted all too well to modernity through unholy compromise. Fundamentalism is therefore always fratricidal: liberals and moderates who fail the test of orthodoxy prove their complicity in the modernist conspiracy and deserve punishment, removal, or even excommunication. One explanation of the origin of the word *assassin* (Arabic for "fundamentalist") suggests one possible means of eliminating unorthodox opponents, though fortunately in today's Catholic Church, execution of heretics is no longer considered appropriate.

Instead, the modern means of punishing the heterodox in the American church is *character* assassination. Its most famous practitioner is the mean-spirited paper *The Wanderer,* which contains weekly vilification of its favorite religious and political enemies. The list of its targets is large, ranging from cardinals to laity, from politicians to academicians. Each is treated as a true villain, rooted in metaphysical wrongness; it is never conceded that these Catholic enemies are also opposed to secularization, are also aware of real dangers to religion and morals, and are also dedicated to the Catholic faith.

Less public fundamentalist-inspired divisiveness is also widely experienced at the grass-roots level, from the parish to the local chancery. One ultra-orthodox group, Opus Dei, recruits followers in a secretive fashion near major U.S. college campuses, promoting the formation of self-righteous cadres free from the oversight of local bishops.[24] Many parishes experience division and confusion when confronted, for example, by claims from CUF that local priests are unorthodox, or when exposed to the cult-like activity of the "Word of God" network.[25] The dissension also reaches into religious life; the fundamentalist magazine *Fidelity*, with the assistance of an anonymous Jesuit, recently exposed the "unorthodoxy" of the Jesuit novitiate in Michigan by devoting a long article to petty retaliatory charges by two angry novices who had been dismissed by their religious superior.[26]

Theologically, the greatest irony in the midst of all the fundamentalist-inspired strife in the Church is that virtually nothing truly *fundamental* to Catholic faith has been seriously at issue in the last decade. Those who cannot abide the traditional doctrinal and moral claims of Catholicism have in large numbers simply left the Church. Those who stay—liberal and conservative alike—willingly profess together weekly at Mass the *genuine* "fundamentals" of their faith in the Nicene Creed. Moreover, the rich tradition of Catholic faith, its veneration of the saints, its holy days and liturgy, its passion for justice and charity, all serve to unite widely varied believers in a manner described long ago as *katholikos*, "according to the whole."

24. See Patricia Lefevere, "Campus Ministers Assess Opus Dei's Campus Role," *National Catholic Reporter*, 2 December 1988, pp. 18-19.

25. See Russ Bellant, "World of God Network Wants to 'Save the World,'" *National Catholic Reporter*, 18 November 1988, pp. 5-21.

26. See Suzanne Rini, "The Jesuits and the Papist Seminarians: A Case Study of the Real Vocation Crisis," *Fidelity*, March 1987, pp. 18-27.

The internecine disputes triggered by partisan fundamentalists, by contrast, have mostly to do with relatively marginal moral issues of the most intricate complexity—either extremely personal psychosexual issues such as birth control, abortion, or homosexuality, or practically intractable global issues such as poverty and oppression. The truly orthodox Catholic Church, in its wisdom, has never included assent to complicated and personal ethical propositions in its creed nor, for that matter, required perfectly successful moral performance in its members. The Church has sought, rather, to bring its sinful members to a common ground of faith that could be celebrated "according to the whole" Church.

Concluding Observations

Though modern fundamentalism has painfully crippled the post–Vatican II Church in many ways, it is far from paralyzing it. Throughout the world over a half billion Catholics worship Christ and perform quiet works of charity untroubled by voices of fear and doom. Indeed, many Catholics have already recognized the fundamentalists for what they are: sincere but overwrought zealots whom we must bear patiently until their panic runs its course, as it inevitably will. There are recent encouraging signs that John Paul II also recognizes how poorly served he is by Integralist curial officials who present him with overwrought and misleading impressions of the Church.

One hopes that the Catholic Restoration Movement ultimately will fail to restore the worst qualities of the nineteenth-century Roman Catholic persona or mood: rigidity, self-righteousness, negativity, and closed-mindedness. For though the fundamentalists describe this spirit as "prophetic witness," in fact it bears little relation to the prophetic message of Jesus, himself the victim of a vicious coalition of Pharisaic fundamentalists and Roman colonial interest. The true prophetic message of Jesus, ultimately the One on whom Catholic faith relies, stands apart from the power plays of politicians and the dogmatism of "true believers." He is the One who not only loved sinners but dined with them, who challenged authorities when they made life hard for the poor, and who could say in the Gospel, "Come to me, all you who labor, and I will give you rest; shoulder my yoke and learn from me, for I am gentle and humble of heart. Yes, my yoke is easy, and my burden light" (Mark 11:28-30).

See also:

Fackre, Gabriel. *The Religious Right and Christian Faith*. Grand Rapids: Eerdmans, 1982.

Jorstad, Paul. *The Politics of Moralism: The New Christian Right in American Life*. Minneapolis: Augsburg, 1981.

Lernoux, Penny. *People of God*. New York: Viking, 1989.

11. The Jewish Face of Fundamentalism

Leon Wieseltier

Before I address Jewish fundamentalism, a word or two about fundamentalism. I do not believe that any term has been more sloppily and more tendentiously used in the political and cultural discourse of recent years than "fundamentalism." Ten years ago, it meant very, very religious. Five years ago it meant very religious. Today it means, simply, religious. Perhaps it was expecting too much of columnists to constrain their usage with history; that is, to use "fundamentalism" to refer to a particular development in American Protestantism. "Fundamentalism" has become a common shorthand for a hostility toward, and a misunderstanding of, religion itself. It was part of the demonological lexicon of a certain coarse secularism (or, when applied to recent trends in Islam, of racism). Indeed, the word was—is—used in a way that makes you wonder whether the fundamentalists' own fantasies about secular humanism have some basis in reality.

There is a difference between being religious, God-fearing, ritual observing, church- or synagogue- or mosque-going, and being a fundamentalist. There is a difference between fundamentalism and taking religion seriously. I suspect that what the sloppy users of the term find so intolerable about the religious phenomenon they are trying to describe is nothing more than the absence of irony. They cannot get past the essential literalness of the believer.

This literalness, this absence of irony about the tenets and the instruments of faith, has nothing to do with scriptural inerrancy. It is something much deeper, something prior. A religious man or woman believes that certain propositions about the nature and the origins of the world are *true*. He or she believes that before a religion is a worldview, or a belief system, or a culture or a form of life, it is a *truth*. Either God exists or God does not. Either God created the world or God did not. Either God revealed the divine self to Moses, or Jesus, or Mohammed, or God did not. For the believer, those who affirm the negative options above are wrong. In the final analysis, all intellectual sophistication notwithstanding, the believer lives as if Marx and Nietzsche and Freud had never lived. For most of us, that is a little hard to imagine, especially at this late date in the history of desacralization.

Almost all of the "fundamentalisms" we hear about, then, are not fundamentalisms, but only a variety of religious phenomena that inspires horror. No faith has suffered more at the hands of this improper usage than has Islam. But Judaism has also had much darkness cast upon it by the fundamentalist fallacy. The occasion, in the Jewish case, has been the new political prominence of the religious community in Israel: of the nationalist Orthodox which, in the form of Gush Emunim and, more generally, the settlers movement in the West Bank and Gaza, has enjoyed international interest for almost two decades. (In a useful study of Gush ideology, Ian Lustick recently argued that it represents "Jewish fundamentalism.")[1] The religious community's prominence is also evidenced in the antinationalist Orthodox, who have emerged as unexpectedly powerful actors in Israeli electoral politics.

But neither Gush Emunim or Agudat Israel can be correctly described as fundamentalists. The Jewish fundamental-

---

1. Ian Lustick, *For the Land and the Lord: Jewish Fundamentalism in Israel* (New York: Council on Foreign Relations, 1988).

ists of today might be more properly referred to as Jewish restorationists. They seem to be agitating for a return, either to a text or to a time. The impulse of return to a text, however, is much weaker and less intellectually and culturally plausible than the impulse to return to a time.

It may be stated, without much controversy, that there is no such thing as fundamentalism in Judaism. Or, to be a little more precise, and to leave room for Judaism's one fundamentalist episode (which lasted, to be sure, more or less a thousand years but with always increasing marginality), fundamentalism is a form of decadence in Judaism. The reason is plain if one studies Jewish tradition. If, taking the American Protestant model, by fundamentalism we mean a religious form which is based on the centrality of Scripture (not of text, please note, but of Scripture), or revealed Scripture, or more specifically, on the inerrancy of Scripture (in the sense of privileging the literal meaning of the text), then Judaism, which is a tradition based upon the authority of commentary—which indeed *invented* the idea of tradition, as Scholem showed, precisely by raising commentary to authority—is not fundamentalist. Rabbinic is the opposite of fundamentalist. When fundamentalism arises in the Jewish community, it is experienced philosophically as a deviation and socially as a sect. I have in mind the phenomenon of Karaism. It was the first and last fundamentalism in Judaism. It inspired the philosophical and polemical energies of medieval Jewish intellectuals almost as much as Christianity and Islam; it was successfully pushed to the peripheries of Jewish life and thought.

It is true that the Gush Emunim has relied heavily upon the Bible, especially upon its geography, in the formulation of their views. They have certainly insisted upon the bearing of Scripture on the contours, the reasons, and the strategies of the Jewish state. To that extent, they appear to wish a return to a text. Are they, then, fundamentalists? Their writings show that, strictly speaking, they are not. Or if they are, the fundamentals to which they refer are the complexities of the Oral Torah as well. Gush ideology rests not on biblical verses, but upon the rabbinic interpretation of biblical verses. One of the central texts, for example, upon which the Gush relies is not Deuteronomy 7:2, but the comment on the verse in the Babylonian Talmud, Yebamoth 10a, which appears in Rashi's commentary to the verse. *Lo tehonnem,* "show them no mercy," says the biblical verse of the nations in Canaan. The rabbis are struck by the similarity between the verbs "to pity" *(hnn)* and "to camp" (or "to settle," *hnh*). In a very familiar rabbinic technique of exegetical punning, they read the verse to mean "do not let them settle in the land." The rabbinic reading, of course, is intended to moderate the meaning of the verse, which might be taken literally as a command to destroy physically the nations. The world of the Bible was a more brutal world than ours. The Gush Emunim use the moderating commentary of the rabbis as a warrant for the immoderate actions of the expropriation of Palestinians. One day, perhaps, they will use the same rabbinic proof text to justify "transfer" as well. (As for the ultra-Orthodox rabbis of Jerusalem and Bnei Brak, it should go without saying that they are the very opposite of fundamentalist—they are the avatars of an enormously complex and highly developed current in modern Judaism. It is not fundamentalist to wish to apply your religion to your private and public life.)

The reason for the impossibility of Jewish fundamentalism goes to the heart of the Jewish view of history. The Jewish tradition is characterized by a fascinating, and finally enabling, ambivalence about origins. On the one hand, rabbinic Judaism is experienced and described as a fall, as a stopgap measure for the period between the destruction of the Jewish commonwealth by the Romans and its restoration by the Messiah. It is the spirituality of the interim. On the other hand, there is in Judaism no hostility whatsoever to the idea or the reality of development. The interim is very long. There is, in fact, a love of development, a commitment to the refinement of religious concepts and practices that allows the Jew to live very fully in the present, even if the present is lived in exile. Indeed, the Jewish commitment to development is so great that Rabbinic Judaism actually came to fear a restoration in the end of days, because it seemed to abrogate and make obsolete much of the massive corpus of philosophy and law that was sustaining Jewish thought through the centuries. Most notably, Maimonides took pains to interpret messianism in a way that reduced the difference between the redeemed era and the unredeemed to a minimum.

Fundamentalism is the very antithesis of normative Judaism, because of all that it proposes to abolish. The present, exile and all, is rather a capacious theater of religious thought and action.

I do not mean to deny, of course, that something is afoot. But it is not fundamentalism. It is, rather, a more general change in the relationship of religion to politics. In the Jewish world as elsewhere, a great reaction is taking place to what some people consider to be the excesses and the exaggerations of the separation of religion from politics. In Israel, most notably, the Labor party has been paying dearly for its shallow, socialist, anticlerical notion of the place of religion in human affairs.

Religion has been accorded a new prestige in politics, and politics has been accorded a new prestige in religion. Neither of these phenomena requires much illustration. Many alarmed observers have noted the damage that religion may do to politics. It is time, particularly for Jews, whose spiritual institutions are becoming centers of agitation and militancy, to worry about the damage that politics may do to religion.

PART TWO

12. From Island to Continent: Is There Room in American Politics for Both Fundamentalists and Their Enemies?

Donald W. Shriver, Jr.

In her remarkably perceptive book on Christian fundamentalism in Amarillo, Texas, A. G. Mojtabai demonstrates an empathy for this version of Christianity along with a critique of it. In one place she astutely identifies one of the severe internal theological tensions in that strand of fundamentalism called premillenarianism: "They live in deferment, not fulfillment." The theological cost of such deferment to Christians, she observes, is the constant downgrading of the redemptive importance of the first coming of Jesus into the world. "Nothing will be solved" in world history until the Second Coming in the great Windup of All Things.

"'But Jesus came,' is my constant refrain," in conversation with millenarians, exclaims Mojtabai. Alas, she adds, "Going from church to church in Amarillo, the impression is unavoidable: some of the most ardent born and born-again Christians are writing Christianity off as something that did not, could not work—at least, not in the First Coming." Christian readers of this book need to remind themselves, with a certain wonder, that its author is a Jew.[1]

---

1. A. G. Mojtabai, *Blessed Assurance: At Home with the Bomb in Amarillo* (Boston: Houghton Mifflin, 1986), pp. 153-54.

Mojtabai's book sets a high standard for a form of interfaith understanding and sociological scholarship which Max
Weber and others titled *verstehen-Soziologie*. She also demonstrates that one can combine understanding with criticism;
indeed, such scholarship purchases its right to criticize in the
energy it expends in understanding. And her major criticism
of fundamentalism in Amarillo (where all the trigger mechanisms for the American arsenal of nuclear bombs are manu-
factured) centers on its "island mentality," which, again, is a
contradiction internal to the Christian faith as well as a contradiction to certain universalistic values of Enlightenment-
derived humanism.

> The extensive missionary activities of Amarillo churches are
> often an expression of an island mentality. While seeming to
> be a horizontal reaching-out to all the nations of earth, the out-
> stretched "right hand of Christian fellowship" is, in fact, ex-
> tended along an ideological axis. This is colonizing for Christ,
> or for a particular Christian denomination—an expansion of
> the enclave of ourselves, rather than a bursting free of all en-
> claves. . . . [For example] the Rapturists dream of rescue, of an
> island safety in the midst of a general conflagration. "This is
> the promise," it is proclaimed at Second Baptist [Church],
> "that Jesus Christ will separate us from all the others who do
> not believe in His name." Separation and exemption is the
> hope. The vision is narrow and preferential; it is island dream-
> ing, special interest dreaming, and the sum of interests as
> divided as these is not community, nor polity, but a city, a
> world, in fragments.

To be sure, she adds the following:

> Another, more inclusive vision does assert itself from time to
> time. I recall San Angelo author Elmer Kelton, speaking [in
> 1982] . . . in Amarillo. "I try to make even my bad characters
> have a reason," Kelton explained, "to be believable." It's true,
> Kelton admitted, that without conflict there's no story, but it
> doesn't have to be conflict between good and bad, between
> white hats and black hats. It can be conflict between the drift-
> ing and the fixed, or conflict within character. Or it can be con-

flict between pretty good people pointed in different directions.[2]

I like that phrase for tagging the promise and the problematic of a democratic political philosophy: "pretty good
people pointed in different directions." How are they, who at
their best are still only "pretty good," to learn to live together
in spite of their "different directions"?

I shall discuss that question from the standpoint of the
democratic political process itself. I want to stress some attitudes
which *religious* critics of religious fundamentalism should bring
as undergirding their criticism of, and opposition to, fundamentalists in our American midst.

A first contribution is cogently embodied in Mojtabai's
book. She is Jewish, but in her months of residence in Amarillo
she exercised a capacity for interfaith *verstehen* which is as rare
as it is indispensable in democratic politics.

An Empathetic Understanding of "The Enemy"

I put quotation marks around "the enemy," for the project of
empathy itself requires one to be provisional about that designation of another. Once, around a table with Christian church
leaders in Moscow, I casually referred to the Americans and the
Soviets as "enemies" in today's world. One of the Orthodox
church leaders, a woman, quickly corrected me, saying, "We
should never use that word about each other." Perhaps so, but
in the ordinary empirical side of human politics, our differences
lead to animosity and crystallize only too often into enmity. And
in a state of animosity or enmity, what are we to do? If we have
even the glimmer of a continuing faith that God creates, judges,
and cherishes this human race as such, we must continue to accord even to our enemies the status of human. And to accord

2. Ibid., pp. 222-23.

them that in practice as well as in theory, we must put our minds and emotions on the road to empathetic understanding.

G. H. Moore remarked once that the success of the democratic political system depends on the ability of voters, when they enter the polling booth, to vote for the interests of some other human group in the society besides their own. No political virtue is more worthy of cultivation in this century, between the Soviets and the Americans, than this virtue. Not enough Americans, for example, have spent so much as ten minutes thinking of what it is like to live there on the plains between the Elbe River and the Urals, remembering centuries of invasion and millions of your people lost in war. Has it not been enough to produce chronic political paranoia? To understand this about the Soviets is not to justify any of the aggressions of their government over the past forty years, but it is to humanize some of it.

Even so with the behavior of many about whom we have written in this volume. I think, for example, of the Ku Klux Klan. As a Virginia-born southerner, I have never had the least occasion to join that organization. I was not born in rural poverty. No one ever called me a "redneck," nor could I come to an early understanding of how necks got red, never having worked all day in a tobacco field. Nor have I ever known what it was to sense that I was somehow in the same economic position of a sharecropping black farmer while being told by a politician running for office that, if I was to save my self-respect as a white man, I had to do my part to "keep the black man in his place." Finally, it has never occurred to me that burning a *cross* on somebody's lawn was a way to testify to my faith as a Christian. But all these differences between myself and many a member of the KKK can crystallize into *contempt*, if I let them do so. Or they might crystallize into an empathy which, far from turning into bland tolerance or naive forgiveness, keeps a bridge open for me toward the humanity of these misguided racists.

Consider, for example, the dispute in some public school districts over the teaching of "evolutionism" and "creationism." Earlier in this volume, Clark Pinnock rightly pointed to the "ontological" differences between a Genesis view of the empirical world and an agnostic view. What if the relation of these two views is ruled out of order in a public school classroom? What do you say and do about your eight-year-old child who gets the impression from her schoolteacher that it is a "no-no" even to mention the name of God in a public school classroom? What if you experience the alleged religious neutrality of public life in America as an antireligious influence in the life of your child?

Christians in America would have a better understanding of the very reasons for a religiously neutral education system if they imagined to themselves the same sort of experience for Jewish families. Empathy for religious differences is an experiential foundation for legal tolerance of those differences. Without empathy, democracy, as a philosophy of public order, may be very difficult to sustain.

That opens the door to another attitude, another political virtue, equally apt for the same sustaining.

The Acknowledgement of Our Own "Fundamentals"

Mojtabai alludes to "conflict between the drifting and the fixed," which is how liberals and fundamentalists often see each other. But, in fact, fundamentalists can be drifters, as when they drift with the tide of American patriotism or middle-class economic aspirations as though these values were divinely inspired. The case for a "closed" fundamentalism, to use Pinnock's term, rears up here: be too open to the shifting tides of human culture, and your religious identity can get sucked into the undertow. The "closed solution" to the salvaging of religious identity has served Jews well from the Babylonian captivity through the modern history of Europe. It has served black American Christians equally well.

But then: liberals have their fundamentals, if by "fundamentals" one means basic convictions about what makes human life "human"—the right to be a citizen of some political entity, for example. The twentieth-century experience of

Jews has convinced many of them that Israel must become the name of a state as well as the name of a people. The twentieth-century experience of black Americans has convinced many that, absent their organization in churches and other organized protection of their integrity, American society will not accord them justice. And for many of us who are not yet ashamed to tag ourselves "liberal," it is a *fundamental* truth of our life to say, with Learned Hand, "The spirit of liberty is the spirit that is not too sure it is right."[3] The freedom to learn, to change our minds, to discover the new truth, is basic for us; it is basic in our very *theology*, if our finite freedom to change our mind is grounded in our obligation to respect God's freedom to effect the change. Freedom, especially the freedom of God, is a fundamental of much theology in my own line of Protestantism, Calvinism. No doctrine was more fundamental to the Reformation-based theology of Karl Barth than the freedom of God.

There is great potential for human collision brewing here, of course. I wrote an article not long ago on the subject, "What Can Liberals and Evangelicals Teach Each Other?"[4] A man from California wrote to the editor saying, "I'm glad that some liberals want to learn from evangelicals. Let them sit at our feet long enough to learn. But we don't have anything to learn from them." Between the two attitudes, surely, lies a great, agonizing gulf. It is a conflict between fundamentals. In your practical political philosophy toward your cantankerous neighbors, do you keep the drawbridge open or do you close it with a clang? Are you a self-contained island, or do you—with John Donne—open up to continental possibilities?

The conflict here need not be a mere collision, however, if the fundamental of inclusiveness stands fast over against the fundamental of exclusiveness. More about that at a later point: for now I merely point out that if inclusiveness in the body

3. Learned Hand, "The Spirit of Liberty," in Irving Dillard, ed., *The Spirit of Liberty: Papers and Addresses of Learned Hand* (New York: Alfred A. Knopf, 1952), p. 190.

4. Donald W. Shriver, Jr., *The Christian Century* 104 (12-19 August 1987): 687-90.

politic is a basic principle of your political stance, you are bound to include the fundamentalists in your continent of humanity even if they do not include you in their island. Nothing is a more difficult maneuver for the tolerant, perhaps, than to strike up a consistent stance toward the intolerant. "I will tolerate anything but intolerance," some will say, intolerantly. That may be all right for verbal logic, but the moral logic would seem to be that true tolerance has in it provisional room for the intolerant. There is great risk to some other democratic and religious values here; there is also a formidable set of practical social problems, as when the intolerant move from attitude to action that threatens the integrity of others in the society. But there has to be room for them in a democratic society, just as there has to be room for sinners in synagogues and churches.

But here again one feels, rising to the surface, one of the deeper fundamentals of a liberal and liberating theology. One of the differences between having fundamentals and being a fundamentalist hinges on whether, even in possession of one's dearest convictions, there is something outside those convictions which prevents them from turning into the intolerance of an "ism." That other something for many of us is God, before whom our convictions, like our knowledge and our virtue, are modest, finite, and often afflicted with sin.

Yet another something transcending our convictions is the concrete presence of our neighbors, who frequently have different convictions. What we share here, says one recent Christian writer, "is a common finitude and a common tendency to forget it."[5] Here, perhaps, is the principal challenge of "biblical realism" about human nature to the very hope of a democratic political theory: can people of deep differences *be* neighbors to each other? No mature person in the twentieth century is likely

5. Peggy Shriver, "World Renewal Is at Hand, U.S.-Style," *The Reformed World* 39 (September 1987): 752. As Director of the Research Department of the National Council of Churches, this author has spent 10 years carefully monitoring various aspects of the resurgence of evangelicals and fundamentalists among Protestants in the United States. I am indebted here and in several places below to the fruits of this research.

to ask that question lightly! But it brings me to a third "political virtue" I would like to promote in this discussion.

The Discipline of Practicing Freedom for the "Thought We Hate"

The phrase, of course, is that of Oliver Wendell Holmes, Jr., for whom religion played no necessary part in the cultivation of the legal or the moral community of a democracy. The history of religion in the world, not to speak of the recent history of religion in America, offers abundant illustration of claims by religious people to freedom which, once exercised, becomes the occasion of clamping down on any equivalent freedom among their neighbors. In politics, religion is a two-edged sword: it cuts out a space for itself by appeal to higher authority; then, with seeming equal authority, it cuts others off from their spaces. No wonder the authors of the U.S. Constitution both feared and respected religion; and no wonder a good theologian will always keep a shrewd eye open for the difference between religion and God.

Such a theologian was one who makes a brief, crucial appearance in the book which Christians call *The Acts of the Apostles*. His name was Gamaliel. His colleagues among the Pharisees wanted prompt action for repressing the Christians. But Gamaliel showed reverential caution. "Men of Israel, be cautious in deciding what to do with these men. . . . Leave them alone. For if this idea of theirs or its execution is of human origin, it will collapse; but if it is from God, you will never be able to put them down, and you risk finding yourselves at war with God."[6] Would that, in the centuries to come, Christians themselves had been theologians after the model of Gamaliel, in their attitude toward the "putting down" of Jews!

Visible here is at least the beginning of a religious grounding for institutionalizing in any society a certain freedom for the

6. Acts 5:35, 38-39, New English Bible.

thought that many, perhaps a majority of citizens, *hate*. And let academics among us be the first to confess that the "thought we hate" is sometimes simply the new thought. A friend of the late Michael Polanyi tells how, after that successful chemist turned his scholarly attention to the study of epistemology, his scientific colleagues at Oxford stopped walking the garden with him at teatime. He had transgressed the boundaries of "real" science, and they no longer had anything to talk to him about. As Polanyi himself was to write, new ideas in science are never acclaimed, but rather resisted, by the majority of scientists.[7]

Perhaps among those who read this paper there are some sobered liberals, six decades or so of age, who have found themselves not a little "hating" the new thoughts which women, homosexuals, native Americans, and Third World people have insisted on bringing to our attention. I remember, with such sobriety, the great line from Oliver Cromwell, spoken to a group of passionate arguing Scottish soldiers: "I beseech ye, by the mercies of Christ, think that you may be wrong!" Such thinking is as hard for liberals as for fundamentalists. It is simply difficult for aging human beings to give up pet ideas. The Greek word for "repentance" means "changing your mind." Mind changing has about it a quality of moral discipline and moral humility. It is hard for all parties to any human conflict, because in conflict intellectual positions tend to harden, unless one brings to the conflict a steady, stubborn *humility* that expects to learn from people of different persuasions from one's own.

And that is one reason why, repentantly, we Jews and Christians in this American society should celebrate, perpetuate, and improve the facilities of this society for effecting cognitive dissonance, contradiction, and the pitting of one credible reality over against its equally credible opposite. Good art, good drama, good literature always does this. So does good politics. With a fourth word about "good politics," I will close.

7. See Michael Polanyi, *Personal Knowledge: Towards a Post-Critical Philosophy* (Chicago: University of Chicago Press, 1958); and Thomas Kuhn, *The Structure of Scientific Revolutions*, 2d ed. (Chicago: University of Chicago Press, 1970).

The Politics of Inclusiveness

Somewhere Kurt Vonnegut has commented that he always rediscovers his extended family when he goes to funerals. So many folk are present there whom he never did like and doesn't like now. But why worry about that? he reflects. Families are not there to be liked; they are just there to be—family.

Is this what Mario Cuomo means when he talks about the "New York family?" I'm not sure. I only know that one of the acid tests of my own personal ability to remain a neighbor to conservative Republicans in the United States of America is my ability to remain on decently tolerant terms with my own *father* around election time. And, a fortiori, if with my father, how much more with that company of strangers who meet me on Broadway between 120th and 110th streets? In this context, elections are good for the isolated souls of us all; they remind us how much bigger, more diverse, and more annoying is the full spectrum of our political neighbors.

I very much like the words of one leader of the National Council of Churches, my own wife Peggy Shriver, who in a sobered and even repentant liberal mood, writes: "A helpful spiritual exercise for the post . . . election blues is to ask ourselves, 'Whom have we passed by on the other side?'" It is a question, she says, applicable to both liberals and fundamentalists in the American political dialogue. "One hope for the religious right's involvement in politics is that it will rub shoulders with other viewpoints and become less arrogant. Perhaps liberal Christians will also become less arrogant if contact with evangelicals improves. We have eagerly delved into complex problems of economics . . . poverty, war, and racial prejudice. But we have only recently, through the window of feminism, taken a hard look at pornography, and we have folded our hands over the increased divorce rate . . . and the destructiveness of drugs. . . . If it is not repressive to urge a lifestyle that diminishes world hunger, why is it necessarily repressive to urge a lifestyle that diminishes drug or sexual abuse?"[8]

8. Peggy Shriver, *The Bible Vote* (New York: Pilgrim Press, 1981), p. 100.

My theory here is that the politics of inclusiveness begins in the spiritual discipline of personal and in-group repentance. Religious assemblies, congregations, like-minded members of prayer groups could do worse, to get ready for democratic politics, than to reflect on their temptations toward exclusiveness.

But, like all repentance, that of all religious folk will be forever incomplete and partially mistaken. We will not always be accurate in seeing *what* we have to repent of. We will continue to collide with others in the public arena, ready to war with them and brandishing as weapons our pet convictions. And here the minds of liberal and fundamentalist religious folk ought to reflect on the spiritual grace which sometimes comes to human beings in the democratic public life itself. As many a politician can testify, one may ride into that arena on the high horse of moral principle, but one is apt to come out a pedestrian. In 1981, Richard Neuhaus said of certain incomplete or frustrated victories on his side of the 1980 election, "I know that we lost, not because we ran away, but because on a number of key issues they were right and we didn't have the imagination or the nerve to come up with convincing alternatives."9 That is about as plain an evocation of the repentant spirit as one might ask for, and I *like* Richard Neuhaus when he speaks *that* way!

Anyone with religious zeal is likely to learn to speak that way if he or she takes conflict-ridden democratic politics seriously, for the ordinary push and shove of democracy is hard on zealots. Max Weber defined the political vocation as "slow boring of hard boards,"10 the sort of hard boards that dull the bright edge of sharp ideological tools. As Bill Moyers said of a meeting of evangelicals in 1980, "It is not the evangelicals' taking politics seriously that bothers me. It is the lie they're being told by the demagogues who flatter them into believing

9. As quoted by Shriver in *The Bible Vote*, p. 51; Richard Neuhaus, *Reform Judaism* 9/4 (March 1981): 11.

10. Max Weber, "Politics as a Vocation," in *Max Weber: Essays on Sociology*, trans. H. H. Gert and C. Wright Mills (New York: Oxford University Press, 1958), p. 128.

they can achieve politically the certitude they have embraced theologically. The world doesn't work that way. There is no heaven on earth." Moyers speaks with Johnson-White-House sobriety when he adds the warning that these pretty good folk will have their "hearts broken by false gods who, having taken the coin of their vote or purse, will move on to work the next crowd."[11]

"Put no trust in princes," says the Hebrew scripture.[12] But when your trust is betrayed, do you retreat into the closed and isolated comfort of separatism? We have seen that many among the fundamentalists remain separatist, for they know that in some measure the world is, indeed, an evil place. To sally forth, to struggle, to retreat back, to gather strength, to sally forth again: that is the dialectic of religious and political association. Some years ago we did a sampled study of citizens in the central North Carolina region, to find out if there was any apparent relation between "ethical maturity," religion, and political participation. We defined maturity as basic trust, as conformity between belief and behavior, as openness to the views of other people, and as a willingness on occasion to sacrifice something of value to oneself for the sake of something valuable to the public at large. What we found was that this version of ethical maturity increases the more a citizen has, in combination, (1) a set of strong convictions, (2) a set of supportive friends, and (3) regularity of public political experience. The most frustrated group in our study was one with high ideals, few friends, and a record of only episodic participation in political life. These folk suffered the highest index of stomach ulcers and insomnia. They were the spitting image of tired liberals on the one hand and closed fundamentalists on the other. In between were the "idealists" with growing capacity to compromise in public while renewing their ideals in more private associations were those of a religious

11. As quoted by Shriver, *The Bible Vote*, p. 83; "Bill Moyers' Journal," television transcript, Campaign Report #3, Show #603, P.B.S. air date, 26 September, 1980.

12. Psalm 146:3, Revised Standard Version.

congregation. But there was a great difference, we found, between these idealists and those overtly religious people who always darken the doors of churches and synagogues but never set foot inside a city council chamber or a political party caucus. Something happens to religion and politics, we found, when the two rub shoulders both privately and publicly.[13]

T. V. Smith was speaking for all idealists, and perhaps all people of faith, when he warned: "There is a special claimant, if not indeed a little totalitarian, hidden in the bosom of every conscientious [person], especially if [that person] be a middleman operating in the name of God."[14] Religious or not, he observed, "Equally honest [people], with causes equally sincere, meet in such manner that neither of them can permit the other to have its way without loss of face and impairment of self-respect. . . . Such a case will but recall to our democratic minds a double fact: the fact, first, that there is no other way of settling such issues as justly as by compromise; the fact, second, that such settlement [usually] requires the presence of a third party. Such settlement is politics; such a third party is the politician," who, in Smith's view, is the architect of the compromises that permit us to go on living another day until our next conflict. In that context, Smith urges us to look again at the *ethical* side of that much maligned word, compromise. Compromise, says he, is a "necessary derivative of finitude."[15] It "establishes an atmosphere of peace and permits each conscience to go back to its groups of likeminded people and there work out its highest promptings unpolitically, for the subsequent improvement of a body politic more sympathetic to one's ideal demands."[16]

My only caveat here is that the religious congregation to which Christians and Jews sometimes repair is not all that "un-

13. See Donald W. Shriver, Jr., and Karl A. Ostrom, *Is There Hope for the City?* (Philadelphia: Westminster Press, 1977).

14. T. V. Smith, *The Ethics of Compromise* (Boston: Starr King Press, 1956), p. 54.

15. Ibid., p. 51.

16. Ibid., p. 63.

political." It may not be quite as full of diversity as the broad
way of democracy, but it is a place where sinners of various
beliefs, ideologies, interests, and orientations collide with each
other around such ordinary human (and political) issues as
budgets, jobs, status, power, and prestige. But the congregation
has a certain discipline for the cure of ills inherent in such col-
lisions: It is the one place I present myself in worship before
"the One with whom we have to do." In other public places I
may try to behave in ways fitting to such worship; and I may
have reason to observe that politics in the church or the synagogue is not radically different from politics in the public
arena. Indeed, for the humanizing of both, I may have something to learn in both arenas—a thought that first dawned on
me powerfully when, within the same twelve months, I attended
the General Assembly of the Presbyterian Church U.S. and the
1968 National Convention of the Democratic Party in Chicago.
The dynamics of conflict in the two meetings were not all that
radically different, an observation that many of my Southern
Baptist friends would be likely to make about the political conflicts which have recently come close to tearing their fourteen-
million-member national convention apart.

In a major national survey sponsored by the National
Council of Churches, conducted by the Gallup organization in
1978 and reaffirmed in a repeat study in 1988, a large majority
of the people who do not attend church or synagogue professed
a set of religious beliefs almost indistinguishable from the spectrum of belief in the American public at large. For the most part,
these nonattenders say that they can "believe without belonging."[17] Theirs is the shaky legacy of that Protestant individualism which afflicts the mind of many a liberal and fundamentalist alike in our culture. The events of the past fifteen years have
perhaps persuaded many individualists on both sides that it is
high time we rediscovered, in the depths of our Hebrew and
Christian roots, the inherent social foundations of even the most

17. See *The Unchurched American* (Princeton: The Gallup Organization,
1978).

personal faith related to these roots. Black Americans, those who have the most reason to remember the history of slavery, are the most certain that individualism does not work for them in religion or in society. Who, more than our black neighbors, knows better that freedom and fairness in society are socially constructed and socially protected realities? The very separation of "church and state" is a separation instituted and perpetuated by law and law enforcement.

If the secular side of American politics is to learn new lessons in the art of democratic inclusiveness, what contributions might *organized* religion make to that learning? Here one circles back to the fundamental divide between the "island" and the "continental" mind in religion itself. Which mind will be nourished inside the religious and secular politics of America? Does the recent entry of many conservative Christians into new public coalitions portend an access of democratic humility and a new appreciation of the ethics of compromise in a world of plural interests and cultures? Can ecumenical Christians— what Martin Marty calls the "public church"[18]—bring their ecumenicity to bear in a welcome of other kinds of Christians into the public debate? And with the help of the long memories of such minorities as the Jewish and the black communities, will other Christians as well as the secularists among us listen to those memories and learn anew that democracy is not merely the rule of majorities but the protection of minorities, down to the last minority of one person?

These are all hopeful questions. They root in a yearning at once religious and political. Whether American politics helps make our religion more ecumenical, or our religious ecumenicity makes our politics more inclusive, makes no difference. The great difference is the choice between the island and the continent. Since none of us is more than a pilgrim from the one toward the other, the religious among us should pray for all the help we can get for continuing this journey.

18. See Martin Marty, *The Public Church: Mainline-Evangelical-Catholic* (New York: Crossroad, 1981).

13. Fundamentalist Involvement in the Political Scene: Analysis and Response

David Saperstein

An analysis of the involvement of the fundamentalist community—the so-called religious right[1]—in the political arena must address the following five questions:

First, what motivates the fundamentalists to become involved in the political system?

Second, what is the political nature of the debate between the religious right and the mainstream American community?

Third, in what manner does the religious right function politically, and how does it differ from the mainstream religious groups?

Fourth, what has the religious right accomplished and what has it failed to accomplish in the past decade?

And finally, and most important, how should we respond to the challenge the religious right poses in American society?

---

1. The term "religious right" is used throughout the article to describe generically the organized, conservative, Republican-oriented involvement of the fundamentalist community in the political system over the past fifteen years. There are important distinctions within the fundamentalist community as to political involvement, as well as regarding theological justification for that involvement; while these distinctions are important to an accurate understanding of fundamentalist involvement in politics, they are not germane to this article.

214

1. Why, then, did the religious right in the United States become involved in the political scene?

It is common wisdom that—with some notable exceptions over the centuries—there has been a long tradition in the fundamentalist communities of remaining outside the political arena. Yet, in fact, they have always been involved. The extreme influence that the fundamentalists typically exert over the political ideology of the areas in which their dense population predominates renders it unnecessary for them to become *formally* involved in politics. No official can be elected who does not ascribe to the basic worldviews of the fundamentalists.

Occasionally, the external sociocultural and political environment encroaches on the fundamentalists; some react by commenting on or supporting forays into the national political scene. The Gablers may be making a presence on the national scene today through their efforts to ensure the teaching of biblical truths, but so did William Jennings Bryan (albeit with different goals in mind). The warning that today "our country is filled with a socialist, radical, lawless, anti-American, anti-god . . . gang, and they are laying the eggs of rebellion and unrest and we have some of them in our universities," might have been the cry of Rev. Tim LaHaye or Rev. James Robison; but in fact it was the warning of Billy Sunday in 1925.

In the past, however, each of these forays into politics eventually ebbed. The groups retrenched to focus on local control of their lives—particularly the lives, values, and education of their children. By and large, they were content to let the world to go on about them—as long as it did not "contaminate" them.

In the past two decades, however, two major factors have caused the fundamentalist elements of the nation to sense that they had lost control of their own destinies. The first factor was the impact of activist Supreme and federal courts which asserted the rights of women and minorities (blacks, Hispanics, the handicapped, Jews, Catholics, and atheists among them) against the views and decisions of the majority. The fundamentalists became increasingly alarmed as these court decisions radically affected their communal institutions, particularly the public schools that trained their children. They found themselves held to a standard that in their view sterilized the religious underpinnings of the value system that had long infused their pedagogic curricula.

But to this problem the fundamentalists had at hand a partial response: the creation of parochial schools. In the past decades, even as the number of Catholic parochial schools shrank substantially, the number of fundamentalist schools skyrocketed.

The second factor, however, totally demolished the ability of these communities to protect their children from the corrosive values of the surrounding society. Technology in general, and dramatic new communications technology in particular, simply reshaped the cultural interaction of America in ways fundamentalists could no longer control. Radio, movies, television, and rock and roll records flooded their children's world with ideas and values that were abhorrent to the community. And all efforts to convince their children to ignore and shun those intrusions were alarmingly unsuccessful. (At a luncheon I had two years ago with Rev. Jimmy Swaggart, he blurted out during his explanation of his call for kids to destroy their rock records, "You know, if only Norman Lear had not put 'All in the Family' into our homes, we would not be facing the problems our nation faces today.")

Gradually, the reality began to sink in: If fundamentalists could not protect their children from the outside political, social, and cultural environment, then it was time for them to change that environment. At its core, the current emergence of the religious right on the political scene is a struggle to protect their children and their communities. The effort to transform America turns out to be an indispensible means of protecting their families and values.

It is interesting to note that one of the techniques which they have adopted to achieve their goal is to co-opt for their own uses the very same technologies and public tactics that threatened them: televangelism, Christian rock music, fellowships of athletes and beauty queens, political involvement, the promise of material success for those who really believe. Whether in the long run such tactics will result in their co-opting the society whose values so trouble them or in having that society co-opt them remains to be seen.

2. *What are the political issues which underlie the debate between the religious right and the mainstream religious and political communities?*

What is at stake in this political debate is nothing less than the fundamental accomplishment of the American revolution. For 2,000 years of Western civilization, prior to the establishment of the United States, the rights that an individual had were rights which accrued from some source beyond himself, that is, derivative rights. They might vest from an economic membership—a class, a guild, or a feudal elite; they might stem from political membership—even the ancient democracy of Athens and the Republic of Iceland which predated our own asserted that the rights of their citizens were those granted them by their governments; they might derive from membership in a religious group—Jewish rights in medieval Europe were those that were granted to each community by its ruler.

The United States turned that notion on its head. The founders of our nation asserted that the rights we have are not granted by any external source but come from within, from the belief that as a God-created human being you were endowed with certain inalienable rights, among them life, freedom (liberty), the right to determine your destiny (pursuit of happiness), the right of speech, of worship, of publication, of association with like-minded people, the right to petition your government for a redress of grievances.

The purpose of government was not to establish those rights but rather to make them secure and protect them. Thus, in the United States, it does not matter if all 250 million Americans believe that what you have to say is wrong, nor does it matter if the entire U.S. Congress, Supreme Court, and the President believe that the way you worship is incorrect; so long as your exercise of your rights does not infringe upon anyone else's or threaten the existence of the society itself, you have the inalienable right to say what you want, to worship the way you want.

And in a democracy, we believe that this right strengthens our nation. We do not affirm freedom and pluralism of ideas only for their own abstract value but because we know that by affirming freedom we avoid mistakes. Only by testing policies and views in the free marketplace of ideas do we ensure that the truth will ultimately prevail.

In the past decade, the religious right has developed a political program based on a different view. They assert that the United States was founded on certain traditional values—specifically Christian values. The purpose of government is to secure those values even if it means determining when we pray in school, what we study in biology (scientific creationism), what we read in our libraries. It is the view represented by:

> I hope I live to see the day when, as in the early days of our country, we won't have any public schools. The churches will have taken them over again and Christians will be running them. What a happy day that will be![2]

> America was founded by Godly men who had in mind establishing a republic not only Christian in nature, but a republic designed to propagate the Gospel worldwide.[3]

> There is no such thing as separation of church and state. It is merely a figment of the imagination of infidels.[4]

> I'll tell you what is wrong with America. We don't have enough of God's ministers running the country.[5]

> Catholicism is a false religion.[6]

2. Jerry Falwell, *America Can Be Saved* (Murfreesboro, TN: Sword of the Lord, 1979), pp. 52-53.

3. Ibid., p. 21.

4. Rev. W. A. Criswell, CBS interview shown 6 September 1984, taped the day after he gave the benediction at the Republican Convention.

5. Rev. Tim LaHaye, Executive Director, American Coalition for Traditional Values, at Religious Roundtable breakfast prior to his speech at the White House, reported, *New York Times* 8 September 1984.

6. Jimmy Swaggart, *Letter to my Catholic Friends* (Baton Rouge: Jimmy Swaggart Ministries, 1982), p. 18.

The Constitution of the United States, for instance, is a marvelous document for self-government by Christian people. But the minute you turn that document into the hands of non-Christian people they can use it to destroy the very foundation of our society. And that's what's been happening.[7]

We will support only "born-again Christians who hold traditional values."[8]

We must have a second Revolution to bring back Christian values to America.[9]

3. How then do the fundamentalists function in the political scene, and how does their functioning differ from that of mainstream religious groups?

The early phase of the latest manifestation of the fundamentalist involvement in the political scene was marked with the use of tactics and rhetoric that resonated with the approach of Max Weber's ultimate politician. Imbued with the certainty that God was on their side, they developed political viewpoints, tactics, and strategies that were quite different from those of the mainstream religious groups.

Among the more significant differences: First, the fundamentalists' concern is not so much with public morality as it is with private morality. While traditionally, mainstream religious groups have attempted to influence what happens on the assembly line, the picket line, the grape farm, the military, the marketplace, and the ghetto, all of which are accepted generally as the legitimate domain of government in the public arena, the religious right advocates legislating issues of personal morality, including those affecting personal conscience, reading habits, religious behavior, the human body, and the bedroom.

A second difference is that the religious right believe that their entire political agenda has been decreed by God and must

7. Rev. Pat Robertston, *Washington Post,* 23 March 1981.

8. Resolution considered by Minnesota Republican county caucuses, 1984.

9. Paul Weyrich, Director, Committee for Survival of a Free Congress.

be obeyed by this nation if it is to save itself; that is, we must be a good Christian nation. This political approach is deeply rooted in the theological duality of the fundamentalist world view described so incisively by George Marsden in *Fundamentalism in American Culture*. Within the quasi-Manichean duality of the fundamentalist worldview is the attitude that what is not specifically Christian, by their definition, is of the devil. Such an attitude is easily manipulated into accepting that political views can also be neatly divided. Hence, when presented with a religious leader's admonition that God mandates support of SDI, opposition to gun control, and prayer in the schools, those who demur must clearly reject God.

It has been argued that the leaders of the religious right are more like the Jewish prophets than are the leaders of today's mainstream religious groups. There is some truth to that assertion. Both the prophets and the fundamentalists believe that they were commanded by God; both types believe that only they have the truthful message; both types are intolerant of those who deviate from what they believe is God's will. But the prophets lived in a theocracy; the religious right live in a secular democracy. The same religious tradition that commanded Jews to live by God's laws rejects the call to "Judaize" non-Jewish nations. Furthermore, the substances of the two messages is radically different. As with the mainstream religious groups today, the message of the prophets was a concern for the poor and the hungry. They were fanatical dreamers of peace. The religious right is deafeningly silent about the plight of the needy, and they invoke God's support for the concept that the pursuit of peace is served by attaining military superiority over the USSR.

The Jewish tradition long ago recognized that those who claimed to speak for God could always undermine the stability and foundation of any society which was based on the exercise of human reason. The admonition of the Talmud that the mantle of insight into God's will passes from the prophet to the community and its leaders could well be taken to heart by the religious right: "We pay no more attention to a Heavenly voice, because You have long ago written in the Torah at Mount Sinai: 'After the majority must one incline.'"[10]

In our own time, on that day when first the words "Judeo-Christian" were hyphenated and used to designate the highest values of Western civilization, the multiplicity of divine revelations and the insufficiency of any one of them was given an imprimatur which it now would be tragic to erase. Therefore, when Jews hear attacks on their legitimacy, as in the judgment that "God does not listen to the prayers of a Jew," and when they hear calls for the "Christianizing of America," the echoes of the past strike genuine concern in their hearts and minds.

The third component of the religious right's approach which differs from the mainstream groups is that they are attempting to impose religious discipline and authority on the voting and political decisions of their followers. Both the American political and legal systems are based on the belief in, and commitment to, the freedom of choice that inheres in every person. But when the late Cardinal Humberto Medieros wrote in a pastoral letter that it is a "sin" for a good Catholic to vote in favor of a candidate who favors the right, he imposed religious authority over the political behavior of his followers, raising the prospect of their having to ask forgiveness for voting in favor of Barney Frank.

But whether we are talking about Cardinal Medieros, about the Lubuvatcher Rebbe telling his followers to vote for Ted Kennedy in the 1980 New York primary, or about a religious right leader who tells his followers that God has instructed him to call on them to write letters in opposition to the Civil Rights Restoration Act—the intrusion of religious authority into politics undermines the unimpeded exercise of conscience which is so essential to a healthy democracy.[11]

10. Babylonian Talmud, Baba Metzia 59b.

11. Indeed, the danger of religious coercion is illustrated by the recent Israeli election—an intrusion that bodes ill for the future of *Israeli* democracy. During the election, the heads of Agudath Israel and Shas repeatedly appealed to Sephardic religious voters that a vote for them was a vote for their rebbe and a vote for Torah. The fundamentalists in Israel, mimicking the U.S. model of

After sustaining repeated defeats in Congress and at the national polls, the religious right has made a demonstrable shift in two key tactics. The trend began in 1986 and accelerated in the 1988 election. The first is the abandonment of public God-oriented explanations of their political agenda, a shift for which key leaders on the right recently called.

The tactical "moderation" of the political techniques of the religious right was reflected in a number of developments in this election. Key religious right supporters moved into the mainstream of the Republican party and did not just stay with Pat Robertson; among them Jerry Falwell, C. W. Criswell, and Ed McAteer, the head of the Religious Roundtable. Gone in this campaign were the religious rhetorical flourishes, like "ambassador for Christ" and "Christian nation" and "Break the back of Satan," that backfired embarrassingly for the religious right in 1986. This time the buzzwords were "traditional values" and "decency" issues. As Robertson aide Michael Clifford observed: "A real challenge for Pat Robertson is to really excite a born-again Christian audience, but also make it mean something to the common man." And that, of course, has always been the challenge of religiously oriented political figures, from Abraham Lincoln to Martin Luther King, Jr.: to take denominational religious ideas and express them within the ideology of our civil religion so as to avoid alienating the mainstream of our nation.

Second, the religious right has begun to focus more and more of its energy and resources on the local and state level as opposed to the national level, where it has suffered widespread

---

using television to transmit their message, broadcast all kinds of promises of religious benefits in exchange for political support. Two parties offered the blessings of charismatic rabbis: Aguda from the Lubuvatcher Rebbe and the Baba Baruch (the son of the revered Moroccan Rabbi Baba Sali), and Shas the blessing of former Chief Rabbi Ovadiash Yosef, who appeared on television dressed in the robes of the Sephardic chief rabbi to ask for support. Rav Yosef threatened at one point in the campaign that those who oppose Shas would be punished on the Day of Reckoning. At another gathering, he told the audience that a vote for Shas was the key to the Garden of Eden in the afterlife because it facilitates the building of yeshivas, synagogues, and mikvaot.

legislative and electoral setbacks. As Paul Weyrich said in his speech before the Family Forum in the summer of 1988:

> So many people first of all, made the assumption that by the election of 1980 and its ratification in 1984 that their work was really over. . . . We had won the battle.
>
> We're not a serious movement because we have failed to organize at the state level and at the local level where things really happen and we became Washington-focused and when you're Washington-focused you must understand that the other side controls the territory. It's theirs. They own it, they run it. They make the rules. They cause you to operate, even people like us, within their framework. and until we can change that it is useless to solely play the Washington game. Now I'm not talking about copping out in Washington. Because if that were the case I'd pick up and leave and go somewhere else. I'm still there and I intend to remain there. What I'm talking about though is building the kind of infrastructure at the state level which is taken seriously. . . .
>
> Where are we losing? The educational battles of the country, we're losing them in the school boards at the local level. Where can you control pornography? At the county boards and commissions, city councils across the country, where can you take cases, even an abortion, to the Supreme Court if you control the city council? You can pass an ordinance, get it challenged, take it all the way to the court, give the chance for these new Reagan appointees to show whether or not they're pro-life. And then when you have the name and experience and the trust of the people, then run for the state legislature and then for the Congress. We'll begin to build the kind of movement that will be taken seriously.

But the truth is much more alarming. They are winning on those levels, taking hold of school, library, and county boards. Censorship cases are up dramatically. The Gablers, who used to be alone in this battlefield, are now joined by Phyllis Schlafley's Eagle Forum, Pat Robertson's National Legal Foundation, Beverly Lahaye's Concerned Women for America and Citizens for Excellence in Education, the first of the groups to make controlling school boards its principal agenda.

This local organizing will be combined with increasing protest, agitation, and civil disobedience over the abortion issue, aimed, as Falwell said in his speech before the Family Forum, at creating a national movement and atmosphere of excitement akin to the impact of civil disobedience in galvanizing the civil rights movement a generation ago.

And the most important legacy of the Pat Robertson campaign is that while he lost in the primaries, his supporters are better organized than ever and have won control of the Republican party structure at numerous local levels—and even have substantial or total control of some state parties (such as Alaska, Iowa, Washington, and Michigan). Indeed, Robertson's campaign to obtain 3.3 million petition signatures before declaring his candidacy, rather than being a simple public relations ploy, turned out to be an exceedingly effective political organizing tool. He had months to develop networks of signature gatherers who were later elevated to campaign workers; and the signators became the backbone of his political donor efforts.

As for the performance of the religious right on the national level, political commentators have failed to notice that of the nine open House and Senate races (i.e., races where there was no incumbent,) in which the religious right groups were backing a candidate, they prevailed in seven. Combine this with the loss of Sen. Lowell Weicker, the Senate's most vigorous champion of church-state separation and anchor of the liberal wing of the Republican party, and it bodes ill for the ability of the pro-church-state separation forces to muster the bipartisan support it has needed in the past to defeat school prayer, abortion restrictions, parochaid, and scientific creationism legislation. With the prospect of more seasoned and experienced religious right operatives coming up through the ranks over the years from the local arena, the religious right now feels that they have hit on an effective two-pronged agenda: Take control of the local arenas where they are in the majority, and thereby develop experienced leadership for national races in the future.

And all of this must be viewed against the backdrop of a court system that has been radically reshaped by the "Reagan

Revolution," with over 45 percent of all sitting federal judiciary (most of the younger members) having been appointed by President Reagan, and the Supreme Court itself having been reshaped sufficiently to lead some of its own members to predict the overturning of basic church-state, abortion, and civil rights ruling of the past generation. With *three* liberal Supreme Court justices 80 years of age and older and all in frail health, probably no decision President George Bush will make will be more important than the type of judges he appoints to the federal bench.

4. *What are the successes and failures of the religious right?*

Let me mention just one of each. They have failed to enact into law even a single item on their social legislative agenda. To date, neither the courts nor the Congress have seen fit to accept the religious right's vision of America or to implement it into law—in no small measure because the American people simply do not accept either their views or their tactics. That they are modifying both is a source of encouragement and alarm for those who oppose them: encouragement to the extent that they are truly moderating those views, alarm to the extent that they are disguising their old agenda in more moderate clothing. Under their Jeffersonian togas they still wear Calvin jeans.

Their greatest accomplishment: To have put on the agenda of mainstream America profound problems about this nation with which other segments of the American polity have not been willing to grapple. Among those problems are the breakdown of family; the rising rates of illegitimate births and abortions; the frightening rates of drug abuse and crime in our streets.

Credit should be given where it is due. The fundamentalists raised these issues more dramatically and forcefully in the public arena than any other segment of the religious *or* nonreligious community. But while few Americans would disagree with any of the questions they ask about American society regarding these issues, most, by far, clearly disagree with all of their answers.

*5. Which leads to the final point: What should be the response of
the mainstream religious community to the religious right?*

The mainstream must address the challenge that it poses
on a number of levels.

It is time for the mainstream churches to address those
systemic problems of American society about which the fundamentalists are so concerned. The mainstream groups are effective when it comes to problems that can be solved by passing
a bill. But talk about the breakdown of the educational system,
the problems of drugs and crime, the breakdown of American
families, the alienation and powerlessness of individuals in this
society—and we just are not there. If the mainstream groups
abandon the arena of public concern on these issues to the religious right, then the right will have deserved the number of
political converts it attracts.

The religious right's analysis of the problems America faces
and the answers they give distract our nation from addressing
these problems realistically and meaningfully. One image
dramatically illustrates this danger. In 1982 Bill Bright, the head
of the Campus Crusade for Peace, stood before 400,000 fundamentalists on the Mall in Washington, D.C., and exhorted
them to political action. He argued that God had been kicked
out of the classrooms of America by the Supreme Court. Look
what has happened since, he observed: John and Robert Kennedy assassinated; Martin Luther King, Jr., murdered; drug
abuse and divorce out of control; people afraid to walk the
streets, more illegitimate than legitimate births in Washington,
D.C. These observations are chronologically correct, albeit a bit
weak on the cause-and-effect side. His answer? Put God back in
the school by passing a school prayer amendment. But when the
talents, energies, resources, and creativity of tens of millions of
people are diverted from addressing the true nature of these
problems to passing a school prayer amendment, then there is
little hope that American society will ever prevent these problems from festering and expanding. The mainstream religious
community must intensify its efforts to lead its members and the
community at large in addressing these pressing issues.

The religious right has succeeded in appropriating the Bible as well as religious ideas and rhetoric in our public political discourse. In recent decades the mainstream groups have tried to frame their rhetoric in general political terminology, thus undermining their uniqueness and moral authority. In the 1980s there has been a demonstrable shift in the rhetoric of the mainstream religious groups. Increasingly they frame their arguments in more distinctly religious form even while expressing them in terms accessible to the majority of Americans. The recent pastoral letters by the Catholic and Methodist churches exemplify this trend. But because the religious right's approach often offers simplistic religious/political answers to contemporary problems, the mainstream groups are at a disadvantage.

The mainstream groups need to recognize the legitimacy of some of the complaints of the religious right. By addressing legitimate issues they raise, mainstream groups can begin to work together with the right in a manner that can build trust and understanding, even while it undercuts the right's overall political distinctiveness. Thus, when the fundamentalists in Tennessee and Alabama and Arkansas complain about the censorship of any mention of religion in our history texts and cultural courses, they are more right than wrong. And those of the mainstream groups who care about the presence of religion in America and believe there are differences between "teaching religion" and "teaching *about* religion" need to monitor our textbooks, work with the curricula developers, and ensure that the religious traditions of our nation find their *proper* place in this nation's schools, textbooks, and curricula. In so doing, the ground can be cut out from beneath the right's political efforts as politically moderate fundamentalists are offered an alternative to the religious right's formulations, an alternative that can address their concerns without weakening the Constitution.

The mainstream groups must begin to deal with, and interact with, the religious right more than they have done. The religious right is not the enemy; its ideas are. And through encounters with mainstream groups they can change and moderate their views. If Jerry Falwell saw fit to stand before the Rabbinical Assembly of America and apologize for what he had said about Jews and about separation of church and state; if Weyrich can say that it is time for us to stop talking about God dictating the right's agenda; if Pat Robertson can stand before the Religious Action Center of Reform Judaism's Consultation on Conscience and affirm his commitment to the Judeo-Christian heritage of this nation and reject the notion of "Christianizing" America, then the inherent moderating phenomenon of the American political system described by political scientists since de Toqueville is still at work.

Forty years ago Billy Graham emerged on the scene as ethnocentric and politically conservative as the new religious right leaders are today. But the mainstream Christian and Jewish communities worked to educate him and expand his understanding of our communities and our vision of America. Today he stands as a public figure committed to pluralism and to a moderate political vision of the nation.

The beginnings in this direction made by the Falwells and Robertsons, whether they are self-serving or not, reflect a fundamental political reality: the more they express such views, the more they are forced to defend them; the more they repeat them, the more their followers believe them (and the mainstream groups cannot reach most of their followers); the more they affirm them, the more they testify to the extraordinary situation of the Jew in America: if you want to be accepted by the mainstream of American society, you cannot be seen as anti-Jewish nor can you be seen as an opponent of those fundamental liberties that have uniquely ensured Jews rights and opportunities in this land that they have known in no other.

At the same time, the mainstream groups have to strengthen their legislative advocacy efforts to defeat the legislative manifestations of the right's traditional agenda. To do so is the constitutional right and political responsibility of mainstream groups. The "wall separating church and state" is a misnomer. It is a "one-way wall," limiting the ability of governments to interfere with the functioning of religious groups and the religious life of the individual, but not limiting religions. The founders always believed that religious groups would play an indispensible role in serving as a goad to the conscience of America.

On that point the mainstream groups and the religious right agree. All such groups have the right to speak out—including the religious right. The Supreme Court in *Walz* v. *Tax Commission* stated clearly: "Adherents of particular faiths and individual churches frequently take strong positions on public issues. . . . Of course, churches as much as secular bodies and private citizens have that right." It is not that the religious right does not have the right to speak and petition the government; it is that from the perspective of the religious traditions of the mainstream religious group, what they are saying is not right. They have forgotten the fundamental values of the Judeo-Christian religious ethic.

Finally, the mainstream groups must retrack their own efforts to begin to address the challenge that the religious right poses at the local level. There needs to be more training for rabbis, ministers, and priests; more courses at our seminaries about social justice and more training in skills for being social action leaders. The mainstream groups need to work in a much closer coalition with each other so that in every area of the nation, whatever the dominant religious group, they will have access to those who share their values and their views—people who can count on the support of the national groups in their efforts to defeat censorship of libraries, manipulation of curricula, and restrictions on freedom of religion for any children—including religious minorities.

14. The Enduring Truth
of Religious Liberalism

Eugene B. Borowitz

In March 1950, the Reform rabbis' association, the Central Conference of American Rabbis, perturbed by the changing religious mood of a postwar world, held an unprecedented assembly for its members, an Institute on Theology. One of its several discussion sections, that on revelation, could not compose a consensus statement. Its report merely indicated the eight problems which engaged the group, many of them related to God's role in revelation.

This notion so startled the chairman of the Institute, Ferdinand Isserman, that he broke into the proceedings with a personal response. He was astonished that the group had made no reference to the Documentary Hypothesis and its understanding of the creation of the Torah. As far as he was concerned, it had settled the matter of revelation. Like most other religious liberals, he considered the Bible a thoroughly human document, though one which was endlessly relevant because of its incomparable account of humankind's spiritual quest.

Liberals also often said that the Torah was inspired by God, but this seemed more deference to traditional usage than a living sense of God's partnership in the process. They had little doubt about the truth of their radically modern view, for it was supported by university research and organic to the Zeitgeist, the social optimism that expected cultural enlightenment to power steady human progress. The rabbis attending the Institute would no doubt have hooted down a suggestion that in a few decades fundamentalism—or, its less terminologically troublesome Jewish equivalent, orthodoxies—would claim best to express the Zeitgeist and win the willing allegiance of many university graduates.

The totally unanticipated resurgence of orthodoxies in the nearly four decades since then has surely had little to do with new findings concerning the biblical text. Rather, it has come as a reaction to the failure of the cultural messianism espoused by liberal religion. With all its many benefits, modernity has also traumatically increased human misery in ways as local as the threat of drugs or the loss of meaning, and as global as unchecked pollution or nuclear destruction. Individuals, institutions, and ideologies so regularly disillusion us that cynicism and depression abound, while hope is uncertain and escapist fantasies are appealing. Insightfully, we call this time "postmodern," for we no longer share the modernists' confidence in humankind's capabilities. In this context, orthodoxies have had great appeal, either to those seeking to replace anarchy with psychic stability or to those who believe that a good God gave us divine instruction to save us from the vagaries of our too free wills.

Specifically, liberalism lost its cultural hegemony largely because of the demythologization of its allies, university rationalism and science. At one time we thought them not only our finest sources of truth but our surest means to human ennoblement. Today the sophisticated know that they deal only in possible "constructions of reality," and the masses sense that they commend ethical relativism more than necessary values and duties. For, having brilliantly unmasked all the ethical cant around us, they abandon us to the randy promptings of the self. And liberal religion, many believe, has been the willing handmaiden of this modernist loss of standards. By turning God's revelation into mere human growth and self-determination, liberal religion helped destroy our faith in stable human values and made us prey to moral anarchy. How, after the human failures of recent decades, can any sensitive person consider liberal religion a worthy faith? Simple morality, if nothing else, should prompt our return to the old religious paradigms of reality with their strong, clear teaching of what a person, a family, a community, and a nation ought to be.

The bankruptcy of liberalism is simply accentuated by the uncertain status today of its former academic cornerstone, the higher criticism of the Torah. My seminary teachers said they were teaching us "biblical science," a method so reliable that one professor regularly assigned a numerical probability to his emendations restoring the original biblical text. My professors, of course, espoused "the Documentary Hypothesis"—but in actuality considered it to be "the facts."

Today, the theory is a shambles. It exists and is used only for want of a better explanation of the messily discordant data. No one can specify an empirically verifiable description of the distinctive language of the Torah's alleged documents, or resolve the doubts as to their century or sequence, or clarify their relation to the redaction process or to the local traditions present in the text, or satisfactorily explain how the oral became the written, or the role of literary coherence in all of this, much less how the distinctive religious vision of the Torah, its most significant characteristic, utterly transforms the cultural images it employs. The older critical work in Bible seems, for all its academic hermeneutic, essentially another midrash, one which tells us more about the author's trendy suppositions than about the text's own apparent concerns. Surely one ought not urge the perplexed of our day to stake their lives on such flimsy grounds. Rather than trim our religion to what one generation or another's celebrated professors teach, should we not rather live by what our religious tradition tells us a good God has graciously made available to us?

Some such case, I believe, grounds the conservative religious Zeitgeist of our day. Hence my focus is primarily on the issue of the consequences of our theory of God's revelation and only secondarily on how we can best understand the biblical text.

To facilitate the central discussion, I shall shortly grant this conservative statement of the case. But I should like to be quite explicit that, in fact, I consider it false when stated so unconditionally and, when properly nuanced, so altered in meaning as to lose its decisive affect. Permit me, then, a few counter-comments.

I know of no major liberal religion that advocates drugs, child abuse, family violence, robbery, hard core pornography, graft, cheating the government, or other niceties of the nightly news. One reason liberals often get tarred with the brush of every social pathology is that they think it morally responsible to confront and talk about the human realities in their midst, from mental retardation to wife abuse. The orthodoxies generally prefer another strategy. First they deny that their communities have such problems, or they simply exclude such sinners and defectives from the community of the faithful; later they admit that such problems do occur among them but suggest greater faith and devotion as the best therapy; and finally, when the humanistic treatments are long established elsewhere, the orthodoxies co-opt them with the guidance of a suddenly more accommodating Scripture and tradition.

Orthodoxies do present a legitimate challenge to liberalism: that its emphasis on individual freedom leads to an impoverished sense of duty and a virtual abandonment of limits, of what in one's freedom a liberal believer must *not* do. Having clarified my response to that charge elsewhere,[1] I shall not say more about it here except for some brief comments toward the end of this paper. Instead I shall approach the issue of moral consequences comparatively, that is, by analyzing the problems orthodoxies can engender as contrasted to liberal religion's approach to the same issues. That should clarify why liberals know their faith to be truer.

Let us begin with historical analysis. Had traditional religions not behaved so badly when they had effective power, lib-

---

1. Eugene B. Borowitz, "The Autonomous Jewish Self," *Modern Judaism* 4/1 (Feb. 1984): 39-56.

eral religion would most likely not have come into being. The rationalists of the Enlightenment scornfully charged that religion, by separating people into the saved and the damned, by its persecutions, inquisitions, crusades, and wars, has created more evil than good. It is a particularly egregious sin, for religions normally proclaim that they seek to bring peace into the world. More important, this divisiveness and controversy arise from fundamental, not peripheral, claims of the orthodoxies. In so far as a faith claims to know in some detail what God wants of all humankind, then loving one's neighbors as oneself can mean hating the one who is not like you and lovingly forcing them to be like you. Thus, Jewish law—and not merely its moralizing homiletics—restricts the neighbor I am commanded to love as myself to the one who is like me in religious observance. Its negative consequence is classically grounded in Psalm 139:21-22. "O Lord, You know I hate those who hate You, and loathe Your adversaries. I feel a perfect hatred toward them; I count them my enemies."

The theology of all such orthodoxies is, by internal standards, logically unimpeachable. God, who alone has every right to do so, has made perfectly plain how human beings ought to live. To do otherwise is not only a rejection of the highest good but a personal affront to God, whose holy law is being spurned. The pious who do nothing about this perversity are deeply implicated in it, for by not opposing evil they teach humankind a false lesson and silently ally themselves with the devil. They thereby retard the coming of God's rule and draw forth God's punishment, on the righteous, alas, along with the sinful. So for God's sake and their own, those who love God should fight and uproot sin.

This limited tolerance, or intolerance, arises precisely from what the orthodoxies claim to be their great strength: against moral flabbiness and uncontrolled freedom, their faith and discipline are certain. And because that knowledge is unqualified and absolute, no argument can logically challenge or refute it. One cannot range human understanding against what God has ordained, since God, who set these standards, is the ultimate ground of all human existence and dignity. One hears this same understanding in the talmudic retort, "The words of the master and the words of the disciple: to which should one listen?"[2]

Indeed, a special horror must greet any serious challenge to God's word. Absolute good is at stake, hence what normally would be a sin can now become a virtue; one kills flagrant sinners to save their souls. Given full social power, or access to it, orthodoxies have been known to utilize it against those demonic souls who deny God. Thus, in the Spanish Inquisition, Jews who had converted to Catholicism but, under torture, confessed that they had reverted to Jewish ways were not spared capital punishment, only executed somewhat more humanely.

I am not arguing that orthodoxies necessarily or inevitably lead to these harsh consequences, and I am not saying that the orthodoxies have learned nothing since the Middle Ages. All the traditional faiths I know have beliefs which could counteract such absolutism, God's love for every creature and God's desire for their genuine repentance being the most notable among them. And there have always been leaders in our religions who have been revered for their compassionate embrace of everyone, even vile sinners. Orthodoxies can be tolerant. That is not the issue between us. Nor is it one of determining which approach to faith is wholly correct and which wholly wrong. Liberal and orthodox faiths share too much of their views of God and humankind for such simplistic judgments. I think it irresponsible to charge that the orthodox ignore human self-determination or that the liberals forget that God is the ultimate ground of our values and being. Both affirm the transcendent preeminence of God and ascribe some independent dignity to humankind. What is at stake between us, then, is a question about proper balance, about the relative weight we attach to God's sovereignty and to human will.

Liberals reject orthodoxy not because, given the power, orthodoxies *will be* intolerant, but that, because of their basic

2. For example, Babylonian Talmud, Kiddushin 42b.

faith, they can generate extremism, zealotry, and fanaticism—
something they have often done in the past and still do today.
These, simple human experience has taught us, desecrate
God's name while claiming to exalt it and therefore are among
the foulest of human sins.

By contrast, liberal religion intrinsically affirms religious
pluralism. It does so because its experience of closeness to God
emphasizes the human side of the relationship and thus the
limited though commanding nature of our human comprehen-
sion of God. Hence liberalism affirms each individual's and each
generation's right to find a better approach to God. Few of us
are wiser at this than our inherited religious traditions. But, in
principle, with none of us able to affirm that ours is the only,
the absolute, way to God, we are led to affirm the rights of others
to go to God in their own way, even if it differs from ours. Such
pluralism as the orthodoxies know is limited to groups and
movements that are loyal to their revelation, though they may
be odd interpreters of it. But to those who differ radically, no
such positive pluralism applies; the orthodoxies draw the circle
of tolerance relatively closely to them while liberalism seeks to
make it ever more inclusive. Traditional Jewish law, for example, tolerantly teaches that one need not be a Jew to know
God and gain the life of the world to come. But it also asserts,
in Maimonides' famous ruling, that in a Jewish state gentiles
must accept this universal religion as a matter of Jewish revelation or be put to death—and that from the greatest of medieval
Jewish rationalists.

Sensitive to this problem, many spokesmen [*sic*] of contemporary orthodoxies have indicated their spiritual unease with
extremism and used their influence to oppose it. While admir-
ing such leadership, I see this as a quiet concession that the liberals' moral-religious concern for pluralism has genuine merit.
But human nature being what it is, we cannot be asked long to
rely on compassionate leaders regularly arising to offset the exclusivist thrust of orthodox religious belief. And if proper leadership can satisfactorily be relied on to offset a religion's shortcom-
ings, then it should also apply to good liberal leadership.

Besides, prudence suggests to liberals that the present more positive orthodox attitude toward pluralism derives more from their lack of effective power than from their principled commitment to pluralism. Were there not so many orthodoxies fighting for preeminence among us, were one of them able radically to influence our country's leaders, their view of how much sin they should be asked to tolerate would most likely constrict. It is this understanding about orthodoxies which deeply distresses most American Jews about the power wielded in the State of Israel by the Israeli Orthodox political parties, despite their minority status. And they devoutly hope these parties never become a majority, for they know that a substantial number of the Israeli Orthodox have had no experience of democratic pluralism and even greater numbers do not accept it as a value consonant with Torah.

Orthodoxies have a principled problem with democracy. One sees it most easily in their internal functioning, but it also carries over to what they tend to find most desirable in a government. As to the former, God being one, indeed incomparably so, any institution properly representing God will speak with hierarchical authority to its members. This is not to deny that the will of the people may have an important role in orthodoxies. At Sinai, for all that God spoke directly to the Jewish people and summoned them into covenant, their willing assent was requested and memorably gained. (One rabbinic midrash explains that the first "commandment" of the Decalogue, God's self-identification as the people's redeemer, was needed so that they would know with whom they were to join in partnership.) For all that, orthodoxies strictly limit the functioning of the individual conscience by what they know is God's own law and institutions.

Consider, for example, the logic of the traditional Jewish laws regarding menstruation. To begin with, they are the only body of the biblically prescribed ritual purity laws now operative despite the destruction of the temple, the focus of all the practices related to ritual purity. In postbiblical times the menstrual laws gained a somewhat surprising addition. Though the Torah prescribes a separation of husband and wife only during the period of the menstrual flow, the later law added a further seven days to the period of ritual impurity. The basis of this ruling is disputed, but most sages came to ascribe it to a custom Jewish women voluntarily adopted. To the extent that custom can occasionally make law in Judaism, something like democracy has a place in it. Nonetheless, wherever Jews have modernized, Jewish women have overwhelmingly abandoned the practice of the menstrual laws; they would thus seem to have retracted their previous decision. Only they apparently cannot do so. The sages of each era, all male, retain the exclusive authority to determine not only the law but which customs can become law and which must be opposed.

Perhaps that issue agitates only a small number of the pious among us. What, then, shall we say of the issues raised by feminism generally? Setting aside for the moment the merits of one specific concern or another, what concerns Jewish feminists most fundamentally is the critical issue in democracy: effective participation in the power of decision making. Little is dearer to the modern spirit than self-determination, having a realistic role in determining the rules by which one is expected to live. In the established orthodoxies I know, God has commanded or God's appointed authorities have long decreed that religious authority is reserved to males. Liberals will surely agree with the orthodoxies that the content of a religion should not be determined simply by ballot. Nonetheless, in principle, the liberal religious spirit accords fundamental respect to human autonomy. Our human self is the medium through which all we know of God is mediated, hence the individual's quest for God concerns liberals as much as does what we discern as God's reach toward humankind—and this partnership, together with our community's historic spiritual experience, becomes the foundation of a religious life that is inherently democratic because of its individualistic emphasis.

By extension, the same contrast in attitude toward democracy may be seen with regard to government. In the Bible, even the introduction of a king is considered a rejection of God's own rule over the people, the most desired state of affairs. Governmental structures which provide the stability of enforcing or at least encouraging what God requires of all people are therefore most congenial to its sense of standards. By contrast, democracies, with their shifting determinations of how people ought to be treated, are far more problematic. Consider, for example, how much easier it would be to resolve our continuing American religious tensions over abortion if we were not a democracy. Were our governmental leaders more independent of the people and congenial to a given orthodoxy, or were one or another of the orthodox faiths decisively in power, the issue would be quickly settled. Surely one reason why no constitutional amendment on abortion could be passed in Congress during the Reagan administration was that our orthodoxies could not agree which view of God's own truth about abortion was correct.

This brings us to an important qualification of the orthodoxies' claim that they would bring order into our society. This would be so if there were only one orthodoxy or if the several orthodoxies could agree on a policy. Orthodoxies often disagree as to what constitutes God's own will, and such disagreements can generate intense social conflict—and do so today as in the past. Traditional Jewish law, for instance, does not consider Jewish abortion murder but rather mandates an abortion when the mother's life, or according to some, her basic mental health is at stake. At the same time, it rules, for reasons which are obscure at best, that gentile abortions are murder.

Let me add that liberals need not necessarily be pro-abortion, though with their high regard for the individual, they will have tended, in this as in other matters, to make the decision of the immediate party involved—in this case, the mother—their primary concern. And this religious appreciation of the individual will makes them, in principle, enthusiastic about democratic governance despite its occasional vagaries.

Some orthodoxies have sought to meet the issues of pluralism and democracy by trying to make room in their midst for "the rights of conscience." It is a quite recent notion, one that only uncommon exegesis might find in Hebrew Scripture, the New Testament, or the Koran. Since such institutional commitments have developed largely as an accompaniment to the rise of rationalism and the Enlightenment, I see them as a silent orthodox acknowledgement of the religious truth that more centrally engages liberal spirituality. Obviously, orthodox faiths which esteem conscience will find it easier to appreciate and accommodate to democracy. But the fundamental problems of blending God's own truth and individual self-determination must not be underestimated. Thus, I see no institutional acceptance of the rights of conscience in either traditional Judaism or Islam. And where it does occur among Christians, in teachings as diverse as those of Roman Catholics and Southern Baptists, those who seek new ways under the promptings of conscience are these days reminded forcefully that in an orthodoxy obedience is the higher virtue.

This orthodox discomfort with sinners and evildoers spills over into another of its characteristic manifestations: the limited moral horizon we call ethnocentrism. The theological grounds of such high self-esteem are clear. Their community alone is fully loyal to God's own truth because often it is the only one to have known God's unique act of revelation. Others do not know, or they ignore, pervert, or even reject God's truth. So orthodoxies tend to tilt heavily in their own direction the balance between the love of all God's creatures and of those in their community. When this sense of cosmic group worth is joined to the common human preference for the known and the familiar over the strange and the alien, the more uncanny, unnatural, and perhaps even inhuman others appear to be. At the extreme, one secludes oneself from a defiling world so that one may share one's life as exclusively as possible with one's sacred kin. Yet even in less self-ghettoized groups, the sense of the universal is often highly constricted; charity, in the broadest sense of the term, not only tends to begin at home but largely stays there.

Modern Jews are often startled to learn about their legal tradition's interpretation of neighborly love, the commandment Rabbi Akiba called the most inclusive generalization in the

Torah. Over the centuries our authoritative sages have said it applied only to fellow Jews (and, essentially, to righteous ones). Among the specific consequences the rabbis drew from this commandment are a regard not only for a fellow Jew's honor and body but for his money. From this, some authorities ruled that in their business dealings Jews should give preference to other Jews, our community's version of the Christian Yellow Pages.

No religious community which hopes long to maintain itself, indeed which believes that, for all its humanity, it contains a true insight into the Divine, can do without some separatism and self-differentiation. In recent years many Jews have reasserted their Jewish particularity, and some have even built a cultural ghetto to do so. But modernized Jews, who are part of this same cultural thrust, believe traditional Jewish law engenders a restrictive ethos which underestimates the sacred quality of the common humanity they encounter wherever democracy truly functions.

All these unhappy consequences of orthodox theories of revelation come to a climax in their necessary subordination of persons to text, interpretation, structure, and precedent. God stands behind just these words and no others, behind just these interpretations of the words and no others, behind just this institution by which proper interpretations are mediated, and behind just this inherited wisdom which largely fixed what is and what is not God's will. Should adherents of an orthodoxy testify that to serve God most responsibly they believe they must significantly depart from tradition, then their authorities will insist that their "conscience" must defer to what their religious heritage knows to be God's will. God knows best, they will be told, and so, as a consequence, do the leaders of one's faith.

To liberals, an alternative explanation seems very much more probable. Rather than function as the privileged channel of God's instruction, religious institutions behave very much more like other human structures. All we have learned about the history of groups, of their transition from charismatic beginnings to institutionalization to bureaucratization, for good and for ill, seems to explain much better than does God's revelation or providence why they act as they do. Few orthodoxies today will deny their institutional humanity, but as God's own legatees they regularly claim to be exempt from the same sort of correction we think appropriate for other human structures. Liberals, too, hope that God's will manifests itself in their activities. But putting the balance on the human partner in our faiths, they deem it a duty, in principle, to be open to those new human experiences which, while deviating from the past, now appear to express its contemporary meaning.

Classic Jewish law, like that of other orthodoxies, contains many rulings where text and precedent are reinterpreted by the law's own means to permit what moderns see as greater personal fulfillment. Thus, the lex talionis is God's immutable law, but the rabbis so interpreted it that it calls for monetary compensation, not physical retribution. To make possible a second marriage, one witness instead of two may be acceptable to the rabbinic court, and that one may be a woman as well as a man. And, perhaps most tenderly of all, though Jewish husbands should divorce wives who do not bear children after ten years of marriage, we have no record of that law being enforced, only waived. Only a caricature would depict religious orthodoxies as without heart.

For all that, the principle of tradition over person substantially maintains itself. The classic Jewish cases have long been the *agunah* and the *mamzer*. The former is a woman who cannot remarry because she cannot legally prove that her husband is dead or has divorced her. The latter is the Jew who was born as a result of adulterous or incestuous intercourse. That Jew may never marry a proper Jew. Liberals cannot understand how such rulings can be understood to be God's will for us today. And they do not understand how those traditional Jews who agree they should be made inoperable continue to be appeased by authorities who say that the legal system has the means to remedy these inequities when, for decades now, these authorities have made no significant change in them.

Permit me one further example, not any the less interesting because the public furor over it was initiated by a hoax. It relates to one of the humane considerations articulated in the earliest document of rabbinic law, the Mishnah, edited about 200 C.E. Should a structure collapse on the Sabbath and someone be buried underneath it, we must immediately set aside all the usual prohibitions of labor on the Sabbath and work as hard as we can to dig the person out. Saving a life supersedes every law in Judaism except the prohibitions of murder, idol worship, and sexual immorality. That certainly seems, as a matter of law, to give human existence proper priority. But the Mishnah specifies that, should we discover that the buried person is a gentile, the Sabbath laws immediately go back into effect and we stop digging. No liberal Jew I know can face such a law without a protest, and at least one Orthodox Jewish legal authority has by some similar sentiment been led to reinterpret the Mishnah rule—but precedent having the weight it does in orthodoxies, we cannot say what proportion of observant Jews would follow this liberalized ruling. To liberals it is perfectly clear that persons, gentile or Jew, have a major claim on the laws and interpretations of the past, and that in this case an old human understanding, not God's own will, is at stake.

Thus far I have sought to show how the deleterious social consequences fundamentalists associate with religious liberalism must be balanced against the evils which can and have arisen from orthodoxies. For liberals, these humane, ethical considerations are generally decisive.

I wish to turn now to the debate over our sacred texts. Orthodoxies are committed in principle to God's authorship of the explicit verbal form in which, all things being equal, we have Scripture. Thus, should we, reading it, be surprised that God stated what seems contrary to presently established fact, or that God enjoined or condones what seems an inhumane act, then our understanding of it must be faulty. As Rabbi Mana said, it is we, not the verse, which is empty.[3] Thus, Abraham, Isaac, and Jacob cannot be charged with what, from the stories in the text,

---

3. Jerusalem Talmud, Peah 1.1, commenting on Deut. 32:47.

we would otherwise consider lying or deceit. So, too, the command to the invading Israelites to kill every Canaanite man, woman, and child of the seven local nations must have religious validity despite its ethical abhorrence. And the apparent duplication of stories in the text, the close parallels the Bible sometimes has to other Near Eastern texts, the statements of the Torah which seem post-Mosaic, the shifting chronology of the narrative, the odd orthography, all must be there to serve a divine purpose. In perhaps the most popular contemporary traditional Jewish commentary to the five *megillot,* the scrolls of the Hagiographa read on special synagogue occasions, the author denies that there is a literal meaning to the text of the Song of Songs. Indeed, he terms it heresy to suggest that the Song of Songs deals with human sexuality and not, as tradition teaches, the love of God for the people of Israel. To the liberal eye, these and other such exegetical strategies seem a defense against what contemporary common sense suggests, that the text is very much more human than divine, though surely a mixture of both.

Liberals hold to their divergent, more humanistic theory of revelation because it gives us a more fully integrated view of the data before us and accords much better with all else we know and have experienced. Once one concedes a considerable role to the human partner in revelation, most of the ordinary difficulties we have in reading the Bible fall away. Few today are still shocked that human beings, even ones with rare human sensitivity to God's will, would express themselves in terms of the worldview and values of their day. However, it is awe-inspiring, literally so, that these same authors often completely transcend their time and culture and speak of ultimate truth and sanctifying duty in words in which we can still hear God addressing us.

Orthodoxies have so full a sense of God's own truth that they often insist that if one does not accept Scripture as entirely God's word then, by making it largely human, one renders it insignificant. Liberals find that dichotomy utterly distorts their religious experience. For them, precisely because rejecting Scripture as God's own truth liberates them from the burden of explaining away the innumerable problems in the text, it frees them to appreciate fully the spiritual genius that produced it.

The critical choice between liberalism and the orthodoxies centers upon their different approaches to religious truth. For the liberals, faith in God needs to be understood as but one aspect, if the crucial one, of the seamless whole of human existence. The orthodoxies assert rather that their Scripture is unique in human experience, something God never fully did before and now will never supersede. Its proper meaning, then, cannot be ascertained by our customary methods of reasoning.

Occasionally, orthodox religious philosophers try to show that reason and the revelation of their faiths are compatible. But there are so many radical discontinuities between sacred texts and scientific data, to give one critical instance, that the more common strategy is to compartmentalize truth. One assigns one's religious truth to one mental chamber, while one's clashing modern knowledge is isolated in another. And some few true believers seek to resolve the tension by rejecting modern knowledge altogether.

Liberals can appreciate the respect for God's uniqueness that lies behind this schizoid existence, but they find it distorted by its lack of a balancing appreciation of every human being's ability to know God. They would agree that God's incomparable indwelling presence must receive its proper due and not be reduced to people's ordinary sense of things. At the same time, liberals reject a compartmentalized spirituality because they believe that the human soul, created in God's image, ought to strive to be one even as God is one. And that means coordinating the discordant elements of one's personality into an ever expanding whole, integrating one's spiritual experience with that of one's faith community and, reaching beyond them, seeking to relate it to the experience of all God's children.

Hence, in the liberal understanding of faith, there is ideally no barrier between what is known in every other human discipline and what is known in religion's self-understanding. Explicating that unified sense of human existence has turned out to be a more difficult task than early liberal religious thinkers estimated. Not the least reason for this difficulty has been the unexpected shifts our modern worldview has taken as people have studied humankind and pondered its recent sorry behavior. Nonetheless, liberals know that this pursuit of the soul's integrity is the only true way they can serve God.

This dedication arises from a compelling sense of what the human spirit can achieve when it is free to use its powers of intelligence and creativity in God's service. In its youth, liberalism was utterly optimistic, as in its heady doctrines of human perfectibility and social action messianism. Today, that liberal confidence seems naive and even destructive. But that does not refute the liberal's sure knowledge of two truths. One, that in some significant if limited ways we can transform the world and make it more just and loving. And two, that we know that God's mandates may still be heard among us, directing us in new as well as old ways. True, the mature self can easily collapse into willfulness or idiosyncrasy. On this score the challenge of the orthodoxies has considerable merit, and postmodern liberalism needs to respond to it. Thus, for me, the Jewish self ought never think of its existence as merely individual but only as existence in Covenant. Hence its autonomy must always be exercised in Covenant with God, with the Jewish community of the present, with the community of the past through its tradition, and with the Messianic Time through the Jewish people's future. Living the Covenant this liberal way will surely not enjoin the stated limits on human freedom that often make the orthodoxies attractive today. But it also cannot, for all its emphasis on human self-determination, be called anarchic, libertine, or uncommanded. It is a liberal Jew's devout response to the imperative arising from the Covenant with God found more directly through the self than through any text or tradition.

The division between liberal religion and the orthodoxies arises, finally, from the different balance of faith and consequence we find most true to what God wants of us. Orthodoxies know the power of God's own word and the warmth of God's own communities, but these strengths engender what liberals see as problems with the rights and integrity of persons. Liberal religion's genius lies in its appreciation of the personal and the universal, but it creates the problems of relativism, indecisiveness, and the question of proper limits of personal freedom.

In the backlash against modernity which has swept across Western culture, the orthodoxies have shown how deeply they still appeal to the human spirit. But despite their continuing power, most people who have tasted the personal dignity modernity has conferred upon them have rejected orthodoxy. I see this judgment arising from their quiet conviction that the secular movement to individualism, pluralism, and democracy has a lasting spiritual validity that cannot be denied. Or, in rhetorical conclusion, that God has spoken to us through the new, personal freedom modernity has conferred upon us, so that, for all that we may have abused it, only in its affirmation and responsible use can we truly serve God.

15. The Religious Challenge of Fundamentalism

Preston N. Williams

The question of the religious response to fundamentalism is both timely and challenging. Timely because Christian fundamentalism, which has existed at least since 1920, has recently become a high-profile worldwide phenomenon and contributed to changes that have led to the reshaping of nation-states, societal ethics, and relationships among religious communities of faith. The increased vitality and vigor of fundamentalism, together with its assumption of a public role, makes it difficult for socially or religiously conscious groups and individuals not to notice it or to avoid interacting with it in the public arena. One cannot avoid being challenged in some way, not only because of the vigor of the movement but also because its influence is making changes and setting trends. To keep one's own orientation, whether as an individual or as a group, one must frame a response to the initiatives of this greatly strengthened social and religious force. Not to do so would be to ignore, if not a revolution, at least one of the most remarkable efforts by religious persons to determine the moral and religious as well as political and social climate of our world.

I shall not attempt, however, to address either the worldwide expression of fundamentalism or the entirety of its manifestation in the United States. If I had been asked to comment upon social or political happenings, I would not shy away from that task. I have been asked, however, to address the religious challenge, and I can only do that from the perspective of my own faith. I shall limit this paper, then, to the appearance of fundamentalism within Protestant and secular America, a subject with which I am a bit familiar from both the outside and the inside. This form of religious piety and practice was present in my Presbyterian and Afro-American Christianity. I have heard debates on the issues for some time and have listened to such prominent spokespersons as Donald Grey Barnhouse, Clarence Edward McCartney, Charles E. Fuller, Harry Emerson Fosdick, and Charles W. Wesley. I developed a perspective on the preaching and teaching of men such as these before I realized the need to sort them out and put them into boxes labeled fundamentalist and liberal, or evangelicals, social gospelers, and conservatives. My own formation, under the tutelage of Christians of the right, center, and left, has determined how I seek to respond to the religious challenge of fundamentalism. An adequate response should be one of moving beyond labels, letting God be God, learning how to read Scripture, how to shun triumphal Christianity, and how to enable persons to become religiously mature.

During much of the period in which nonfundamentalists and fundamentalists have been in conflict, it has been the habit of the former to look with condescension upon the latter because of their anti-intellectualism, their class status, their unwillingness to surrender unsophisticated styles of piety, and their willingness to affirm doctrines of revelation and scriptural interpretation which intellectual Christians believed to be in error and contrary to the best knowledge and science of the modern world. This attitude of superiority is still widespread today, even though the acceptance of fundamentalist views is less embarrassing in much of contemporary public discourse than it was several decades ago. This belief of nonfundamentalists that their faith alone was rational and intellectually respectable led them to become religious despisers of their fellow Christians. The attitude of the fundamentalists toward their coreligionists was one characterized by hatred

and hostility. It was an attitude that promoted division and alienation rather than union or cooperation. Members of both camps
seemed to feel that their faith required separation from and con-
quest of the other rather than reconciliation. Unfortunately, attitudes similar to these continue to be prevalent today between the
fundamentalist and nonfundamentalist. Consequently, the first
religious challenge from fundamentalism is the challenge for religious persons and groups to learn to love each other and to accept other religious persons and groups, often one's coreligionists, in spite of the grave differences they may have in respect to
faith and its practices. At the core of the faith that Christians share
with each other is the commandment to love the neighbor as the
self. The advent of fundamentalism as a social and religious force
should cause us to realize that the conception of neighbor includes the several parties or divisions within the faith as well as
all other children of God. Neighbor includes one's religious
enemy as well as all other enemies.

The past history of crusades, religious wars, and divisions
among communities of faith indicate the unpleasantness and
destruction that can come from seeking to obliterate those with
whom one differs. We need to learn from that past. The more
recent experiences of ecumenism and pluralism point to ways
to live together as communities of faith without demanding that
others deny their faith. Further efforts to develop these positive
ways of relating to our differences need to be explored and developed. This should be the first response to the religious challenge of fundamentalism.

One needs to begin here in order to overcome the ill-will
and stereotyped ways of thinking about and relating to each
other that have developed between the fundamentalist and
nonfundamentalist. The task is an exceedingly difficult one because one has to overcome more than a half-century of con-
certed attacks by one group upon the other, in which deliberate
distortions of the position of the opponent were common practice and in which deeply embedded negative symbols like that
of the Scopes Trial were planted in the culture.

In spite of the convictions of some that fundamentalism is

characterized by absolutes and separatism, those who have lived through much of its history know it to be in many ways porous. Martin Marty reminds us of this:

> Today the word "fundamentalism" is often casually applied to people who are intransigent about change, advocates of resistance to modernity anywhere in the world. More properly, it should be applied to a loosely organized cluster of allies that could unite for certain causes in America.
>
> They never even agreed on exactly what made up the fundamentalists, differing in their acceptance of five or nine or fourteen of them depending on who was counting—and often not bothering to count.[1]

While it is true that most fundamentalists will espouse an absolutist posture and seek to isolate themselves in certain ways from the world or the Church or both, it is nonetheless true that this movement has been marked by great change and inventiveness, and that it has never rejected all of what we term the modern world or liberal religion. Cooperation with fundamentalists may be difficult, but it is not impossible or undesirable. It can be prepared for, and accomplished, if we rid ourselves of our notions of superiority and set aside our stereotypes of these religious adversaries. We must approach fundamentalists with love and with openness, and embrace them as people, as well as adherents of a particular creed.

The interdependent and interrelated nature of our society makes it extremely difficult for any groups or individuals to separate themselves and live in isolation from all that goes on about them. This is why the fundamentalists have joined the liberals in creating a social agenda and entering the world of politics. This is why Jews and Christians have increased their dialogues with each other and have come to recognize more adequately the existence of other world religions. Our interdependence and interrelatedness requires that we cease pretend-

---

1. Martin E. Marty, *Protestantism in the United States' Righteous Empire,* 2nd ed. (New York: Charles Scribner's Sons, 1986), pp. 211, 212.

ing that separation, isolation, or absolutism makes cooperation with fundamentalists impossible. The first religious challenge, then, that the fundamentalists present to us is that we prove the credibility of our claims to be called loving persons, open, inclusive, and willing to accept diversity as one aspect of God's created order. If one can accept the particularities of social class, sexual, ethnic, and individualized perspectives in religion; if one can turn toward the East or to Africa and find there insights that are compatible with our faith; if one can see our faith as not being inconsistent with a wide variety of scientific and unscientific worldviews—then it should also be possible to turn to the right and find there some wisdom and truth.

The problem that inhibits a serious attempt at rapprochement may not be the question of the truth or falsity of religious perspectives but that of power. Power cannot, and must not, be overlooked or dismissed, but it also must not be determinative for our response. We must be mindful of the fact that not only are great social and religious issues at stake, but that love is a form of power and God is Love.

The first response to the religious challenge of fundamentalism is, then, the response of love—of learning to see and to know the fundamentalists for who they seek to be and what they seek to do, and of attempting to relate to them in a positive and constructive fashion. This does not mean that we accept their position as true, but it does mean that we recognize them to be persons deeply committed to what they consider the true statement and living of their faith. Our differences, then, are true differences, and we must sympathetically but firmly deal with them. This requires one to relate to fundamentalists as if they were faithful servants of God acting according to their best lights, even if we have grave and profound doubts about their faith and their understanding of God's will.

There are, to be sure, risks involved in this type of approach, risks to our faith and to theirs. Our vaunted openness and reasonableness will be put to the test, and we will engage them in respect to their certainty and their desire to convert others. The risks may be threatening but no more threatening than that of permitting Catholics, Jews, secular humanists, Muslims, and the vast variety of sects and cults present in America to have full freedom of thought and action. I am not persuaded that the fundamentalists, who could not, during the last sixty or seventy years, destroy the religions they despised, can now uproot and destroy them. Nor am I persuaded that the threat they pose for faith is more menacing than a thousand other seductions that result daily from our encounter with the world.

Love and openness is the first response to the religious challenge of fundamentalism in America because, in the first instance, fundamentalism is a division in the Protestant religious community that requires healing and because a deeper, more authentic practice of the Protestant understanding of the Christian faith on the part of fundamentalist and nonfundamentalists is necessary if the division is to be overcome.

While it is necessary to be in dialogue with Catholics, Jews, Muslims, and other communities of faith about the issues involved and the most desirable religious outcomes, the controversy regarding fundamentalism must be seen as being a uniquely and distinctively Protestant conflict or debate. Fundamentalism in America is a challenge for Protestants to come to some consensus regarding the boundaries of their understanding of, but not agreement about, the nature of Christianity. It would be unwise for Protestants prematurely to address fundamentalism as it manifests itself in Roman Catholicism, Judaism, or Islam, not to mention its worldwide presence, if the concern is with the religious challenge. Most Protestants, even the educated ones, do not know enough about these other groups as communities of faith to undertake refined analyses of how they ought to come to terms with the religious dimension of the fundamentalist phenomenon. Moreover, in that the Protestant division has influenced the rest of the American culture and religions, it would be better if they would address first the problems of internal rather than external division when seeking the proper response to the religious challenge of fundamentalism.

A second response that Protestants might make to the re-

ligious challenge of fundamentalism may, in spite of my reti-
cence to speak about the expression of fundamentalism outside Protestantism, furnish the basis for a more general response by communities of faith. Religiously, fundamentalism
challenges us to distinguish between the absolute and the relative, religion and culture, and the world or the creatures and
the creation of God. Now this distinction may not exist in all
religions or worldviews, but it is of the essence of Protestantism
as well as Catholicism, Judaism, and Islam. Since all of us are
born into a particular culture and ofttimes a religion as well, it
is important that we strive not to absolutize the relative. Nonfundamentalists are quite frequently more sensitive to this than
are fundamentalists. The conscious and deliberate utilization
of extrareligious sources of knowledge like science and the historical-critical approach to Scripture makes nonfundamentalists aware of how religion is embedded in culture and stimu-
lates them to distinguish between religion and culture.
Fundamentalists are more apt to identify religion and culture,
and to advocate the absolutizing of the relative because of their
acceptance of biblical inerrancy and direct intervention by God
in history, and because of their tendency to reject much of
science and higher criticism. Fundamentalism itself might be
a new idea called into existence by modernity, but it is set forth
in a fashion that leads to the obscuring of the difference between faith and culture and the absolute and the relative. If
the two divisions of Protestantism can come to speak the truth
to each other in love and with care and consideration, and
come to know and appreciate each other's message and goals,
then it may be possible for them to aid each other in discover-
ing how their faith is entangled in culture and what might be
done to reduce some of these attachments. The association of
nonfundamentalists with the dominant high culture often
causes them to fail to see their cultural and class accretions just
as the fundamentalist's effort to restore or save the old-time religion obscures the cultural deposits present in that faith.

Or again the nonfundamentalists' tendency to accept pluralism might awaken them to their continuing practice of in-

tolerance and exclusiveness, while the concern of the fundamentalist with the correct dogma and practice might orient them to an uncritical acceptance of cultural mores.

Be that as it may, the problem is that both the nonfundamentalist and the fundamentalist have a faith that is embedded in culture, and if they speak to each other in love about their differing perspectives on the one God that they worship they may be able to aid each other to see their cultural attachments and to undertake the task of distinguishing between the relative and the absolute.

The civil rights revolution, for example, enabled Jerry Falwell to better distinguish between the folk mores of the South and the biblical teaching with respect to race. More recently he has changed the nature of his participation in politics. In both instances, what we observe is that fundamentalism does change and that it does, on occasion, accommodate itself to practices of civility and pluralism. In both these instances it appears also to have adopted a better understanding of what is culture and what is religion; in a way, it has been critical of itself and has, in the light of that criticism, altered its nature. We need to continue to seek to dialogue with fundamentalism in the effort to bring about more of these changes.

No religious response to fundamentalism can omit an in-depth discussion of how we are to read Scripture and what we are to seek there. Fundamentalism began with a concern about how one was to understand a scriptural text and how sufficient that text or collection of texts called the Bible were for the understanding of life and the world. The confidence the fundamentalists have in the inerrancy or infallibility of the Bible remains a source of division and fear in respect to the religious challenge of fundamentalism. Fundamentalists seem unable to see how a historical-critical approach to Scriptures can sustain the truth of the faith. Only the doctrine of inerrancy, they think, is able to support and preserve proper piety and precise doctrine. I must confess that I do not know how one can even focus on this problem unless one can first speak the truth in love and then accept the fact that many of our conclusions about proper piety and precise doctrine may be matters of indifference to the God whom we serve. If we can agree with these statements, then it might be possible to set aside or bracket the question of inerrancy in the same way we set aside the doctrine of the infallibility of the Pope. We can understand how the teaching came to be, what it is intended to safeguard, and what it means to those who accept it, without accepting it ourselves or feeling the need to condemn those who believe it. More importantly, we might point out to all, that whatever their attitude toward the doctrine, it is unable, even when utilized by the ones committed to it, to achieve the religious purposes intended.

The ample testimony of history ought to be able to persuade us that neither the method of the scholars of biblical inerrancy or that of the historical-critical school can guarantee the truth or sufficiency of Scripture. Scientifically, the new theories of literary criticism and historical discovery alert us to the fact that both biblical inerrancy and historical-critical studies embody significant elements that prevent the recovery of full truth concerning the biblical text and its meaning. Doctrinally, the Protestant communities of faith asserted, and deeply embedded in their faith, the belief that any person could discover the truth of Scripture if they read Scripture in the light of their own reason and under the guidance of the Holy Spirit. This teaching undercuts the concept of inerrancy and makes tentative the conclusions of historical-critical studies of Scripture. The Bible has an uncanny way of reasserting its truth in the face of false interpretations. The truth of the Scripture somehow transcends the teachings of the various schools of scriptural interpretation. The religious challenge of fundamentalism is the challenge to discover how to convey this truth about Scripture together with a robust confidence in Scripture.

The scholarship of the historical-critical school seems to be indispensable to a serious reading of Scripture, whether by Protestant, Catholic, Jew, Muslim, or secular humanist. We can not hope to understand the texts without knowing as much as we can about what they meant in their own time and in their own setting. Historical-critical scholarship is most valuable in ruling out certain errors of interpretation, but it is less valuable in helping us, nonfundamentalist and fundamentalist alike, to find what we want most from Scripture: namely, an understanding of the positive faith of the ancients and guidance toward a positive faith for ourselves and for this age. Modern critical scholarship is a better guide to the leading orientations in intellectual, political, and cultural thought than it is for the spiritual or religious life and the reactions of that life to every aspect of personal and social living.

The historical-critical method owes its existence to the desire of biblical scholars to be a part of and acceptable to the scholars of the cultural and natural sciences as well as the demands of truth. We should not be surprised to discover that, even today, there is tension and conflict between this orientation and the unearthing of truths necessary for fruitful religious living. In some instances pursuit of cultural and academic respectability has been detrimental to religious life. The hoped-for harmony of scientific and religious truth is not always present. Fundamentalists have perceived the presence of these disharmonies, but have unfortunately sought to protect themselves and their churches from them by inventing a distortion: the concept of the inerrancy or infallibility of Scripture. In a sense, the notion is not new because every individual faith and every community of faith formed around Scripture invests a portion of its energy in trying to guarantee the correctness of biblical teaching. None, however, has gone quite to the extent of the fundamentalists in declaring the Bible to be inerrant. The fundamentalist error, like that of the nonfundamentalist, is an error of logic, reason, and modern thought. Perhaps a continuing conversation about each other's goals and aspirations (our first suggestion), even at this late date, will cause the two groups to recognize this.

Crucial to the development of this approach to reconciliation is the recognition by fundamentalists that their doctrine of inerrancy is a doctrine that can not be enforced, because scriptural truth is always to a considerable degree in the hands of the interpreter. Even in a tightly controlled church such as that desired by the conservative Southern Baptists, the purity of Scripture will be polluted by the attachment to it of cultural perspectives by those certified by the denomination as fit teachers. The religious challenge that must be made clear to fundamentalists is contained in this perceptive insight of Daniel Meeter: "No formula of inerrancy or infallibility can limit in advance the inevitable and sinful desire of preachers, teachers, and writers to escape the scandal of the Bible."[2] The difficulty about what I am recommending is attested to not only in the contest among Southern Baptists but also elsewhere in our religious world where Christians fear each other more than they fear their secular and humanistic culture.

We must come to recognize that whatever the nature of our scheme for being faithful to Scripture, our sinful natures and the errors of our communities of faith permit inerrancy and historical-critical methods to go astray. They can neither guarantee the truth of Scripture nor make possible the extraction of only truth from Scripture. Knowing this, perhaps we can learn to tolerate the existence of methods of scriptural interpretation other than our own and stress the need to pursue truth in every effort made to know and to apply the teachings found in Scripture. The key to success in this dialogue is our ability to respect each other, to learn as much as we can about Scripture and its context at the time of its origin as well as the history of its interpretations, and to communicate the insights of Scripture, with as little distortion as possible, to other persons, to our religious communities, and to our world. In this type of activity the nonfundamentalist and the fundamentalist are equals differing only in respect to the cultural or nonbiblical elements they tie to Scripture. The greater the effort to detach the absolute from the relative, the greater the likelihood that persons and groups will possess the insight needed to identify the essentials of religion and the will required to separate the religious from the cultural.

2. Daniel Meeter, "Bowing before the Text" in *The Reformed Journal* 38 (Jan. 1988): 10-11.

An additional religious challenge posed by fundamentalism is the need for both major divisions of Protestant Christianity to surrender or greatly modify their practices of triumphal Christianity. It has long been the practice of Christianity to seek to annihilate its foes. This was true under the Roman popes and emperors, the reformers on the Continent and in England, and among the Puritans in New England. The sectarian character of Christianity in America has enabled this characteristic to remain as a mark of American religion in spite of the separation of church and state. Both Protestants and Catholics had visions of winning America and the world for Christianity—and these visions have not yet died completely. The vision is rooted in the concern of Christianity to be an inclusive, universal religion and to be a faith established on pure doctrine. The current inordinate fear of fundamentalists rests upon the belief that they are too committed to this vision and are willing to impose it by state regulation. Nonfundamentalists are also troubled by the fact that their willingness to be more inclusive in respect to doctrinal perspectives has often led to particular and exclusive claims in respect to reason, class, ethnicity, race, and gender.

The willingness of the nonfundamentalists to revise the statement, if not the substance, of doctrine in order to be more inclusive and universal has often ended in their being more bound by culture, class, race, and gender. The failure of the strategy practiced by the nonfundamentalists should not obscure their intention to be triumphal.

When Harry Emerson Fosdick preached his historic sermon, "Shall the Fundamentalist Win," he stated that a pluralism of doctrine within Christianity was desirable to preserve the total community of Christians and a vital Christian mainstay in society.[3] Certainly that pluralism has come within the fundamentalist and nonfundamentalist communities of faith. It has

3. See H. Sheldon Smith, Robert Handy, and Lefferts A. Loetscher, *American Christianity: An Historical Interpretation with Representative Documents*, vol. 2: *1820-1960* (New York: Charles Scribner's Sons, 1963), pp. 294-301.

come with the National and World Councils of Churches, denominational mergers among Lutherans, a beginning recognition of African-American religion, and the many cooperative movements between fundamentalist and nonfundamentalists. It will continue for some time in the future because both, even today, seek to win and because unanimity among Christians on matters of mission and doctrine is highly unlikely.

It is interesting to note that today the center of controversy seems to be in the area of social policy and not theology. It is questions of abortion, school prayer, and government support of religious education and not the nature of revelation, Scripture, and Jesus Christ that are being contested. Fundamentalism is a threat because of its consequences for social policy and stability, not its religious teaching. It appears now that for both fundamentalist and nonfundamentalist, social salvation is as important as personal salvation, and victory in the theological circle as well. Just as riches were once the presumptive sign of personal salvation, so now victory in respect to social issues is taken as the presumptive sign of doctrinal purity. The relative success of fundamentalism in creating social instability, if not social change, alerts us to the religious challenge to both fundamentalism and nonfundamentalism. Christians must learn to rid themselves of triumphalism in respect to each other and in respect to those who are not Christians. Fundamentalism alerts us to the danger, but the danger is widespread in most of Christianity.

The movement of nonfundamentalist Protestantism in the direction of a universal inclusive faith, which tolerated genuine doctrinal differences, was a step in the right direction. The ecumenical movement among this branch of Christianity was an even further step because it abandoned Fosdick's concern with who shall win. Fundamentalist and evangelical Christians as well as Vatican II Roman Catholics have taken similar steps in this direction. The dialogue that presently exists between evangelicals, those who call themselves neo-fundamentalists, and Pentecostals as well as other Protestants, may contain an opportunity to widen the dialogue to include those we still call fundamentalist, the residual category of persons who cling to nineteenth-century Christianity.

The religious challenge for those who are not fundamentalist is to keep alive the possibility for a conversation by refusing to create a wholly negative and evil stereotype of the fundamentalist. We must see the fundamentalist as one like ourselves, both possessing the truth and seeking a fuller truth, and therefore one whom we do not seek to convert or to conquer but rather one with whom we seek to share our faith and mission in society. Some of this new attitude already exists. It is not fully recognized because we do not always analyze the supportive constituency of the conservative social agenda or the belief structure of nonfundamentalist Christians. Yet closer scrutiny will reveal that many bridges do bind fundamentalist and nonfundamentalist in matters of mission and faith. What one needs to do now is to build upon this by removing the fear of fundamentalist absolutism and nonfundamentalist permissiveness, and enlarge their participation in the cultural, social, and political world they desire to shape.

The building of such relationships will lessen the tendency of Christians to conquer those they consider to be less than fully Christian. Fundamentalist and nonfundamentalist might come to see the social positions, beliefs, and rituals they share as well as those on which they differ. The common commitment of Christians to love God and their neighbor will lead to a greater toleration of doctrinal differences and a greater faith in God's ability, working through all humankind, to fashion a more just society. Fundamentalists and nonfundamentalists will be more prepared to believe that the existence of the other will not lead to the radical distortion of human nature and all human institutions. They will recognize that Christianity can be influential without being triumphal and that God, not they, will become all in all. Triumphal Christianity must be abandoned by both fundamentalist and nonfundamentalist in favor of a Christianity that sees as its goal the proclamation of love, justice, and humility. Such a response is the proper response to the religious challenge of fundamentalism.

As we outline these several understandings, it becomes increasingly apparent that one of the most important is the need for the better education of religious persons by communities of faith. Our current fundamentalist-nonfundamentalist controversy arose when Protestant Christians sought to adjust the central core of their faith to the basic religious tasks of culture, society, and personal living. Today, both great divisions of Protestantism face this task anew. The modern age, many tell us, has or is passing. A postindustrial, nuclear age has come. A few years ago, we were told the Protestant era had passed. In America today, not only Protestants, Catholics, and Jews seek freedom and influence but also Muslims, Buddhists, and worshipers of native American and African religions. At the turn of the century, many religious persons and groups sought to preserve a Victorian Anglo-American culture in the face of a great influx of new immigrants and new technology. As the century closes, America seeks to preserve the West even as many of its citizens turn East and a new immigration of non-European people arrives on its shores.

Communities of faith must learn to educate their members for change as well as stability. During the twentieth century, nonfundamentalists and fundamentalists did not fully accomplish this task. The challenge of fundamentalism is to undertake it anew with a deep concern not only for the spirit of the age, which will in time pass, but also with a concern for the verities that endure even in a secular age and that require commitment and not just casual loyalty. This requires people and groups willing to work at understanding each other in a fair and loving manner while practicing diverse approaches to God. If one meets the religious challenges which this paper suggests that fundamentalism highlights, then some measure of success will be obtained in the endeavor to create mature persons for life in a religiously plural world.

Contributors

PATRICK M. ARNOLD, S.J., is Assistant Professor of Theology at the University of San Diego and has taught at the Jesuit School of Theology (Berkeley, California), St. Louis University, and Candler School of Theology, among other places. He has also pastored in various parishes. He is the author of *Gibeah: The Search for a Biblical City*, and he has also written several articles on archeological and theological topics.

EUGENE B. BOROWITZ is the Sigmund L. Falk Distinguished Professor of Education and Religious Thought at the New York School of Hebrew Union College-Jewish Institute of Religion where he has taught since 1962. He is the founder and editor of *Sh'ma: A Journal of Jewish Responsibility*, and has written a number of books, most recently *Exploring Jewish Ethics*. He is also the author of the article on "Judaism" for the recent *Encyclopedia of Religion*.

NORMAN J. COHEN is Dean of the New York School of the Hebrew Union College–Jewish Institute of Religion and Director of its Rabbinic School. He also serves as Professor of Midrash and has written numerous articles in the field.

JAMES M. DUNN is Executive Director of the Baptist Joint Committee on Public Affairs. He has served as a pastor, a campus minister, a college teacher, Executive Director of the Christian Life Commission, and President of Bread for the World.

RIFFAT HASSAN is Professor of Religious Studies at the University of Louisville. She was formerly Deputy Director, Bureau of National Research and Reference, Ministry of Information and National Affairs, Federal Government of Pakistan. She has participated in numerous interfaith discussions and lectured widely on interfaith dialogue, and has written many articles on this subject.

JAMES DAVISON HUNTER is Professor of Sociology and Religious Studies at the University of Virginia. His best-known book is *Evangelicalism: The Coming Generation,* which won the Distinguished Book Award from the Society for the Scientific Study of Religion.

GEORGE M. MARSDEN is Professor of the History of Christianity in America at The Divinity School, Duke University. He has written and edited several books, including the award-winning *Fundamentalism and American Culture* and *Reforming Fundamentalism: Fuller Seminary and the New Evangelicalism.*

RICHARD JOHN NEUHAUS is Director of the Institute on Religion and Public Life, New York City. A Lutheran clergyman, he was senior pastor for a parish in Brooklyn for seventeen years. He has been a leader in many organizations dealing with civil rights, peace, international justice, and religious ecumenism; he has accepted presidential appointments in both the Carter and Reagan administrations; and he is a board member of the United States Institute of Peace. Among his best-known, most recent books is *The Naked Public Square.*

MORTIMER OSTOW is Sandrow Visiting Professor of Pastoral Psychiatry at the Jewish Theological Seminary of America, where he has taught since 1953, and President of the Psychoanalytic Research & Development Fund. He practices psychoanalysis and psychiatry in New York City and has written several books and many articles on psychiatric, psychoanalytic, and neurologic subjects, some dealing with the psychology of religion. His most recent book is *Judaism and Psychoanalysis*.

JAROSLAV PELIKAN is Sterling Professor of History at Yale University, where he has taught since 1962. He is a leading scholar in medieval intellectual history, has authored and edited many books, received numerous honorary degrees, and has held many distinguished positions, including Chairman of the Council of Scholars of the Library of Congress.

CLARK H. PINNOCK is Professor of Systematic Theology at McMaster Divinity College, where he has taught since 1977. He has authored several books, including *The Scripture Principle*.

A. JAMES REICHLEY has been a Senior Fellow in the Governmental Studies Program of the Brookings Institution since 1977. He has written *Religion in American Public Life*, among other books. Before coming to Brookings, he served on President Gerald Ford's White House staff.

DAVID SAPERSTEIN is Co-Director and Counsel of the Religious Action Center of Reform Judaism. He is also adjunct professor in comparative Jewish and American Law at Georgetown University Law School. He serves on the boards and executive committees of over thirty national organizations, including NAACP, People for the American Way, Common Cause, and the Leadership Conference on Civil Rights.

DONALD W. SHRIVER, JR., is President of the Faculty at Union Theological Seminary, New York, where he is also Professor of Applied Christianity. He was formerly Professor of Ethics and Society at Candler School of Theology. He has written ten books, including *Beyond Success: Business Ethics in the Nineties*.

LINCOLN CHRISTIAN COLLEGE AND SEMINARY

LEON WIESELTIER is the Literary Editor of *The New Republic*. He is the author of *Nuclear War, Nuclear Peace,* and has written various articles on literary, political, and Jewish subjects.

PRESTON N. WILLIAMS has been Houghton Professor of Theology and Contemporary Change at Harvard Divinity School since 1971. He is an ordained minister in the United Presbyterian Church in the U.S., and has been a college chaplain. He has also served on several boards of professional and religious organizations, as President of the American Academy of Religion, and as President of the American Society of Christian Ethics. He has contributed articles to several journals and scholarly publications, including *The Westminster Dictionary of Christian Ethics.*